HER
LOTUS
YEAR

HER
LOTUS
YEAR

China, the Roaring Twenties,
and the Making of Wallis Simpson

Paul French

ST. MARTIN'S PRESS
NEW YORK

First published in the United States by St. Martin's Press,
an imprint of St. Martin's Publishing Group

HER LOTUS YEAR. Copyright © 2024 by Paul French.
All rights reserved. Printed in the United States of America.
For information, address St. Martin's Publishing Group,
120 Broadway, New York, NY 10271.

www.stmartins.com

The Library of Congress Cataloging-in-Publication Data
is available upon request.

ISBN 978-1-250-28747-2 (hardcover)
ISBN 978-1-250-28748-9 (ebook)

Our books may be purchased in bulk for promotional, educational,
or business use. Please contact your local bookseller or the
Macmillan Corporate and Premium Sales Department
at 1-800-221-7945, extension 5442, or by email at
MacmillanSpecialMarkets@macmillan.com.

First Edition: 2024

10 9 8 7 6 5 4 3 2 1

For Beatrix Anne and Ernest James

CONTENTS

A NOTE ON NAMES, SPELLINGS, AND LANGUAGE

Names in this book reflect the spellings most commonly used in the first half of the twentieth century. Hence, Peking and not Beijing; Canton and not Guangzhou. Where names and spellings have changed, I have mentioned the current or commonly used name in parentheses after first use.

Where Chinese people were commonly known by Western names to foreign audiences, these are used rather than either the older Wade-Giles or the more recent pinyin systems of romanization. Additionally, I have used the best-known variations of some Chinese names rather than their more modern variants, such as Sun Yat-sen rather than Sun Zhongshan, and Chang Tso-lin as opposed to Zhang Zuolin (though, where applicable, contemporary pinyin names are included in parentheses at first use).

For Shanghai, I have used the former road and district names of the International Settlement and French Concession within the text as they were in 1924. Additionally, many roads, particularly those of Beijing's Legation Quarter and Guangzhou's Shamian Island, were popularly known by various European names by foreigners at the time, and I have used these. For all roads, the current name is given in parentheses after first use.

As the *New Yorker* writer, China sojourner, and onetime ardent "Shanghailander" Emily Hahn once commented when tackling the question of rendering Chinese into English, "This writer has done her best but knows it is not good enough, and meekly bends her head before the inevitable storm." I too bow my head.

Wallis, as well as many of her biographers and commentators, were men and women of their times. Various outdated terms, such as *coolie* (meaning "laborer"), *boy* (meaning "servant"), and *Chinaman*, are used occasionally in contemporary quotes. These terms are derogatory and insulting to us now, and in using them in original quotes, I reflect the languages, assumptions, and foreign mores of the times. Such language is itself the result of colonialism and Western privilege in China and reflects the realities of the period in which the younger Wallis Spencer lived.

However, we should not think that the use of such terms at the time was wholly accepted and went unchallenged. For instance, the term *Chinaman* in particular must be framed and contextualized. The term was widely used in the nineteenth century as a pejorative, usually with generally derogatory overtones, but not always intended as malicious. By the 1920s, a vigorous debate was beginning to occur over the use of the term both in the United States and in Britain.

From the mid-1920s, American writers and "China Hands," such as the Missouri-born Shanghai-based journalist and advertising agency owner Carl Crow, began to criticize people using the term *Chinaman*. Crow and others—academic Sinologists, Chinese students in America, and diplomats at the Chinese Embassy in Washington, DC—engaged with newspapers and authors as well as entering into long correspondences with the compilers of the *Oxford English Dictionary* concerning the term.

Eventually, in 1938, the editors of the *OED* in England accepted the argument that *Chinaman* had gone out of fashion and was now a derogatory term and therefore offensive. The *OED* said that they would consider revising their entry. Crow was encouraged enough to fire off letters to the compilers of other English-language dictionaries in America, such as Merriam-Webster, encouraging them to alter their entries too.

What was without doubt the most delightful, the most carefree, the most lyrical interval of my youth—the nearest thing to a lotus-eater's dream that a young woman brought up the "right" way could expect to know.

—Wallis, Duchess of Windsor,
The Heart Has Its Reasons

INTRODUCTION

The many biographies of Wallis Simpson have tended to focus almost exclusively on the love affair that forced the constitutional crisis of the abdication of King Edward VIII in December 1936 and the challenging years of exile for the Duke and Duchess of Windsor that followed. The earlier part of Wallis's life, her first disastrous marriage to Commander Win Spencer, her escape from that relationship, and the pivotal year she spent in China across 1924 and 1925 have been the subject of much rumor but relatively little close study. *Her Lotus Year* reveals a different Wallis Simpson from the one so often presented.

Early-twentieth-century Chinese history is complicated and undeniably confusing, while rarely being the province of royal historians. And so Wallis's China sojourn of the mid-1920s tends to be noted solely in terms of salacious gossip and innuendo rather than her actual experiences of the country. Many nefarious stories surrounding her China sojourn emerged around the time of the threatened abdication a dozen years after Wallis had left China. They formed the substance of what would come to be known as the "China Dossier." The elite ruling clique of the English Establishment, including the then government of Prime Minister Stanley Baldwin and the British intelligence services, sought to use Wallis Simpson's time in China to denigrate her moral character, making prurient and baseless assertions. These were given weight by the prevailing Sinophobic narratives in British society that associated single white women in the

Far East with sexual impropriety and were designed specifically to derail her relationship with King Edward VIII.

In the first half of the twentieth century, images of the "heathen Chinee," the fleshpots of the Far East, the "Yellow Peril," and "white slavery" east of Suez were rampant. The notion that sojourners in the East somehow jettisoned their moral compasses as soon as they stepped ashore reached the common reader and cinemagoer through countless plays, short stories, novels, and films. Travelers in the East, especially white women, went bad out there, if they weren't already prone to moral rot and therefore attracted to the Orient in the first place.

With this image of China so prevalent in the imagination of audiences on both sides of the Atlantic, it was easy for the British Establishment to perpetrate the rumors of Wallis's supposed descent into (take your pick of any or all of the suggested rumors) prostitution, opium addiction and dope dealing, modeling for pornographic photographs, fronting for a gambling syndicate, endless love affairs (mostly with married men), lesbianism, living as a "kept woman," drunkenness, sexual ménages à trois, exotic massage techniques to encourage ejaculation, and (perhaps most famously and endlessly repeated to this day on a thousand websites fascinated by Wallis) her supposed technique, learned in a low Chinese brothel of course, of the "Shanghai Grip."

The rumors were used to blacken Wallis's name in London society. Originally, the insinuations were proffered to offer some explanation (as opposed to any notion of character, style, sophistication, or fashion sense) for Edward VIII's obsession with her. A justification for her hold over him. The lurid rumors hung around Wallis like a bad smell for the rest of her life and continue to be recycled in the tabloid press today. Crucially, however, it seems that while the gossip circulated wildly among the upper echelons of British society, Queen Mary, the then Prince Albert (later King George VI after the abdication) and his wife, Elizabeth (later better known as the Queen Mother), senior government ministers, the clergy, and so on—nobody ever actually read a physical copy or held an actual document in their hands. In fact, nobody has ever seen the purported document. Richard Aldrich and Rory Cormac's book *The Secret Royals: Spying and the Crown, from Victoria to Diana* claims that Edward VIII's close confidant and royal insider Kenneth de Courcy knew the "document" was "totally false." The authors conclude that the dossier did not exist. Further to that, the top civil servant of his day and private secretary to three prime ministers (Chamberlain, Churchill, and Attlee), Jock Colville, had never come across the dossier.* When word of the dossier eventually reached Wallis, she understood the allegations to be "venom, venom, VENOM."[†]

Her Lotus Year offers a very different account of Wallis's time in China from the version suggested by the rumors put about by the purported China Dossier. Having written about China and the country's convulsive interwar history between the world wars for a quarter century, I became intrigued by the fact that Wallis Simpson had spent time in China in the mid-1920s. I began to trace her footsteps, discovering her experiences of Hong Kong's Kowloon district, Canton's Shameen Island, the Shanghai Bund, or Peking's ancient hutongs. I was struck by the events she would have witnessed, given what a chaotic, uncertain, and often dangerous period it was in China's history. I would find myself in places I knew she had once stayed—Shanghai's Palace Hotel, the old building of the Grand Hôtel de Pékin, the traditional hutong lane where she lived with friends. At these random moments, Wallis's China sojourn would come within reach.

Rather than the rumors and allegations, casually repeated and to

---

* Richard Aldrich and Rory Cormac, *The Secret Royals: Spying and the Crown, from Victoria to Diana* (London: Atlantic Books, 2021), 345, 617–618.
† Joe Bryan and Charles J. V. Murphy, *The Windsor Story* (New York: HarperCollins, 1979), 22.

any China historian obviously false, the journey she took across the country in such perilous times was revealing of a fast-disappearing world of cosmopolitan glamour, political intrigue, and unashamed colonial excess. This I discovered was what was truly formative in shaping the Wallis Simpson the world would come to recognize, and far more fascinating than the tawdry rumors put about by the China Dossier.

In the summer of 1924, Mrs. Wallis Warfield Spencer, having just turned twenty-eight years of age, boarded a United States Navy transport ship bound for Hong Kong. She was traveling to the Far East in the hope she could save her failing marriage. Her husband, US Navy pilot Earl Winfield "Win" Spencer Jr., was an abusive drunk with a temper, and their marriage had been troubled for some years before he was posted east to serve with the US South China Patrol. He begged her to follow him; he swore he'd given up the booze; her family urged her to try to repair the relationship. So she went . . .

After a seemingly idyllic reunion in Hong Kong, Win soon slipped back into his old ways—drinking to excess and abusing his wife verbally, emotionally, and physically. At this point, Wallis decided to leave him. *Her Lotus Year* tells the story of what happened next.

Wallis left Win and Hong Kong for the cosmopolitan delights of 1920s Shanghai, where she effectively began her life over. From there, she journeyed to Peking, where she immediately became entranced with the ancient Chinese capital. She was to stay in China for approximately a year.

It was a period Wallis herself later referred to longingly as her "Lotus Year," invoking the lotus-eaters of Greek mythology, Homer's *Odyssey*, and Alfred, Lord Tennyson's poem. Homer describes the lotus-eaters, a tribe encountered by Odysseus during his return from Troy, as having become "forgetful of their homeward way."

Pleasantly marooned on an island, in an altered state and isolated from the rest of the world, they live a life of indolence and peaceful apathy, free of practical concerns.

> *Let us swear an oath, and keep it with an equal mind,*
> *In the hollow Lotos-land to live and lie reclined*
> *On the hills like Gods together, careless of mankind.*
>
> (Alfred, Lord Tennyson, "The Lotos-Eaters," 1832)

This was how Wallis viewed her China sojourn. It was a year that would affect her in significant ways. She discovered she could mix easily in sophisticated international company, where the conversation was immeasurably more interesting than the middle-class Baltimore dining rooms or drab US naval base society she had known previously. Over the course of her stay, she would develop a lifelong appreciation of traditional Chinese style and aesthetics, developing the exquisite taste for which she became renowned.

An adventurous, curious, active, and independent woman, she traveled across the country during a time of great political turmoil in China. In the power vacuums that followed the collapse of the 267-year-old Qing dynasty and the problematic emergence of the first Chinese Republic, warlord battles threatened to plunge China into full-blown civil war. These self-proclaimed leaders of large armies controlling vast swaths of territory skirmished and fought for power all around her as she moved from Hong Kong north to Shanghai and then farther north and inland to Peking. Even though she remained largely in the safe confines of the International Settlements in Hong Kong, Canton, Shanghai, and Peking, disease, natural disaster, and banditry were never far away. She made lifelong friends and enjoyed a genuine love affair.

Wallis was aware of the chaos engulfing China, the revolution of Dr. Sun Yat-sen, the violent jockeying for position among the warlords, just as she was aware that most of her time in China was spent in a form of privileged isolation from the confusion and mayhem out-side the enclaves of colonial Hong Kong, the foreign treaty ports and concessions of Shameen Island, Shanghai, and Tientsin (Tianjin), or the protected Legation Quarter of Peking. Looking back thirty years later, by then the Duchess of Windsor, she would write: "In later years I was to reflect upon how much I missed China."*

---

* Wallis Simpson, *The Heart Has Its Reasons* (London: Michael Joseph, 1956), 119. Wallis's autobiography is ghostwritten. It was reputedly a rather torturous affair. The project was started with Charles J. V. Murphy, a former Washington bureau chief for *Fortune* magazine, who also wrote for *Time* and *Life* and had previously ghost-written the Duke of Windsor's *A King's Story* (1947). The process was not smooth, and Wallis fired Murphy. She then hired the American author and critic Cleveland Amory, but he also soon departed the project.

HER
LOTUS
YEAR

Prologue

BACK TO THE BEGINNING

THE VILLA LOU VIEI
NEAR CANNES, THE FRENCH RIVIERA
DECEMBER 2-11, 1936

Don't worry. It never happens . . .
>   —Wallis's motto, according to the Duke of Windsor

FLIGHT TO OLD FRIENDS

On December 2, 1936, the long-running and much-gossiped-about affair between the American double divorcée Wallis Simpson and King Edward VIII dramatically became public. Wallis, two years younger than Edward, had met the then Prince of Wales in 1931, becoming his mistress a few years later. The king demanded to marry Wallis, who had recently divorced her second husband, Ernest Simpson. A constitutional crisis of unprecedented magnitude loomed.

The traditional restraint of Fleet Street in not reporting the private lives of the Royal Family was shattered as one of the Establishment's best-kept secrets was revealed to all for the price of a tabloid newspaper. The foreign media, free of any need to display deference to the Court of St. James's, had been gleefully running the story for quite some time. Of course, those in the know in British society—the so-called Establishment of politicians, senior clergy, the intelligence services, as well as the aristocracy in their town houses, country estates, and London clubs—had long spoken of the affair. Largely, they had tolerated the former Prince of Wales's infatuation with the twice-divorced American woman formerly known in her native Baltimore as Bessie Wallis Warfield, then Mrs. Earl Winfield Spencer and, until her most recent divorce, Mrs. Ernest Simpson. This tolerant attitude changed when the prince became the king.

Edward had become the monarch following his father King George V's death in January 1936. Wallis had begun divorce proceedings from Ernest Simpson in October, received a decree nisi, and was now required to wait six months before the decree was made absolute, thereby legally ending her marriage.[*] She would then be technically free to marry the king.

For Wallis, the drama and media frenzy became simply too much. Edward was said to be threatening suicide (and reminding her that he slept with a gun under his pillow) if he was unable to marry Wallis.[†] Her photograph was magnified on the front page of every newspaper—unbearable for a woman who cared so much about her appearance. The pictures were accompanied by generally hostile captions. She received floods of hate mail; she could not easily move around the city. She needed to escape, to get away from London and the intrusions of the press. But where to go?

After careful thought, Wallis decided that there was only one place, the Villa Lou Viei—"the only sanctuary within reach," as she wrote much later in her memoirs.[‡] It was over eight hundred miles

---

[*] A decree nisi being a preliminary statement that the court does not see any reason why the couple cannot divorce.

[†] Emily Chan, "How 'Needy' King Edward Left Wallis Simpson Trapped," *Daily Mail* (UK), November 21, 2017.

[‡] Wallis Simpson, *The Heart Has Its Reasons* (London: Michael Joseph, 1956), 261.

from London, a fifty-five-hour journey by car and ferry. Situated in the hills above Cannes in the South of France, the villa, a twelfth-century converted monastery, was the stunning home of Herman and Katherine "Kitty" Rogers, a wealthy American couple. Wallis had known Kitty since before the First World War, back when she was married to her first husband, Commander Earl Winfield "Win" Spencer, a US Navy pilot, and when both Wallis and Kitty had been "navy wives." Wallis cabled Herman and Kitty in France asking their assistance. Herman replied immediately, "Of course, you must come to us."*

After a dash from London, a powerful Buick car arrived at the villa at two in the morning. In the front seats were chauffeur George Ladbrooke alongside Police Inspector Evans of Scotland Yard. In the rear, Wallis, in a three-quarter-length sable fur coat, crouched on the floor, a rug thrown over her by her other traveling companion, the British peer, lord-in-waiting, and close friend of the king's, Perry Brownlow (sixth Baron Brownlow). The car sped through the swiftly opened wrought iron gates into the sanctuary of the Villa Lou Viei.

Inspector Evans made arrangements with the French police to guard the villa. Wallis's maid, Mary Burke, had arrived ahead of her mistress to prepare. Shortly afterward, sixteen trunks and thirty-six suitcases of luggage turned up. The villa was in some disarray. The Rogerses had been in the midst of redecorating when a desperate Wallis had asked for refuge.

The next morning, Herman, with Perry Brownlow, sat down on the villa's terrace to help Wallis compose her famous "untenable" letter on December 8. Wallis stated that she was willing "to withdraw from a situation which has become both unhappy and untenable." It did nothing to sway the opinion of the king. Edward replied, "You can go anywhere, to <u>China</u> even, Labrador or the South Seas. But

---

* Simpson, *The Heart Has Its Reasons*.

wherever you go I will follow."* The king's specific mention of China was not accidental. Wallis really had thought of fleeing to China. Perry Brownlow said he would accompany her if she so decided. But Edward had made the decision to abdicate before any such plan came to fruition, if indeed she was ever serious. But clearly the notion of escaping at a time of crisis to China was in her mind. And there was good reason for this.

This was not the first time that Wallis had sought sanctuary with the Rogerses. She had once before been a recipient of their largesse and friendship—on a freezing-cold New Year's Eve 1924, in Peking, China. The independently wealthy Rogerses had decided to live in the Chinese capital for a few years and occupied a beautiful tradi-tional courtyard home on one of the city's distinctive narrow lanes, an ancient hutong.† The then Wallis Spencer was a lone woman traveling through warlord- and bandit-racked Chinese hinterlands, having fi-nally felt compelled to leave her hard-drinking and physically abusive husband in Hong Kong.

Her funds running low, her hotel room only affordable for a few more days, the city frozen and surrounded by bandit armies and a typhoid epidemic, it was perhaps the lowest point of Wallis's life. Until she met Kitty and Herman in Peking. The couple had been her saviors before, and so it seemed they would be again.

On December 11, 1936, the three of them and Perry Brownlow gath-ered around the radio to listen to the king's abdication broadcast.

---

* Charles Higham, *The Duchess of Windsor: The Secret Life* (New York: McGraw-Hill, 1988), 156.

† *Hutong* (a corrupted borrowing from Middle Mongolian *quddug*, "water well") re-fers to the narrow streets or alleys then to be found crisscrossing and proliferating throughout Peking. First developed during the Yuan (or Mongol) dynasty (1279–1368), hutongs are uniquely found largely in Peking as well as some other northern Chinese locations.

Wallis recalled: "I was lying on the sofa with my hands over my eyes, trying to hide my tears. After he finished, the others quietly went and left me alone. I lay there a long time before I could control myself enough to walk through the house and go upstairs to my room."[*]

Wallis would spend nearly six months at the Villa Lou Viei with Kitty and Herman before embarking on her third marriage in June 1937, when she became Wallis, Duchess of Windsor, wife of a former king. Throughout this time, she was besieged by the international press camped at the villa's gates, a pile of mostly hostile letters arrived each morning with the breakfast tray, and her reputation was increasingly trashed in the English newspapers that arrived every lunchtime.

Wallis's dramatic scramble from England to the Riviera was both an escape and a reunion. It's inconceivable that once within the safety of the confines of the Villa Lou Viei, the three friends did not reminisce about their time together in China, a time Wallis was to claim had begun at a low point but ultimately became the happiest of her life. Her self-proclaimed Lotus Year.

---

[*] Simpson, *The Heart Has Its Reasons*, 278.

The USS *Chaumont*

1

THE YEARS BEFORE
AND THE VOYAGE EAST

USS *CHAUMONT*
THE SOUTH CHINA SEA
JULY-SEPTEMBER 1924

So be it, I thought. Win and I have failed in the West. Perhaps in the East we can find our way to a new life together.

—Wallis, Duchess of Windsor, *The Heart Has Its Reasons*

BEFORE CHINA

When Wallis decided to head to the Far East, she had just turned twenty-eight, hoping for adventure, but also aiming to rekindle her estranged marriage. Her husband had been posted to the British Crown Colony of Hong Kong with the US Navy's South China Patrol, and Wallis hoped their relationship might revive in a different environment, especially if her husband had, as he claimed, quit his heavy drinking. Wallis's Baltimore upbringing had been relatively staid, a home of strict conventions, fixed opinions, and one in which divorce was not just scandalous but inevitably seen as a failure on the woman's part. And so Wallis Warfield Spencer felt compelled to try again. She also admitted to her mother shortly before deciding to leave America for Hong Kong, "The truth is, I suppose, I still love him."* It was ultimately to be a doomed attempt, and she was to eventually break free of the conventions of her upbringing. But she departed America with some hope.

Her father, Teackle Wallis Warfield, had died of tuberculosis in 1896, aged just twenty-seven, barely three months after Wallis was born in Blue Ridge Summit, Pennsylvania. She later maintained she'd been raised in "relative poverty," though Wallis's widowed aunt Bessie Merryman declared that it was "not exactly Tobacco Road." Teackle was "a retiring, ailing boy who worked insignificantly as a clerk in Baltimore, but the family had what were called 'good connections.'"† Until the age of six, Bessie Wallis Warfield (she dropped the "Bessie" early, so her biographer Diana Mosley claimed, as she considered it a "cow's name") lived with her wealthy railroad baron uncle, Solomon Davies Warfield, "Uncle Sol," at his home, Manor Glen, eighteen miles outside of the city.‡ Later, her mother, Alice, decided they should move in with Aunt Bessie back in Baltimore.

Thanks to the continued largesse of Uncle Sol, Wallis attended the prestigious, private all-girls school Oldfields, which elevated feminine decorum over an inquiring mind. She did not excel academically but did become an accomplished equestrienne.§ Wallis formally came out as a debutante on Christmas Eve 1914, a celebration rather dampened by the start of the war in Europe.

Two years later, in April 1916, Wallis went to visit her married cousin and close childhood confidante Corinne Mustin (née DeForest

---

* Wallis Simpson, *The Heart Has Its Reasons* (London: Michael Joseph, 1956), 102.

† James Laver, *Between the Wars* (London: Vista Books, 1961), 205.

‡ Diana Mosley, *The Duchess of Windsor* (London: Sidgwick & Jackson, 1980), 24.

§ In 2023, it was announced that Oldfields was closing after 156 years. Most reports noted Wallis as the most famous former pupil.

Montague) in Florida.* Corrine's husband Henry was a pioneering US Navy aviator who commanded the Pensacola air base. There she was introduced to Earl Winfield "Win" Spencer Jr. Eight years older than Wallis, Spencer was a naval aviator. Tanned and handsome, he looked good in his uniform and had an engaging smile. "I have just met the world's most fascinating aviator," she wrote in her diary.† He was attracted by her "sapphire blue eyes and contagious laugh."‡ It was a whirlwind romance, and they married in Baltimore that November. Wallis was just two years out of school, barely twenty, and naive. The newlyweds honeymooned at the popular Greenbrier Resort at White Sulphur Springs in West Virginia.

The son of a Chicago stockbroker, Win Spencer had graduated from the US Naval Academy, becoming a pilot, but had been (maybe due to his excessive drinking) denied an opportunity to go to the war in Europe. Instead, he was left behind in San Diego to establish the Naval Air Station North Island, training other pilots to go to France. Win's constant griping about being left out of the war and stuck in the backwater of Coronado meant that Wallis also came to resent being stuck in California, particularly as she had to endure Win's tantrums and ragings.

The problem was that Win drank . . . heavily. He had a quick temper, which was accelerated by his frustration at his stalled career. The couple lived in regulation married quarters for what felt like a very long four years. Wallis's life was, she openly admitted, boring.§ Endless evenings of navy talk with other navy wives over endless rubbers of bridge (a talent that would come in useful later in China)

---

* Corinne was the great-granddaughter of Commodore Arthur Sinclair (1780–1831), who was an early American naval hero and who served in the United States Navy during the Quasi-War with France (1798–1800), the First Barbary War, and the War of 1812 against Great Britain.

† Caroline Blackwood, *The Last of the Duchess* (London: Vintage, 2012), 64.

‡ Blackwood, *The Last of the Duchess*, 106.

§ Simpson, *The Heart Has Its Reasons*, 72.

and gin. Some of the wives became good friends. The Spencers were close to Kitty Bigelow and her navy pilot husband, Ernest. But then Ernest was posted to France in 1917, and Kitty followed him to Europe as a nurse. Wallis was left alone as Win drank and fumed about being stuck in California while other men were seeing action. The situation was not helped by the fact that Win's younger brother Dumaresq, known as "Stuff," was a volunteer pilot with the Escadrille de La Fayette, a unit of the French air force composed mostly of American volunteers. Dumaresq Spencer crashed and died in France in January 1918.

Coronado was a notoriously tedious place. In his debut novel, *This Side of Paradise*, published in 1920, F. Scott Fitzgerald's main character, Amory Blaine (who does serve in the US military in World War I), recalls his mother spending time there: "Coronado, where his mother became so bored that she had a nervous breakdown."[*] It was an incestuous atmosphere ripe for combustible rows and angry shouting matches.

Wallis had first discovered Win's temper on their honeymoon, when he'd found out the Greenbrier was a "dry" hotel. He'd had to resort to surreptitiously swigging from his silver hip flask. Win's drinking was immense—his regular tipple was a large consommé bowl filled entirely of dry martinis.[†] Then in Coronado, things got worse, spiraling into what was to become an all-too-familiar cycle of anger and violence followed by abject apology and apparent remorse. Wallis would recall that Win would sometimes force her into the bathroom, lock the door, and switch the lights off, leaving her there till morning, telling her she was in "solitary."[‡] He was a mean drunk. While his behavior was intolerable, Wallis was a young woman of a

---

[*] F. Scott Fitzgerald, *This Side of Paradise* (New York: Charles Scribner's & Son, 1920), 4.
[†] Blackwood, *The Last of the Duchess*, 165.
[‡] Blackwood, *The Last of the Duchess*, 165.

certain time and upbringing, and at this point, she questioned her own, rather than her husband's, behavior. The prevailing ethos, instilled in Wallis from childhood, was that marriage was for life and a wife should accept her condition and try harder to please her husband. But though she stayed with Win, it was clear to her that the marriage was falling apart.*

Win eventually escaped Coronado. He was assigned to the navy's Bureau of Aeronautics in Washington, DC. This appointment, it seems, was probably arranged by the bureau's first assistant chief, Henry Mustin, the husband of Wallis's cousin Corinne, and so it is entirely possible that Wallis herself pulled some strings to get them out of the rut of Coronado.

But it didn't improve his temperament much. The bureau was another no-flying, deskbound job. Win continued to drink heavily enough for their neighbors to complain to the management at the Hotel Brighton of their constant arguing. Still, Wallis sought to avoid scandal and stayed with Win. They fought; he took to locking her in the hotel bathroom. His drinking, the anger, violence, and occasional blackouts came to a head when he deserted Wallis for four whole months without explanation. But still Wallis couldn't leave. She consulted her aunt Bessie in Baltimore but found little support—"Divorce! It's unthinkable."† Win returned, and the marriage limped along until February 1922, when he was reassigned to the US Navy's South China Patrol stationed in Hong Kong.

With Win gone to Asia, Wallis moved back to Baltimore. But she regularly paid social visits to neighboring Washington, mingling on the fringes of the capital's diplomatic circle, staying with cousin Corrine, and evidently enjoying her newfound freedom from Win. "I was often out quite late. Whatever the hour, my mother was always waiting for me, sitting up in bed, reading or sewing when I came in.

* Simpson, *The Heart Has Its Reasons*, 82.
† Simpson, *The Heart Has Its Reasons*, 87.

She never failed to ask me where I had been, what I had done and with whom. I always told her."[*]

But perhaps not everything that went on. Before long, Wallis embarked on an affair with a Latin American diplomat. Felipe Espil was the thirty-five-year-old first secretary at the Argentine embassy, a slim, well-dressed, handsome man, noted conversationalist, and a wine connoisseur.[†] Some biographers of Wallis have pondered why the debonair and stylish Espil was attracted to the relatively unsophisticated Mrs. Spencer. Yet a newspaper society page report, noting her appearance in the capital, suggests she was already keen on fashion and making a striking impression. Remarking that "Mrs Winfield Spencer is on a visit to the city while her husband is stationed in China," Wallis is reported to be wearing "a lovely gown of cream lace and georgette . . . long bodice and no sleeves. A cane-like effect of georgette hanging from the shoulders fell into a short wispy train at one side."[‡]

The liaison with Espil was intense but short-lived. He was a devout Catholic (at least in some respects) and would not consider marrying a divorcée. Wallis was heartbroken when he ended the affair.

Win had been in Asia for over two years by the summer of 1924. The US Navy's South China Patrol was constituted of only two gunboats—the USS *Helena* and the USS *Pampanga*, commanded by Lieutenant Commander Win Spencer. The *Pampanga* was nominally based in Hong Kong but regularly patrolled the coast from the

---

[*] Simpson, *The Heart Has Its Reasons*, 100.

[†] Anne Sebba, *That Woman: The Life of Wallis Simpson, Duchess of Windsor* (London: Weidenfeld & Nicolson, 2011), 42–3.

[‡] Mary Louise Love, "Short Skirts and Many Tucks Mark Present Ultra Advanced Capital Costumes," *Corsicana Daily Sun* (Texas), July 19, 1924.

British colony as far as the Pearl River estuary and up to the Chinese city of Canton (Guangzhou). Unfortunately, as with Coronado and Washington, DC, the South China Patrol did not prove a happy posting for Win. Though a navy man, he was a flyer by choice and interest. While he was promoted to lieutenant commander in Hong Kong and handed command of the *Pampanga*, the ship was a rather aged vessel, and there was no aviation component to the job. Named after a Philippines province, it had started service with the patrol in 1919, though it had been built for the Spanish navy back in 1887 before being captured during the Spanish-American War in 1898.

Additionally, Win didn't much like the intense humidity of southern China. He found the summers brutal and complained that conditions on board the small boat were squalid and the "gobs" under his command coarse.[*]

Still, after his disappointment at missing out on the fighting in Europe in the Great War, he did see some action in China. There were regular anti-piracy patrols up and down the China coast and in the waters between Hong Kong and the Portuguese colony of Macao. Then, in late 1923, political agitation in the city of Canton, ostensibly over a customs dispute, meant the *Pampanga* was sent up the coast from Hong Kong to moor off the foreign enclave of Shameen (Shamian) Island to ensure the safety of the approximately five hundred American nationals living, working, and proselytizing in and around the city—more than any other nation at the time. Several gunboats of the Royal Navy, a squad of French soldiers, as well as a hundred US Marines deployed from Manila were ready to evacuate foreign nationals if the situation deteriorated. In the end, apart from a crowd that gathered to throw some stones and tell the "foreign devils" in no uncertain terms to leave, the situation eventually calmed.

---

[*] US Navy slang for an enlisted ordinary seaman.

Still, a clash between French troops and Chinese nearby at the Bocca Tigris Fort on the Pearl River left forty Chinese and five Frenchmen dead.[*]

A few months later, things got difficult again as the *Pampanga*, still under Win's command, was ordered back to Canton and then farther inland to Wuchow (Wuzhou), almost on the border with Vietnam and the French Indochinese empire. It was a challenge to Win's navigation skills, as the river got extremely narrow as it approached Wuchow. But he had to stay at full steam if possible; it was an urgent mission. Two American missionaries, two Europeans, and twenty Chinese were being held captive by an estimated three hundred bandits in the hills outside Wuchow. They were demanding $2,000 in gold (over US$3.6 million in 2024 money), a hundred pistols, a thousand rifles, and a large quantity of ammunition. It seems the approach of the *Pampanga* and the prospect of armed bluejackets storming the bandit lair led the kidnappers to cut their losses and release the hostages.[†]

Later, in 1924, the South China Patrol and the *Pampanga* were back on the Pearl River again, once more heading up to Canton. In June, the crew of the *Pampanga* was involved in protecting the foreign enclave of Shameen after Vietnamese independence activists hurled a bomb into the dining room of the British Concession's Victoria Hotel, attempting to assassinate the visiting governor of French Indochina.[‡] A few weeks later, in August, the *Pampanga* was back at Shameen yet again as various warlord factions skirmished,

[*] Junius B. Wood, "Allies May Land Men at Canton," *Wilkes-Barre Record* (Pennsylvania), December 27, 1923; Junius B. Wood, "French and Chinese in Clash at Canton," *Wilkes-Barre Record* (Pennsylvania), December 27, 1923. The Bocca Tigris was also known as the Bogue and now as Humen.
[†] "Two Missionaries are Released," *Des Moines Register*, June 5, 1924.
[‡] Paul French, "How Vietnamese Revolutionary Leader Ho Chi Minh Was Inspired by a Guangzhou Hotel Bomber's Anti-Colonial Spirit," *South China Morning Post Magazine*, November 19, 2022.

threatening an American Baptist mission close to the city. All the missionaries and their families were safely evacuated.[*]

These were febrile times in Canton—labor disputes raged, factional fighting intensified, and banditry was on the rise in and around the city of two million people, surrounded by a province, Kwangtung (Guangdong), of many millions more. Win and the *Pampanga* were back in Canton again in September as the strikes and fighting escalated and took on an increasingly anti-foreign complexion. Several American bluejackets were wounded rescuing stranded Americans in the city.

Southern China may have been uncomfortably hot and humid for Win, but he couldn't complain that he wasn't kept busy and seeing his fair share of action and challenging situations. But what he wanted was for his wife to join him in Hong Kong.

Thirty years later, looking back with a certain nostalgia, induced perhaps by the passing of time, Wallis claimed that she suffered extreme loneliness after Win had left for Asia. Presumably, though, life hadn't been all bad. The affair with Felipe Espil in Washington was followed by her first trip outside the United States, to Paris to visit her recently widowed cousin Corrine. The ever-dependable Uncle Sol paid her fare. Diana Mosley claimed Wallis did seriously consider divorcing Win in France, but it would have cost a lot of money, and she couldn't afford it.[†] Meanwhile, a stream of letters and telegrams from Win arrived in Paris. He wrote that he was lonely, that he missed her. Couldn't they try again? He vowed to Wallis in his letters that he had quit drinking in Hong Kong.

Wallis was perhaps feeling fragile after the disappointment with

* "US Gunboats off to Canton," *Reno Gazette*, October 16, 1924; "Fighting in China," *Orlando Sentinel*, August 16, 1924.
† Mosley, *The Duchess of Windsor*, 23.

Espil. She couldn't stay in Paris with Corrine indefinitely. She was still married, even if reluctantly. If she went to China, then the navy would arrange the transportation. Win wrote repeatedly claiming six months of sobriety, begging Wallis to come to Hong Kong and try again. Wallis wondered if, perhaps in a strange and exotic environment on the other side of the world, they could perhaps reset their marriage. It was a big decision. Not only the task of trying to reboot a failing relationship on the other side of the world, but with Win in China for nearly two years already, she could not have failed to see the alarming news in the newspapers of the strikes and troubles in Canton that had at times spilled over into Hong Kong, as well as the ever-present scourge of piracy in the South China Sea. The American press reported the *Pampanga*'s involvement in various missions; Commander Spencer was frequently mentioned. But if she had been reading the papers, the news from southern China didn't deter her.

Wallis later wrote in her memoirs, "So be it, I thought. Win and I have failed in the West. Perhaps in the East we can find our way to a new life together."* She agreed to sail to Hong Kong and booked passage east as a naval officer's wife on the US Navy transport ship *Chaumont*.

THE SLOW BOAT TO CHINA

In her memoir, *The Heart Has Its Reasons*, published in the mid-1950s, many eventful years after her Asia sojourn, Wallis looked back on herself as a relatively inexperienced young woman bound for Hong Kong on the "original slow boat to China."† The USS *Chaumont* certainly wasn't in a rush, nor was it much in the way of a stylish ride—a barebones US Navy transport ship that meandered down America's East

* Simpson, *The Heart Has Its Reasons*, 102.
† Simpson, *The Heart Has Its Reasons*, 102.

Coast, through the Panama Canal, and then across the vast Pacific, making stops at the American naval bases at Honolulu and Guam.

The *Chaumont* had been launched into service in 1921 from the Philadelphia Naval Shipyard. Transports typically had just two classes of accommodation: first and second. As the wife of a serving officer, Wallis sailed first class, but on a navy transport, that was still fairly basic. The *Chaumont* was essentially a refitted cargo ship rather than an ocean liner, and so the accommodation was rudimentary. The *Chaumont* could, at full capacity, carry 1,300 troops with an additional couple of hundred crew and civilian passengers. In 1924, when Wallis boarded the *Chaumont*, it was serving as a designated transpacific troop carrier sailing between the United States and the US naval base at Manila in the Philippines.

The *Chaumont* embarked for its six-week voyage from the navy yards at Norfolk, Virginia, on Thursday, July 17, 1924. It was scheduled to take a very long and roundabout route to the Philippines via the Panama Canal. The main cargo on this voyage was actually almost exclusively navy wives and children sailing to join husbands and fathers at their postings. Cabins were assigned according to the rank of the husband. As the wife of a lieutenant commander, Wallis was assigned a mid-rank cabin on the second deck, which she shared with two other women—the wife of a captain stationed in the Philippines and another woman traveling to China to marry an officer in the Marine Corps. The privileges, or the misfortunes, of rank extended throughout the ship. The higher your husband's rank, the closer you were seated to the captain's table in the dining room.

The voyage was initially a rotten experience for Wallis. She spent the first week confined to her cabin with a feverish cold and nausea. She described herself as "half-dead," barely able to rise from her bunk, suffering terribly from seasickness. She avoided the communal areas of the ship, as everybody was smoking, which accentuated her nausea. By the time the *Chaumont* had crawled down the Eastern Seaboard of the United States and reached the Panama Canal,

Wallis was no better and had a high fever. But the ship's doctor prescribed nothing more advanced than dry toast and ginger ale with a little chicken broth or beef tea for dinner. She continued to suffer severe seasickness all the way to Panama City.

Kay Manly, an old friend and fellow navy wife, was stationed with her husband in the Panama Canal Zone and found a physician for Wallis.* After two days' recuperation ashore at the Manlys' home, Wallis declared herself much improved and was able to rejoin the *Chaumont* for the next leg of the voyage—out across the Pacific to Hawaii, arriving for a few days' stopover in Honolulu. On what must have been a rather slow news day, a nationally syndicated social column that ran in numerous newspapers across America noted:

Mrs Wallis Spencer has been sick for a week.[†]

Fortunately, after Hawaii, Wallis's seasickness receded, and things aboard got rather better. Many of the higher-ranking officers' wives disembarked, their husbands stationed at nearby Pearl Harbor, and so Wallis was moved up to a better-situated cabin.

By the time they completed the eleven-day transpacific voyage to the naval base at Guam in the western Pacific, Wallis and a few of the other wives had forgotten their initial seasickness but were now suffering serious cabin fever. Though ostensibly not permitted, a group of them insisted on going ashore while the *Chaumont* discharged supplies for the base. The adventurous gang rented a thatched hut on the

---

* Kay's husband, Commander M. E. Manly, had been appointed captain of Panama City's Balboa Port, located at the Canal's Pacific entrance, in 1923. In the introduction to his edited collection of the letters between Wallis and Edward VIII, Michael Bloch argues that this illness was the start of a lifetime of stomach-related problems for Wallis, but it seems to be no more than regular seasickness. Michael Bloch, ed., *Wallis and Edward: Letters, 1931–1937: The Intimate Correspondence of the Duke and Duchess of Windsor* (London: Summit Books, 1986).

† *Vermont Union Journal*, October 8, 1924.

beach at Apra Harbor for the two-day stopover. It may have seemed exotic, but Guam was in fact a closed port operated by the navy and more like a vast dockyard than an island paradise. The women were perfectly safe in contrast to some heightened reports that they had disappeared into the jungle and gotten lost!

In the few days the *Chaumont* was anchored at Guam, Wallis found time to lunch with the outgoing governor and former navy captain Henry Bertrand Price. Price was not exactly scintillating company, being quite obsessive and known to discourse at great length about his twin passions of modern highway technology and self-sufficient agricultural techniques, both of which he desired to implement on the island. Wallis was introduced to breadfruit, mangoes, and custard apples.*

Eventually, in late August, the *Chaumont* reached its final destination, Manila Bay. After a couple of days in the heavily American-influenced Philippines capital, Wallis transferred to a much better-appointed Canadian Pacific Steamship Company liner, the RMS *Empress of Canada*. In 1924, the sleek, white-painted *Empress* had barely been in service for two years since her construction and was by far the largest passenger vessel sailing the transpacific routes from her base in Vancouver, with stops in Japan, the Philippines, Hong Kong, and China. Just a year before, the liner had arrived at Tokyo Harbor a day after the Great Kanto Earthquake, which devastated Tokyo, Yokohama, and the surrounding hinterland. The liner immediately converted into an evacuation ship and rescued nearly a thousand refugees, transporting them to the safer port of Kobe 250 miles away from the quake zone.

Most of those joining the *Empress of Canada* in Manila were what the crew dismissively referred to as "Army and Oil," either being in the military or working for one of the big American oil companies

---

* Again, this contact with Price may have been due to his acquaintance with (the recently deceased in August 1923) Henry Mustin, husband of Wallis's cousin Corinne.

selling into China—Socony, Texaco, Asiatic Petroleum. Wallis had just two days of comparative luxury on the *Empress of Canada*, largely remaining in her well-appointed cabin before she stepped out on the deck and found they had sailed into Hong Kong's Victoria Harbour on September 5. She had been at sea for just over six weeks.

VICTORIA HARBOUR, HONG KONG

To arrive by ship at Hong Kong in 1924 was a formidable experience. Liners approaching from the South China Sea converged into a harbor tightly packed with a veritable flotilla of similar boats, plus sampans, barges, tugs, and cross-harbor ferries, the occasional junk, packet steamers, tramp cargo ships, and warships of any one of a half dozen nations. The floating confusion forced big ships, like the *Empress of Canada*, to constantly blow their foghorns to alert smaller craft who risked being sunk in their wake.

Hong Kong was a dramatic harbor by any standards. The imposing cluster of European stone buildings along the Praya water frontage extended away toward the more densely populated Chinese districts of Kennedy Town and Sheung Wan.* Behind the Praya, the land suddenly rose steeply, verdant and lush, up to what the British dubbed "The Peak," scattered with the houses of the wealthy and the colonial elite.

On the other side of the harbor lay the bustling Kowloon peninsula, dominated by the clock tower at the terminus of the Kowloon-Canton Railway that ran all the way up through the New Territories, across the border into the Republic of China, and

---

* The Praya (from the Portuguese word *praia*, meaning "beach," though used to indicate a waterfront road in Hong Kong at the time) was subsumed sometime after by land reclamation and the creation of the extension of Des Voeux Road (in today's Central District).

up to the metropolis of Canton. Behind the station was the cluster of working-class districts that formed Kowloon—Tsim Sha Tsui, Yau Ma Tei, Mong Kok, Sham Shui Po, Wong Tai Sin, and others that morphed one into another.

Over Hong Kong flew the Union Jack, the island a British Crown Colony wrenched in perpetuity from the Chinese by an unequal treaty in the aftermath of the First Opium War in 1842, with an additional ninety-nine-year lease on Kowloon and the New Territories to follow.*

The novelist Stella Benson, married to an Anglo-Irish functionary of the Chinese Maritime Customs Service in China, had arrived in Hong Kong a couple of years before. Sailing into Victoria Harbour, she captured the beauty and chaos of the scene Wallis would have experienced too: "Alive to the bland blue outlines of the Peak against the sky. Every scarlet and gold flutter of the paper prayers on the importunate sampans that raced for the liner with messages, cheap trinkets, and gifts, begging bowls . . . the heat like stagnant steam."[†]

Despite the imposing gunboats and the giant billboards advertising British and European products that lined the passenger liner docks, what Wallis would have realized was that, British colony or not, she was now in the Far East. At the disembarkation dock, Win, wearing his uniform, rushed forward to greet her as she came down the gangplank. Wallis recalled he looked fit and clear-eyed. He claimed not to have touched a drop of alcohol since he'd heard she was sailing to be with him again.[‡]

He had organized a taxi. They were to have a second honeymoon,

---

* It was of course the expiration of that lease on Kowloon and the New Territories, under the Second Convention of Peking in 1898, that forced the issue of the handover of Hong Kong in 1997. The cession of Hong Kong Island was in perpetuity though ultimately proved impracticable to retain once the lease on Kowloon ran out.

† Stella Benson, *The Poor Man* (London: Macmillan, 1922), 155.

‡ Simpson, *The Heart Has Its Reasons*, 103–4.

to ease Wallis into Hong Kong life. Win ensured that the porters gathered up Wallis's trunks and cases and loaded them into a taxi, and he and Wallis headed for a few nights of luxury and reacquaintance before the reality of navy life in the Far East really began—dull, uninspiring lodgings, a stodgy colonial society, and Win constantly away at sea.

Win, it appeared, was genuinely trying. Attentive, sober, and having organized this romantic vacation. By the time they arrived at their exclusive hotel on the far side of Hong Kong Island, Wallis was already entranced by the East, by Hong Kong—"the almost unreal. Don't-touch-it quality of the island itself."[*]

What was to become her yearlong sojourn in China was beginning.

---

[*] Simpson, *The Heart Has Its Reasons*, 103.

2

A BEAUTIFUL VISION

THE REPULSE BAY HOTEL
HONG KONG ISLAND
BRITISH CROWN COLONY OF HONG KONG
SEPTEMBER–OCTOBER 1924

Mrs E Winfield Spencer has arrived in Hong Kong, China, where her husband, Commander Winfield Spencer, is stationed.

—Announcement in the Washington, DC,
Evening Star, September 6, 1924

After disembarking they took a taxi to the Repulse Bay Hotel. They left the teeming city behind, the taxi rising and dipping across the hilly terrain. Soon cliffs of yellow-and-red soil flanked the road, while ravines opened up on either side to reveal dense green forest or aquamarine sea. As they approached Repulse Bay, the cliffs and trees grew gentler and more inviting. Returning picknickers swept past them in cars filled with flowers, the sound of scattered laughter fading in the wind.

—Eileen Chang (Zhang Ailing), *Love in a Fallen City*

SEPTEMBER 5, 1924–REPULSE BAY

The Barren Rock or the Fragrant Harbour? Just which epithet you chose to apply to the British Crown Colony of Hong Kong in 1924

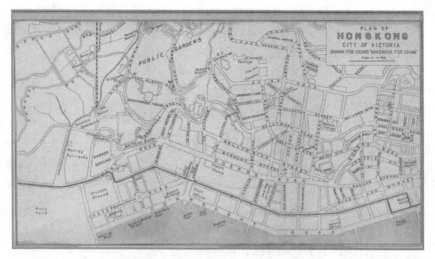

The City of Victoria, Hong Kong Island

Hong Kong and Kowloon

tended to be decided by how you initially experienced the place. Or more precisely from which social strata you were able to observe the colony. Even though Wallis would experience events rendered tumultuous, both by the difficulties of Chinese politics and of her own personal situation in Hong Kong, she later recalled her first glimpses of Victoria Harbour and the island rising up behind as a "beautiful vision."*

The end of September and early October are typically pleasantly warm in Hong Kong, with gentle breezes and a welcome easing of the spirit-sapping humidity of the summer months. The worst of the monsoon season has generally passed, the typhoons receded, the weather usually dry. The skies are invariably a brilliant and cloudless azure blue. It's a different warmth to the uncomfortable mugginess of late summer in Baltimore or the rasping dry heat typical of Coronado. September is perhaps the best time to be a new arrival, to explore the Europeanized streets of Hong Kong Island and what was then called the Victoria City District (today's Central District), to take the funicular tram that angles at times back by a disorienting twenty-five degrees, up to The Peak, and enjoy the views across Victoria Harbour to the peninsula beyond and the densely packed streets of Kowloon-side. Stella Benson took the Peak Tram up the vertiginous hillside and then fictionalized the ride in her 1922 novel, *The Poor Man*:

> The car lifted them all up the hill. Dense dull shrubs bordered the steep track. The houses seemed to lean against the hill. The harbour was unrolled at the foot of the mountain. A fringe of ships, like tentacles round a jellyfish, radiated from the shore. Kowloon, backed by crumpled hills, stretched out a corresponding fringe towards Hong Kong Island.†

---

* Wallis Simpson, *The Heart Has Its Reasons* (London: Michael Joseph, 1956), 103.
† Stella Benson, *The Poor Man* (London: Macmillan, 1922), 158.

Wallis was also to take the funicular up to The Peak, traveling in the first-class cabin as befitted an American officer's wife. Afterward, she and Win walked back down to the harbor along the winding Magazine Gap Road, the gardens of its affluent dwellings heady with tropical blossoms. Wallis became aware that she was a privileged person in the British Empire—white, American, and the wife of a ranking naval officer.

She was now what Great Britain's Royal Navy China Station, which had responsibility for everything from Hong Kong down to Singapore and up to the anchorage at Weihaiwei (Weihai) in northern China, termed a *China Bird*. A wife dutifully following her husband from posting to posting, putting up in a succession of boarding-houses and long-stay hotels, and moving around by navy transports. Additionally, China Bird or not, simply on account of the color of her skin, Wallis had leaped up the social ladder several rungs the moment she disembarked from the *Empress of Canada*. What is more, by virtue of the enhanced pay for officers in overseas postings and the very favorable exchange rates to the US dollar coupled with the wide availability of cheap domestic labor, the Spencers were significantly better off financially than they had been in California.

Win told Wallis he wanted to give her time to adjust to her new Asian home. Hong Kong might not be China proper and may appear to be familiar in many ways, but it wasn't Washington, DC, Baltimore, or San Diego. It was British-run, and the rigid class conventions of its colonial ruler persisted in the colony. It may also have been the case that Win was nervous about how Wallis would react when she saw their relatively small and cheerless US Navy–issued hotel lodgings in Kowloon. So it was in the interests of softening the blow, and no doubt making a genuine effort to reconnect with Wallis, that Win booked them in for a "second honeymoon" at the Repulse Bay Hotel.

Certainly, a trip to Repulse Bay was a good start to any sojourn in Hong Kong. Wallis was to recall that she found her first two weeks reunited with Win to be "utterly satisfying" and, at least initially, she saw the best sides of both Hong Kong and Win.* The new start to their marriage appeared to be working.

The taxi ride to Repulse Bay was effectively Wallis's introduction to tropical climes. The taxi drove through Victoria City passing the racecourse at Happy Valley and then on into the lush green hills of the central belt of Hong Kong Island. Past the cliffs of yellow-and-red soil flanking the road, the ravines on either side scarred with cut channels to allow for water runoff when the intense rains came during typhoon season. Midway across the island, sitting on its spine, was the high point of Jardine's Lookout. In the days of the China clippers, a constant watch was maintained to catch the first glimpse of the sails of the legendary Scottish trading firm of Jardine Matheson's ships arriving from India with opium.

Then the road dipped down toward the southern shore of the island, dense green forest giving way to the curvature of Deep Water Bay and the sparkling South China Sea. The taxi followed the coastal Island Road round to Repulse Bay, a curving half-moon inlet of sandy beach that sloped down to aquamarine waters. The Repulse Bay Hotel sat almost on the beach and was famed as one of the most romantic hotels in the Far East. Beds of fragrant flowers lined the footpaths that twisted throughout the hotel's secluded grounds. There was nothing to disturb the peace at night but a few fishermen's lanterns out at sea and the sweep of the occasional car headlights on the road.

Repulse Bay had been developed as a beach resort early in the century. The hotel had opened for business just four years before the Spencers checked in. The establishment was one of the many luxury properties owned by the wealthy Baghdadi-Jewish trader

---

* Simpson, *The Heart Has Its Reasons*, 104.

and hotelier Elly Kadoorie. With business interests from Baghdad to Shanghai via Bombay and Hong Kong, the Kadoorie portfolio included Hong Kong's major power supply company, China Light and Power, as well as the Peak Tram. They had just broken ground on a large waterfront site in Kowloon, close to the terminus of the Kowloon-Canton Railway and the cross-harbor Star Ferry pier. Kadoorie had designed what he believed would be "the finest hotel east of Suez"—it was to be called the Peninsula. But until Kadoorie's dream hotel was completed, the Repulse Bay Hotel was his landmark property in the colony, looked after by his handpicked American manager, J. H. Taggart.

The hotel was equally popular with international travelers on the grand tour of the East as with expatriates in Hong Kong wanting weekend escapes from the humidity of the central business districts or the claustrophobic clamor of Kowloon-side. It was a favored honeymoon destination for Europeans residing across the Far East, attracting newlyweds from as far afield as northern China and Manchuria and from expatriate communities in Yokohama, Kuala Lumpur, and Singapore.

On arrival, guests passed through the well-laid-out flower gardens with their tinkling fountains to enter the reception at the top of a flight of stone steps. These opened out onto an ornamental rock garden and more low-level hotel buildings and guest bungalows hidden away along winding gravel paths lined with oleander and hibiscus bushes. The rambling establishment was built in what was termed *British Colonial style*—relaxed, genteel, and with an abundance of indoor greenery to cool and refresh the space. None of the hotel buildings were more than a couple of stories tall. Lush, jungly hills rose up behind, while the beach and sea were directly in front with rows of straw-clad, cabana-style huts, each with its own attendant. The curving bay meant the sea was calm. Even in September and October, the sea was easily warm enough to swim comfortably. The bay was dotted with wooden rafts moored in the water for swimmers to rest up, dip their toes in, watch the white-painted paddleboats pass by, or just feel the sun on their skin.

All in all, it was the perfect spot for a voyage-weary Wallis to relax and recuperate. Her trunks were taken to their room and their contents stowed in wardrobes by soft-slippered Chinese porters in American-style bellboy uniforms. The suites had balconies with vine-clad trellises; those overlooking the busy bay caught the sun during the day. The bay itself, with its lovely sandy beach, was said to be a lucky and dragon-friendly spot.* Just offshore could be seen the pleasure boats that circumnavigated Hong Kong Island, stopping at Repulse Bay for beach picnics, the hotel's highly regarded tiffin, or a swim.† Private yachts came and went between Victoria Harbour and Stanley on the far southern side of Hong Kong Island, while wealthy guests arrived by seaplane.

But in the evenings, the bay became quiet, the day-trippers and tourist boats departed, the seaplanes not able to land at night. The hotel gardens were lit with naphtha flares and bamboo lanterns, citrus-smelling incense burned to discourage the mosquitoes. Cocktails were served on the veranda at tables facing out across the bay as the big red sun went down. Wallis was introduced to the Far East colonial tradition of the sundowner, marking the transition from day to evening with a gin and tonic (Hong Kong was always said to be too hot for whiskey).

---

* Considering the flow of dragons, air, and energy is part of the much larger phenomenon of feng shui, widely practiced then and now in Hong Kong. Repulse Bay is thought to have exceptionally good feng shui ("wind-water") and sometimes Chinese geomancy, the ancient Chinese traditional practice, that claims to use energy forces to harmonize individuals with their surrounding environment.

† Wallis would come to know and enjoy the colonial tradition of tiffin in Asia. From an Indian word for a "light meal," in Hong Kong and China tiffin was the localized equivalent of afternoon tea. It could be very filling and often involved alcohol too.

The couple's suite was open to the bay. Gentle nighttime breezes wafted through the mosquito nets that covered the bed; the sound of lapping waves drifted into the room. They took breakfast late in the morning and tiffin by the beach. The hotel's sumptuous evening buffet, which always included a curry, was a Hong Kong institution.

Win had chosen well. Repulse Bay was the perfect place for a second honeymoon, an ideal locale in which to rekindle an ailing marriage. Wallis was hopeful. There had been a time when they were very much in love. When she first met Win in Florida, she'd found him instantly charming, reckless, and brave—the early flimsy US Navy planes crashed regularly in both the sea and on land, and fatalities were not uncommon. Wallis witnessed two bad crashes while at Pensacola.

But Wallis would remember that their first honeymoon at White Sulphur Springs had initially gone well too. West Virginia was a dry state, but then Win had smuggled in some gin, and soon his morose, aggressive, and abusive side revealed itself. This time around, Win largely stayed off the booze and remained good-tempered.

LIFE KOWLOON-SIDE

The newly reunited Spencers couldn't stay ensconced in their Repulse Bay idyll, listening to the cicadas and sipping sundowners indefinitely. Win had secured only a brief leave for Wallis's arrival. Now they had to move into their assigned lodgings before Win returned to the *Pampanga*. This would be something of a comedown after the luxury of Repulse Bay.

Back to Victoria City, then the cross-harbor ferry to the jostling, densely packed Tsim Sha Tsui district in Kowloon, distinctly more Chinese in flavor than what Wallis had seen of Hong Kong Island.

The Kowloon Hotel—the Kow Loon Chow Din to the locals—provided what would now be called a long-stay apartment, with a communal dining room and washing facilities. Even in Coronado, the Spencers had had their own quarters. Gwen Dew, an American newspaper correspondent in Hong Kong some years later, recalled the Kowloon Hotel as a "very second-rate hostelry."[*] It had been built just the year before, in 1923, the third hotel on the same site on Kowloon's Hankow Road, which ran north for three blocks up from the harbor close to where the newly excavated construction site for Elly Kadoorie's Peninsula Hotel was just beginning work. Next door were the Delin Apartments (called the Tak Lun building in Cantonese), and opposite was Tkachenko's Restaurant and adjoining cake shop run by some Russian exiles from the Bolshevik Revolution.[†]

Their rooms were cramped, utilitarian, rather dank and dismal, with only limited natural light. Those facing the alleyways at the rear of the building had to keep their windows closed to prevent malodorous breezes wafting in. Human waste was often left out in buckets for the night soil collectors. It would be over the border and fertilizing the fields of Kwangtung by dawn. Though the smells weren't all bad—the more enticing aromas of coriander, anise, soy sauce, and barbecued pork wafted in from the street-food vendors. But the regularly backed-up drains could be overwhelming. Those residents in the know kept camphor-scented handkerchiefs ready if they had to venture to the back of the hotel.

In Coronado, the newlyweds had lived in functional, unaesthetic, but spacious navy accommodation. Land was not, of course, at such

---

[*] Gwen Dew, *Prisoner of the Japs* (New York: Alfred A. Knopf, 1943), 130. Admittedly, Dew saw the hotel a dozen or so years after Wallis had lived there. But all indications are that it was never anything special.

[†] Interestingly, not that far away and on the other side of the Kowloon peninsula linking Mong Kok and Kowloon Tong was the recently finished Prince Edward Road, named after the Prince of Wales following his brief 1922 visit to the colony.

a premium in California as in Hong Kong. In Coronado, they had a living room, three bedrooms, two bathrooms, a kitchen, and a cleaning maid. Hong Kong was just one bedroom, a living room, one bathroom, a small kitchenette, and a "number one boy" to assist with the chores around the apartment.* While Hong Kong was a step up in Win's career, it appeared to be a step down on the accommodation ladder.

Win reported back for duty, and Wallis was left to contemplate their new home. Inside, the rooms were hot and dark with no views out the windows to speak of. Clothes-washing facilities were shared, or clothes could be sent out to small laundries behind the hotel, while "sew-sew women" set up their stalls on the rear alleyway, mending or adjusting clothing.

She would hear the chatter of rapid-fire Cantonese on the streets downstairs, the voluble spitting and loud clearing of throats, the constant clack-clack of mah-jongg tiles, the hawker cries in the markets. And in those markets, there was a host of new sensations to taste—Cantonese *yum cha*, delicate porcelain bowls of green tea and dim sum, *garoupa* fish dumplings, peeled kumquats and lychees, pastries filled with red bean paste, *pastel de nata*–style egg tarts inspired by nearby Portuguese Macao, hot napkins always proffered before and after meals.

Wallis valiantly tried to make friends with the Scottish woman who acted as the Kowloon Hotel's housekeeper.† Mrs. Blake was in her midfifties and referred to herself as the hotel's "matron." She lived there with her husband, who managed the Victoria Cinematograph Theatre on Des Voeux Road across the harbor in Victoria City. Mrs. Blake directed her to local stores that sold European and American supplies. Wallis was able to purchase what she needed to cook small

---

* "Boys" in Hong Kong and along the China coast could often be men in their forties, fifties, or older.

† Wallis remembered her as English, though she was Scottish.

meals in their rooms, though given the heat, the butter was invariably rancid while the milk always tasted off.

Already by the 1920s, Hong Kong was losing out as a way station for the China trade to the brasher, more rapacious, more freebooting International Settlement of Shanghai 750 miles up the coast. This left the colony increasingly as a garrison town, a Royal Navy–dominated port of shipbuilding, dry-docking, and maritime insurance as the old businesses of opium and tea ebbed away.

Wallis seems to have spent much time alone in Hong Kong in her first weeks there. In Coronado, there had been a bevy of fellow navy wives available for dinner, drinks, bridge, the sharing of gripes and gossip. But in Hong Kong, the number of US Navy personnel was relatively small—the South China Patrol, really just a couple of small gunboats—and most of the crew single men and not officers.

Wallis had an initial shock when tidying their rooms to find two empty gin bottles in the bathroom. She asked the number one boy about them, but he had little to no English, and Wallis had not a single word of Cantonese. Eventually, he made a brushing motion across his mouth and Wallis realized, with a sense of relief, that the gin bottles were intended for the sterilized water necessary for brushing your teeth. The servant took them when they were empty and refilled them, making sure the water had been boiled.

Wallis had found herself Kowloon-side, in the general area of Tsim Sha Tsui, a bustling district, facing across to Hong Kong Island and only a twenty-minute ride on the regular Star Ferry. It was, then as today, a commercial and shopping district, with a few pockets of light industry. However, in those days, there were many more street markets than today, replaced by modern shopping malls. Wallis could wander past the various itinerant vendors claiming their roadside pitches—letter writers, fortune tellers, the ubiquitous cobblers and sew-sew women, as well as earwax removers and (a service few foreigners ever recorded trying) eyelid scrapers. If Wallis needed reminding that disease was ever present, even in British Hong Kong, she would daily pass the metal rat bins affixed to lampposts where citizens could deposit dead rats to be tested, allowing the authorities to rapidly monitor any possible outbreaks of bubonic plague, which still occasionally appeared in Hong Kong in the 1920s.

All the colony appeared to be a frenetic construction site in 1924, a previously unprecedented rate of new building, land clearance, and reclamation as the mainland hills of Kowloon and the New Territories were leveled and the earth used as landfill. Massive construction projects were underway right on Wallis's doorstep on Hankow Road, creating the new districts we now know as Yau Ma Tei and Mong Kok. The intrepid American travel writer Harry A. Franck visited Hong Kong in 1924, after an absence of a decade, and noted, "Slowly the hills of the mainland, as of Hong Kong itself, are being chopped and blasted away to fill in the hollows and give place to expanding Kowloon and its many suburbs, cluttered with elaborate bamboo scaffolds."*

Farther north up into Kowloon, things became noticeably more rural, less developed, and distinctly more low-rise than today. A young British schoolgirl in the 1920s, Barbara Anslow and her family moved to the district just a few years after Wallis, taking a lease on a first-floor flat on Cameron Road, not far from the Kowloon Hotel. The young Barbara recalled huge flying cockroaches, centipedes ten to fifteen centimeters long, and a mostly Chinese and Portuguese (Macanese) community.†

---

* Harry A. Franck, *Roving Through Southern China* (New York: Century, 1925), 212.
† Barbara Anslow, *Tin Hats and Rice: A Diary of Life as a Hong Kong Prisoner of War, 1941–1945* (Hong Kong: Blacksmith, 2018). Anslow's family moved to Kowloon in 1927.

COLONIAL SOCIETY

In those first few weeks in Kowloon, Wallis was never quite sure when Win would be at home and when he'd be at sea. The South China Patrol was not much perhaps compared to the size of the Royal Navy's China Station, but the US Navy's growing strength in the South China Sea was generally welcomed by Great Britain as a supportive alliance of Western power along the China coast. Win was often at sea or on river patrol, but the *Pampanga* typically only went away for a few days between Hong Kong and Canton. Still, Win claimed he was bored with his command. He described the aged *Pampanga* as the "lousiest ship in the navy."* He still saw it as an exile from his real love, flying.

With Win so much away at sea, Wallis was left to make her own way in the British colony. Aside from the street markets, the night markets, tailors' shops, and a few parks, there was little to recommend Kowloon-side to Wallis. As she would discover later, Hong Kong's social life was incredibly staid compared to her future experiences of Shanghai and Peking. Her time was spent with one or another navy wife playing cooncan rummy or alone playing solitaire.

Win was not much for socializing beyond drinking and carousing in taverns. On the few times they went out socially, then more often than not, the Hongkong Hotel bar was their destination.† Wallis could sit and observe the hotel's large ballroom, famously formal, though (annoyingly to Wallis, who loved to dance) Win refused to step onto the dance floor. Passing through the colony a couple of years earlier, W. Somerset Maugham had noted that preferred drinks were brandy and soda for men, gin and Angostura bitters (a pink gin) for the ladies. Sparkling Moselle or Asti Spumante were

---

* Charles Higham, *Wallis: Secret Lives of the Duchess of Windsor* (London: Sidgwick & Jackson, 1988), 30.

† Spellings of Hong Kong as *Hongkong* were common up until the early 1950s.

served as substitutes for champagne. Wallis might have preferred the livelier and more ethnically mixed, Parsi-run King Edward Hotel (opened in 1902 and named for Edward VII) on neighboring Des Voeux Road, but Win, it seems, preferred European company.

Maugham stirred the pot of Hong Kong gossip with his novel *The Painted Veil*, first serialized in *Cosmopolitan* magazine in November 1924, just as Wallis arrived in Hong Kong. The novel caused a sensation, and it's safe to assume it was pretty much the main topic of conversation in the Hongkong Hotel bar that winter.

Kitty Lane, a pretty upper-middle-class debutante, approximately the same age as Wallis at the time, is married to the rather "odd" and dry Dr. Lane. She is bored in the colony and indulges in a potentially scandalous affair with the handsome and urbane assistant colonial secretary, Charlie Townsend. A Hong Kong couple, not known to Maugham but who by chance were of the same name, brought a libel case against the publishers and won. Subsequent editions changed the name to Fane. Then, equally outraged, the actual assistant colonial secretary in Hong Kong also threatened legal action, and Maugham had to change the location from Hong Kong to the fictional town of Tching-Yen for several editions. But the point, of course, was taken by readers. Hong Kong was a place where bored white women indulged in afternoon trysts with men who weren't their partners while their husbands were away running the empire in one form or another. East of Suez was where moral compasses started to malfunction.

How Wallis coped with the suffocating British class system that underwrote social mores and manners in colonial Hong Kong is not clear. Mostly, she managed to avoid it. The American community in Hong Kong was small but perhaps just about enough for the short time she was there. The self-important Peak social whirl existed in its own airy rarity of British Establishment exclusion, and Wallis as an American naval officer's wife wasn't going to penetrate it even if she wished to.

Wallis did cross the harbor on the Star Ferry on her own. She visited Victoria City, the new-style department stores, the charming Mid-Levels streets of local emporiums and antique stores. She would get out of the midday heat into the European-style hotels for tiffin. The main throughfare of the Queen's Road offered modern retail stores alongside traditional Chinese funeral directors, gold dealers, and medicine stores. There were the steeply rising side streets of market stalls up to the Mid-Levels to explore—Pottinger Street (known to the Chinese as Stone Slabs Street for its cobbled steps) along with the fragrant Flower Street (Wyndham Street) crowded with florists. Des Voeux Road was a mass of clanging trams, automobile horns, and bells from passing rickshaws. Chater Road was lined with Chinese bookshops as well as having the best English-language bookstore in Kelly & Walsh, surrounded by myriad newspaper stands. Jardine's Arcade was home to curio shops selling ceramic finger bowls and tin spittoons. Pedder Street provided some arcaded shade from the sun but meant circumventing many beggars, often children, and refugees from the infighting and strikes still growing around Canton. The rise in street beggars from the mainland was to be the first indication of the extent of the chaos in Kwangtung, a situation that would soon become all too apparent to Wallis and Win.

Regular stops included Watson's pharmacy for toiletries, the Lane Crawford and Sincere department stores for imported goods, Whiteaway, Laidlaw & Co. for light raincoats and sandals suitable to the Hong Kong climate, and then into the alleyways of inexpensive tailors behind Pedder Street for handmade summer dresses. Finally, the colonnaded frontage of the Hongkong Hotel, its fans, and some cool air.

The Hongkong Hotel, modeled on the latest London establishments, was the most reputable place for a white woman dining alone or with friends in the 1920s (though the hotel banned Chinese women from the restaurant and the dance floor at the time).[*] Wallis

---

[*] Chinese women were barred according to Francis Rose's memoir *Saying Life: The Memoirs of Sir Francis Rose* (London: Cassell, 1961), 273.

met other navy wives for a cocktail in the bar before tiffin, or, if Win were ashore, for dinner in Gripps, the hotel's famous restaurant. Gripps was cavernous and kept passably cool by huge ceiling fans on constant rotation. Barnlike and open, everyone could see everyone, and in this tight-knit colony, everyone knew everyone. This is where the tittle-tattle of Hong Kong's petty social vendettas played out, where affairs were discussed and careers destroyed just as Maugham portrayed so scandalously in *The Painted Veil*.

November is a relatively temperate month in Hong Kong, so the roof garden and tearooms at the Sincere department store on Des Voeux Road was another popular spot for navy wives—the fare was light, and the terrace afforded a view. But mostly, Wallis dined at Gripps when escaping Kowloon-side for Victoria. It was welcoming, she was in the company of other navy wives, and it was respectable, even if the food was distinctly British-style—"boiled, boiled, and then boiled once again for luck," as a visiting American remarked.[*] However, Wallis—always a great people-watcher as well as enjoying being seen—liked the place.[†]

There were also day trips. Back out to Repulse Bay and the next cove along, Deep Water Bay, for swimming. Down to Big Wave Bay or slightly farther to Shek O on the southeastern tip of Hong Kong Island for Sunday lunches of grilled prawns by the sea and tennis (a game Wallis enjoyed but claimed she never mastered). The bustling fishing village of Aberdeen with shoulder-to-shoulder sampans crammed into the typhoon shelter harbor, whole "sea gypsy" families aboard, three, sometimes four generations down to the newborn

[*] Franck, *Roving Through Southern China*, 213.
[†] The Hongkong Hotel and Gripps Restaurant that Wallis knew were largely destroyed in a fire in 1926. Despite a pledge by the colonial authorities to improve fire safety and the strength of the fire brigade in Hong Kong, a second fire consumed the hotel in 1929, with over a dozen fatalities. Incidentally, in 1926, Royal Navy sailors in port helped the fire brigade tackle the blaze. Among them was Prince George, Duke of Kent, the younger brother of Edward VIII and George VI.

babies strapped to their mothers' backs. Silver Mine Bay Beach on Lantao (Lantau) Island also offered a pleasant breezy ferry ride and a hike to a beautiful waterfall.

And then back across the harbor. Home to the waiting rickshaw pullers at the Star Ferry Terminal and to Hankow Road and once again the confines of the Kowloon Hotel.

TROUBLE IN KOWLOON

One night, Win announced that they had been invited to dine with colleagues of his at their lodgings. They had spent little time in company together since arriving. Wallis was excited, both to meet Win's fellow South China Patrol officers and to make more of an inroad into American society in the colony. At the time Win had said he'd be home to accompany her to the party, he failed to appear. Wallis had bathed and dressed. She sat waiting patiently in their rooms. She waited . . . and waited. No word came, and no sign of Win either. Eventually, Wallis sent the number one boy over to their hosts with the excuse that Win had been unexpectedly delayed and that they should not wait for them to start dinner.

Perhaps inevitably, Win's self-proclaimed dry spell was ending dramatically. Wallis had noted that after their few days at Repulse Bay, he had become increasingly "moody, jealous and impossible" once again.[*] She also noted the financial hit his carousing made to his pay packet. As was the convention along the China coast from Hong Kong to Shanghai and up to the north China naval anchorages at Weihaiwei, Win could sign for drinks with chits (promissory notes recording sums owed to establishments) collected at the end of the month and which saw a considerable amount of his pay deducted by his creditors.

---

[*] Simpson, *The Heart Has Its Reasons*, 105.

It all came to a head in the early hours of the morning when Win eventually arrived back at the hotel. He staggered through their rooms, knocking over ornaments and clattering into the furniture, quite obviously thoroughly inebriated. Wallis, who had waited up, managed to put him to bed where he promptly passed out. The next morning, hungover and morose, Win offered no explanation for his disappearance the night before. After having slipped off the wagon (if he had ever truly been on it) and losing his self-control, as Wallis recalled in her memoirs, "he seemed incapable of regaining it."* It was a downward spiral of drunkenness and meanness.

When in port, Win began to stay out later and later and return to the hotel less and less frequently, even when Wallis knew he was ashore. Where he stayed these evenings is unclear—the unproven intimation is that he was with prostitutes. When he did return to Kowloon, he was usually paralytic and increasingly abusive (at this stage, it appears verbally rather than physically). Several times, he dragged Wallis along, embarrassing her by taking her to sailor bars in the red-light district of Wan Chai or, as Wallis says in *The Heart Has Its Reasons*, "sing-song houses" in the Mid-Levels, where he caroused with the girls.

It is often said that Win dragged Wallis through Hong Kong's brothels. Some biographers of Wallis have suggested that these were humiliating tours. Caroline Blackwood claims that Win frequented brothels in Hong Kong, forced Wallis to accompany him, and even fondled prostitutes while Wallis watched. However, while his tastes for low bars and his verbal and physical violence are attested to, this is not substantiated.†

---

* Simpson, *The Heart Has Its Reasons*, 105.
† Blackwood makes these assertions, with no sources, in *The Last of the Duchess* (London: Vintage, 2012), 169. Certainly such accusations were part of the China Dossier gossip but were perhaps not considered printable prior to the 1990s, when Blackwood originally published. It does seem Win frequented and forced Wallis on a number of occasions to visit some fairly rough bars.

Others interchange the terms *brothel/bordello* and *singsong house*. It's important to understand the difference. Singsong house women were entertainers and worked in these establishments by choice rather than coercion, perhaps (though of course there are many cultural differences) more akin to a geisha establishment in Japan. This was definitely not the same as brothels (licensed and legal in Hong Kong in 1924) that employed prostitutes who may or may not have been working there voluntarily.* Rather than the later-concocted China Dossier legend of Wallis as possibly a prostitute in Hong Kong, the basis for these stories was the embarrassment of Win drinking to excess and Wallis being uncomfortable in the surroundings of their tedious late-night bar crawls.

TROUBLE IN CANTON

Perhaps then it came as a relief when, in early October, the South China Patrol was issued with urgent new orders. Fierce fighting had broken out in Canton between Nationalist forces loyal to Dr. Sun Yat-sen, the father of China's republican revolution, and those loyal to the city's merchant guild. Skirmishing was occurring throughout the city, fires were being set and spreading fast in the higgledy-piggledy backstreets of the mostly wooden old town, accusations of Russian communist involvement were being bandied about, orders supposedly coming to Sun direct from Moscow. The vulnerable foreign concessions on the small enclave of Shameen Island had erected barricades, closing off the two narrow bridges that connected them to the main metropolis.

Douglas Jenkins, the American consul general in Canton, was

---

* European-staffed brothels were not outlawed in the colony until 1932, and Chinese-staffed establishments followed in 1935, after which, of course, clandestine venues remained outside the law.

a stocky and tough diplomat who rarely minced his words. Originally from South Carolina, Jenkins had trained as a journalist before entering the State Department. He'd served in Riga during the Russian Revolution and then the Manchurian city of Harbin as it overflowed with Russian refugees from the Bolsheviks before being posted to Canton in 1921. Jenkins declared the situation in the city as "critical" and "extremely tense," emphasizing the anti-foreign nature of many of the protests threatening the small European and American community on Shameen.* Jenkins was concerned for his safety and the safety of all Americans in Canton. So he called up the South China Patrol.

Win received his orders to sail for Canton on October 8. The *Pampanga* was ready to depart a few days later. It was a month since Wallis had arrived in Hong Kong. Now Win was about to leave for a lengthy river patrol with the *Pampanga* up to Canton, where the strikes and rioting might mean the foreign community needed armed protection, or possibly rapid evacuation.

Wallis, who appears to have always attempted conciliation and hoped things would change, recalled that their original plan had been to enjoy dinner with friends and then spend the few days of leave together before he embarked. Instead, for the next couple of nights, Win headed out on the town on a two-day drunken spree. Finally, he returned rather more sober, though apparently no less morose, in order to pack his kit bag for the voyage.[†]

Wallis decided to confront Win. She asked him if his fall off the wagon, his return to the bottle, was somehow her fault. What had changed since their idyllic few days in Repulse Bay just a few weeks previous? She claimed his answer was that he couldn't explain what made him drink to excess: "It's just me. Something lets go—like the

---

* "American Hit in China Clash," *Detroit Free Press*, October 17, 1924.
† Simpson, *The Heart Has Its Reasons*, 104.

control cables of a plane."[*] It was also the case that Win's drinking was exacerbated just before he embarked on the *Pampanga* or just after he'd returned to port. The simple reason for this was that in 1924, US Navy ships (unlike Royal Navy vessels) were dry, with no alcohol allowed aboard. While this rule may not always have been rigidly observed, for an officer to be seen drinking, and certainly to be drunk, would have been a serious issue.

In hindsight, it was perhaps fortuitous that Win was ordered to Canton. His drunken rages had been escalating, his verbal abuse more frequent, the degrading nighttime bar crawls becoming more commonplace, and it was perhaps only a matter of time before his behavior escalated and he started to use his fists again.

The next day, Win left to begin the *Pampanga*'s patrol up the coast to the Pearl River Delta and the besieged enclave of Shameen.

Then a strange decision was made. Wallis began making arrangements to follow Win to Canton. In her memoirs, Wallis acts as if this were an everyday thing—for a navy wife to follow her husband into a seriously deteriorating political situation in southern China. But this is something that would have been quite out of the ordinary at the time. Indeed, it was a matter of principle among the foreign powers that white women and children were promptly evacuated from potential danger spots.

A plausible explanation is that Wallis was being employed as an informal courier for the US Navy in China. Though the American consulates in Hong Kong and Canton could still just about communicate by radio telegram, postal services between the two cities were highly erratic and unsecure, the rail lines were disrupted, the coastal sea routes prone to seaman strikes and random—often extremely violent and deadly—pirate attacks. New ways of moving information between America's consulates were urgently needed. Navy

---

* Simpson, *The Heart Has Its Reasons*, 104.

wives were one potential answer to the problem—trusted, assumed "cleared" as officers' partners, and readily available. They became informal postmen, taking documents between US diplomats, embassies, and consulates around the region in the face of a collapsing transport and telecommunications infrastructure. Quite simply, the only way for US Navy intelligence in Hong Kong to send documents to their counterparts in Canton, and vice versa, was by hand.

This appears to be the first—though not the last—time Wallis was entrusted with carrying documents between various outposts of the US diplomatic presence in China. These were ad hoc arrangements, informally arrived at, and though it has been hinted at by other biographers (notably Charles Higham), there is no paper trail that has so far come to light.* However, I would suggest that there is ultimately no other sensible way of explaining Wallis's itinerary across China from Hong Kong in late 1924 and 1925 than the suggestion that she agreed to transport documents for the US authorities in Hong Kong and mainland China.

Wallis was about to leave the safety of the British colony of Hong Kong for the growing chaos and fratricidal infighting of republican China. The country had been a republic for barely a decade. The messy process of bringing the imperial reign of the Qing dynasty to a close and forging China's first republic was still ongoing with factional infighting across the country.

From the far northern plains of Manchuria bordering the newly Sovietized Russia and Japanese-occupied Korea, across to the wild and restive western lands of Muslim Sinkiang (Xinjiang), the entire eastern region of China radiating from Shanghai and up the mighty Yangtze River, and down into the fertile tropical southern provinces

---

* Higham, *Wallis*.

around Canton, warlords and republican troops supporting one faction (often referred to as *cliques* in China) or another skirmished constantly, interfering with business, taxing local merchants, disrupting logistics and communications, and destroying crops.

Into the national power vacuum stepped all manner of kidnap gangs, pirates, bandits, and mercenaries for hire. And all the time, the foreign powers—the European "Great Powers" as well as Japan, the Soviet Union, and the United States—hovered, demanding additional treaty port rights and land grabbing. Western arms dealers fueled the conflicts by making fortunes arming the warlord-generals.

The situation in southern China, accentuated by a growing anti-foreigner rhetoric, could turn extremely nasty for the relatively few Europeans and Americans resident in the city, just as it had done slightly less than twenty-five years previously during the Boxer Uprising in northern China. Many questioned whether China, as an entity, would hold together or might fracture apart into multiple civil wars among warlord-controlled states, each constantly at the throats of the others.

Win was sailing into this chaos, and Wallis was about to follow him.

Wallis was never to really know Hong Kong in the way she came briefly to know Shanghai and, during her slightly longer sojourn, Peking. In Hong Kong, she was a US Navy wife, a China Bird, and so confined mostly to US Navy company and the drab long-stay Kowloon Hotel, left to her own company and devices most of the time.

Additionally, Win was a man of rather base tastes—low sailor bars, backstreet taverns, middling hotel taprooms, and chophouses at best. Wallis never even got to live in Victoria City but was confined to the more working-class and cramped Kowloon-side. Apart from their brief early stay at the Repulse Bay Hotel, Hong Kong was for

Wallis a dreary posting with no social elevation, limited intellectual company, and little opportunity to explore.

But though she didn't know it in October 1924, Hong Kong was to be a mere transitory way station on the road to further adventures in distinctly more cosmopolitan and less class-bound cities than Hong Kong. Adventures she would embark upon alone but find willing companions along the way.

3

AN ISLAND AMID
REVOLUTIONARY FERMENT

BRITISH CONCESSION
SHAMEEN ISLAND
CANTON
MID-LATE OCTOBER 1924

At 5 P.M. an additional wireless message appeared:
SHAMEEN. THE ELECTRIC LIGHT HAS FAILED. THE
WHOLE CONCESSION IS IN DARKNESS. THE BRIDGES
FORTIFIED & PROTECTED BY BARBED WIRE. THEY ARE
LIT BY SEARCHLIGHTS FROM THE GUNBOATS.
—André Malraux, *Les Conquérants*

There can't be any gossip or scandal on Shameen, because we all live
in one another's pockets and know one another's history from the
day we or our ancestors landed in China.
—Harry A. Franck, *Roving Through Southern China*

OCTOBER 1924–NORTH TO CANTON

After sailing at full speed from Hong Kong, Win had arrived in
Canton at night on Wednesday, October 15. Now the *Pampanga* and
its sister ship the *Sacramento* were moored up alongside the foreign

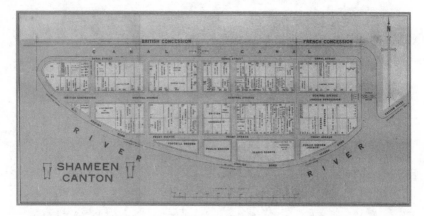

Shameen Island

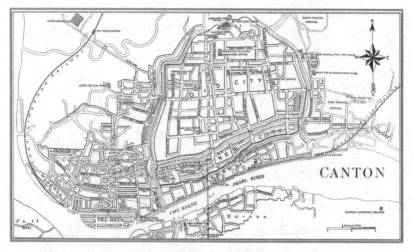

The City of Canton

concessions on Shameen Island, prominently flying the Stars and Stripes. Their guns pointed across the canal toward the crowded central districts of Canton.

Barely a fortnight later, at the end of October, Wallis, who had remained in Hong Kong, received her official permission from the

South China Patrol to follow Win up the coast to Shameen. The city was in the grip of violent strikes and daily street fighting. The so-called Canton Merchants' Volunteer Corps was battling it out with the Sun Yat-sen government–backed Nationalist Revolutionary Army in what became known as the 1924 Canton Merchants' Corps Uprising.

The corps of approximately thirteen thousand men had originally been formed by local merchants in 1911 to protect their premises, homes, and godowns during the upheavals as the Qing collapsed and the new Republic of China was formed. In the dozen or more years since, the corps had largely remained politically neutral, but since the start of 1924 had become concerned that the republican government was too sympathetic to communism and too influenced by the Soviet Union.

The imposition of additional government taxes led to the corps establishing a defense headquarters. Throughout the summer, the situation became tense, with corps-purchased munition shipments seized, the arrests of key members, and a nighttime curfew imposed throughout Canton. Many of the city's districts decided to join the anti-tax movement in support of the Merchants' Corps. The situation appeared to calm in late summer but flared up again in early October when local communists pledged support for Sun's government and issued the rallying cry, "Beat the Merchants' Corps." The corps retaliated with posters urging their supporters to "Beat Sun's Government." Fights broke out between labor activists and corps members, rooftop snipers from both sides picked off enemies, the Nationalists set strategic fires, and things escalated dangerously. The US consulate on Shameen estimated a thousand dead. Various threats were issued to foreigners in Canton (believed to be generally siding with the corps), and many in the city retreated to the relative safety of Shameen, now bolstered by the British, American, and French navies from Hong Kong and Indochina.

As Wallis arranged passage north to join Win in Canton, the

city was reportedly eerily quiet as a standoff emerged between the Merchants' Corps on one side and Sun's government, backed by Sun's new Nationalist Revolutionary Army, led by Chiang Kai-shek and his Whampoa Military Academy cadets, on the other.

Sorting out how exactly to get Wallis from Hong Kong to Shameen had required some time. Canton was linked directly to the British colony by a train line, the Kowloon-Canton Railway, or KCR. However, the strikes, fighting, and socialist revolutionary ferment around the great Cantonese city meant train services were severely disrupted, prone to sudden cancellation, track damage, and even bandit attack. What had previously been a comfortable and safe journey—a day trip or weekend break, from Kowloon Station up through the New Territories, across the border at Shum Chun (Shenzhen), and on into Canton—was erratic and, when operating, had become potentially perilous, and by late 1924, it was no longer considered suitable for unaccompanied white women.

The second option was coastal steamer. Wallis first contacted the offices of the Hongkong, Canton & Macao Steamboat Company to try to board the regular passenger service up the coast. But as with the trains, the steamers were erratic, added to which that area of the South China Sea was commonly described as "pirate-infested." Republican China had little naval power and left pirate suppression largely to the Royal Navy. The passenger steamers sailed up to the Pearl River Estuary unescorted and so were easy prey for the pirates who holed up in the legions of bays, inlets, and barely mapped coastal villages of Kwangtung Province.

The early 1920s had also seen the emergence of a new and alarming pirate tactic—the "passenger ploy." Wallis cannot have failed to have read about this, as it was so regularly employed at the time and demands for stern action to curtail the practice were regular and vocal with almost daily op-eds in the Hong Kong newspapers demanding action. After a period of relative calm since a peak in pirate activity around the time of World War I, it seemed by 1922 that the South China pirates were returning in force. And they were moving with the times. The Royal Navy and the Hong Kong Marine Police now had significantly more and faster boats, as well as submarines, to counter the pirates' outdated traditional junks. So, as ever when organized crime is faced with advances in crime-fighting techniques, the pirates switched tactics. Catching up with or waylaying steamers, boarding, and raiding them became passé, a fast route to imprisonment at best and a swift beheading at worst. Hence the passenger ploy.[*]

The case of the *Sui-an* was typical. On a Sunday afternoon in late 1922, the coastal steamer SS *Sui-an* had departed Macao for its regular journey to Hong Kong, fifty miles away. The ship was at capacity, carrying four hundred Chinese and a further sixty European passengers. An hour or so out of Macao, several dozen Chinese passengers, both men and women, revealed themselves to actually be heavily armed pirates. Their leader, wearing a Western-style tailored suit and accompanied by a smartly dressed woman on his arm, strolled out of first class, pulled a revolver, fired it into the air, and took command. The *Sui-an*'s crew put up a fight. But the pirates were ruthless. Two armed Indian guards were killed, their bodies thrown overboard. Other crew members and a couple of resisting passengers were badly beaten. The passengers were then systematically robbed of their money, jewelry, and any valuables. The pirates changed course away from Hong Kong and headed up the Chinese coast, where they rendezvoused with a number of sampans and then promptly disappeared into the bewildering array of inlets along the coast.

---

[*] Paul French, "History of Real Pirates Who Dressed as Passengers to Hijack and Plunder Hong Kong Ships in the South China Sea," *South China Morning Post Magazine*, May 29, 2022.

Wallis would have taken little comfort in the fact that new regulations aimed at countering the passenger ploy meant coastal steamers now had more armed guards and claimed to be searching boarding passengers (at least Chinese passengers) more thoroughly. Despite these new protocols, ships continued to be targeted by pirates posing as passengers and commandeering them at sea. Things had certainly deteriorated dramatically since Wallis's fellow American in China, ever-upbeat Shanghai advertising man Carl Crow, updated his bestselling *Travelers' Handbook for China* just a couple of years earlier in 1921:

> For the benefit of timid persons who may forego the pleasure of a visit to China because of alarming stories it may be well to point out that these dangers are very small. It should be remembered that China covers a very large territory, and brigands may ravage some parts of it without in any way disturbing the sections ordinarily visited by foreigners. All in all, travel is as safe in China as in any other part of the world. Robbers and pirates exist, of course, and there is usually a revolution or rebellion going on in some part of the country, but these things add zest rather than danger to the journey.[*]

With recent incidences of both steamer guards and passengers being shot, beaten, or thrown overboard at sea, Wallis could not have felt quite so blasé about the threat of piracy.

But ultimately, it didn't matter. Because of the strikes and street fighting in Canton, all coastal steamer services were suddenly suspended, and the SS *Kinshan* had been ordered to remain in port, whereupon the majority of its Chinese crew had promptly deserted to join the strikes. To leave British-controlled Hong Kong and enter

---

[*] Carl Crow, *Travelers' Handbook for China* (Shanghai: Hwa-Mei Book Concern, 1921).

the Republic of China now required her to secure a special US Navy travel pass to ease border controls.

In the middle of this maelstrom, the US Navy appears to have devoted considerable effort to ensuring Wallis Spencer could get to Canton. With the KCR considered too dangerous and steamer services suspended, she would have to travel as a passenger on a naval vessel. But there was a slight complication with this seemingly obvious idea. US Navy regulations strictly forbade women aboard warships.[*]

Consequently, a hasty arrangement appears to have been reached with a friendly British captain to transport Wallis up to Canton on a gunboat of His Majesty's Royal Navy. There was no shortage of British ships in port in Hong Kong that October, as the colony was the winter base of the Royal Navy China Station. Additionally, and crucially, the British were willing to carry her and had, as Wallis later noted, "no such stuffy attitude towards women on-board."[†] Again, in her memoirs, Wallis does not suggest this was an extraordinary situation. Yet the effort to get Wallis to Canton, employing the Royal Navy (and them to agree) seems excessive simply for a wife to visit her husband.

Wallis set sail for Canton.

THE VICTORIA HOTEL–SHAMEEN ISLAND

When the early foreign China traders returned to Canton after the First Opium War (1839–1842), they found their factories and residences burned down. Under the unequal postwar Treaty of Nanking

---

[*] And continued to do, with some exceptions for nursing staff, until 1994.
[†] Wallis Simpson, *The Heart Has Its Reasons* (London: Michael Joseph, 1956), 105.

(Nanjing) between the defeated Qing dynasty and Great Britain, Shameen was forcibly ceded as a place of foreign residence, a so-called treaty port. In reality, it was little more than a sandy mud flat separated from the western suburbs of Canton by a narrow canal. Indeed, *Shameen* literally means "sandy surface." Occupied by the foreign traders and new consulates, Shameen soon developed. Wooden piles were driven into the river and filled with sand. On these foundations was constructed an embankment of solid granite, which eventually developed into the island's recreation ground with a few streets laid out surrounding it. Tiny Shameen became Canton's only defendable foreign enclave. If times were calm, it was quite a pleasant location of tree-lined shady streets. But when riots and strikes in Canton confined foreigners to the island, it could feel claustrophobic.

One-third of the island was controlled by the French and two-thirds by the British. The concessions were really only two main thoroughfares with a half dozen narrower cross streets. There were two pedestrian bridges to the mainland—the English Bridge, and the French Bridge—as well as some open land for a soccer field, which ran down to a sampan landing stage, several tennis courts, and a public recreation park with spreading trees for shade and benches between bright flower beds.

Shameen's streets were planted with banyan trees to provide shade for the island's residents as they made their way from the small consulates to the customs house, a couple of banks, a police station, and a post office. A number of decent-size merchant residences had been built, often in the Italianate style, with deep, shady verandas. There were some lodging houses for the mostly single foreign men who worked for the local *hongs*, which included the Hong Kong businesses of Butterfield and Swire and Jardine Matheson, as well as a number of European and American trading firms—Standard Oil, the high-end Manhattan furniture and rug store W. & J. Sloane, New York's General Silk Importing Corporation, and the architect-engineers Purnell & Paget. Many had offices with their residences above in a "shophouse" style more redolent of Singapore than China. And, of course, as with anywhere the British settled overseas, a club. If Shameen had been larger, then surely a racecourse would have been the second British objective, but the island was unfortunately too small. Shameen was car-free and the preserve of pedestrians, rickshaws, bicycles, and the occasional donkey-drawn cart.

There had been tense times. In September 1883, a demonstration against a European customs officer suspected of killing a local Chinese man had descended into a full-blown anti-foreign riot. The few foreign troops guarding Shameen proved inadequate against the crowd, who began burning foreign residences. In a few hours, the rioters destroyed one-third of Shameen's private houses. Since then, the foreign powers had beefed up their military presence with regular naval visits as well as a police force made up of British coppers, French *flics,* and Sikh constables recruited from India.

By 1924, at least in shape and form, Shameen hadn't really changed since the Reverend B. C. Henry of the American Presbyterian Church mission in China had visited around 1886 and seen the newly rebuilt structures on the island after the troubles of a few years before:

> Formerly a mere sandbank in the stream, it has been surrounded by a strong wall, and elevated above the reach of the highest tides, and shut off from the native town by a canal spanned by two bridges. Elliptical in shape, and evergreen in its grass and foliage, it presents a perfect ideal of retirement and comfort. Park Avenue runs through the centre from east to west, shaded by rows of noble banyans. The bund [raised waterfront] on the riverside is the favourite promenade, being open to the south, whence it receives the full benefit of the refreshing south-east monsoon through the

summer. The consulates, each with its ensign floating, the church with its bell and spire, the merchant houses, spacious, comfortable, and richly furnished, the flower-gardens, tennis-lawns, and shady walks combine their varied interests and charms.[*]

Wallis's Royal Navy vessel from Hong Kong followed the same well-plied eighty-mile route as the coastal passenger steamers. From Hong Kong, her ship followed the coast north before entering the Bocca Tigris, or Tiger's Mouth, where the Pearl River discharges into the South China Sea. A little farther on, she could see Whampoa, where the famous clipper tea ships of half a century before had dropped anchor while loading before starting on their race back with the first tea of the season to the Boston, Salem, Liverpool, and London markets. This was of course a well-trodden route for the opium clippers too. Wallis would have seen no clippers but possibly Chinese navy barges—since May 1924, Whampoa had been home to the Republic of China's military academy under its first commandant, Chiang Kai-shek.

Journeying from Hong Kong to the city just slightly earlier than Wallis, the American author and travel writer Harry Hervey described the approach in his 1924 travelogue, *Where Strange Gods Call*:

As we pressed closer to Canton I felt the luxuriousness inspired by Hong Kong giving away to a melancholy profound as the rain-packed sky overhead...the houses multiplied, and suddenly, too suddenly, we were gliding past ramshackle dwellings and go-downs; grass-thatched house-boats, sampans, junks, and lighters, and millions of roofs that were flung in uneven terraces against the sky. The piles of houses, the swarming river, and docks, in-

---

[*] B. C. (Benjamin Crouch) Henry, *Ling-Nam: Or, Interior Views of Southern China* (London: S. W. Partridge, 1886).

stantly gave me a sense of tremendous and baffling energy. Canton was at once, and always will be, too stupendous and too indefinite to be sheathed in words.[*]

Before reaching Shameen, Wallis would glimpse Canton City itself from the Pearl River. The southern Chinese liked to say that "everything new originates in Canton." That was perhaps not as true in 1924 as it had been previously. Shanghai had emerged to eclipse Canton as the China coast's major trading center and entrepôt port. Still, it was a bustling commercial town, a population of two million in the city and many millions more in the surrounding hinterland.

Though it had teeming slums and working-class districts that merged housing with light industry and craftsmen, Canton was in some districts a very wealthy city, by far the wealthiest in southern China. This was thanks in part to the fact that Canton and the surrounding Kwangtung Province was still, as it had for a long time, providing the bulk of immigrants to the Americas (North and South) and throughout Southeast Asia. These migrants sent back ideas and inventions as well as remittance money. They built villas and mansions, and their families opened businesses on the funds remitted. Sun Yat-sen had hatched revolutionary plots and spread modern ideas of republicanism from Canton, and of course, it had become home to his Southern Government after 1911 in opposition to the Northern Government in Peking that was beset by warlord infighting and would-be emperors.

By 1925, Canton was well advanced by Chinese urban standards. It had begun to pave its streets, had built an electric tramway system, opened the massive North Railway Station, and eagerly adopted the motorcar, the airplane, and the department store. The impressive Da Sun department store opened in 1922, the dream of Chong Choy, a

---

[*] Harry Hervey, *Where Strange Gods Call: Pages Out of the East* (London: T. Butterworth, 1925), 206.

Kwangtung man who had made his fortune in Sydney, Australia, in the 1890s. The city was a center for medicine and modern hospitals and had several highly regarded universities.

Shameen appeared a natural haven in the midst of this cacophonous, dynamic metropolis. Hervey had visited in 1924 during a period when the situation was somewhat calmer.[*]

> From the wharf... I was rickshawed violently over the bridge and upon Shameen, an island southeast of the old and new cities, where the Europeans live. There I found myself in another world, a pleasant if somewhat conventional sphere of brick houses, sidewalks, and lush camphor-trees and banyans that cast a green dusk. The quiet of Shameen, after the confusion of the riverfront, gave me an opportunity to recover my equilibrium, and by the time I reached the hotel I was in the mood for exploration.[†]

Just a few weeks later, Wallis arrived by the same route and checked into the same hotel—the island's only one—as Hervey, the Victoria.

The US Navy didn't maintain regular quarters on Shameen but preferred to use the Victoria Hotel, which faced north toward Canton City. It was in the British-controlled section, next to the small police station and just a block away, no more than a few minutes' walk, from the American consulate on Shameen's main street. The small

---

[*] Hervey (1900–1951) had lived all over the South, from Texas to Atlanta to Savannah, and long dreamed of visiting Asia. He had written a couple of imagined novels of the "East" and would later pen a film treatment that attracted Josef von Sternberg's attention, eventually becoming the 1932 Marlene Dietrich and Anna May Wong movie *Shanghai Express*. In the autumn of 1924, on his first visit to China, and after some time sojourning in Hong Kong and Macao, he reached Canton and Shameen Island.

[†] Hervey, *Where Strange Gods Call*, 207.

consulate was the heart of what constituted the American presence in Canton, housing Consul General Jenkins and his staff, visiting soldiers and navy personnel, and the few residents representing American companies, along with a missionary or two. In fact, it was one of America's longest established consulates in Asia and its oldest in China, dating back to 1843 and the heady days of the tea and opium trade.

The Victoria, though, was nothing special. Certainly not as swanky as the Repulse Bay or the smarter hotels of Hong Kong's central districts, and maybe not much different from the Kowloon Hotel. By 1924, the British-owned two-story Victoria was considered to have become slightly shabby, gloomily filled with blackwood furniture and serving famously atrocious food. Built in the 1880s originally as the Shameen Hotel, it had been renamed some time before Wallis arrived, perhaps to sound grander and more overtly British, but its reputation was terrible. Guidebooks at the time note it as the island's solitary hotel, but they rarely if ever recommend it. The French on Shameen, forced to use it for banquets due to there being no alternative, loathed the place and cursed the kitchens!

In calmer times, it was possible to take a walk across one of the bridges or take a sampan to Canton City for dinner and avoid the Victoria's kitchens. But when Wallis arrived, that option wasn't possible due to the perceived threat to the concessions. British Indian Army sepoys stood guard with a mounted machine gun while French Annamese colonial troops patrolled the streets along the canal banks and small sampan jetty outside the Victoria to prevent anyone coming ashore without authorization. Around the edge of the island, trenches had been dug and barbed wire rolled out in case of a concerted attack.

Tensions were already high since, the previous June, a secret cell of Vietnamese anti-colonial activists had infiltrated Shameen and bombed the Victoria's ballroom in an attempt to assassinate the visiting governor-general of French Indochina. He survived, but several guests at a banquet in his honor died. The assassin drowned trying to flee. By the time Wallis checked in, the ballroom was still in a state of disrepair—charred timbers, shattered glass not yet replaced, no laborers able to get to and from Shameen to do the repair work. The bomb damage surely added to the general nervousness Wallis must have felt with the occasional sounds of rifle shots, fire engine bells, smoke from fires across the city, and constant noisy street demonstrations by one side or the other.

In the time Wallis spent on Shameen, she was never able to cross to the city of Canton; the situation was just too unstable and the risk of violence for a foreigner, particularly a Westerner, deemed to be too great. Wallis's entire Canton trip was to be spent on Shameen.

ISLAND LIFE

If indeed she was a courier, then presumably Wallis delivered her package of documents to Consul General Jenkins at the consulate. After that, there was little to do on Shameen. Wallis could walk around the island, up and down the wide grass circular road of about a mile and a half, sit on the public benches in the shade of the banyans. It was still just about warm enough to eat the ice cream sold by the Cold Storage Company (until they ran out) from their bicycle vendor or use the tennis courts. But Wallis couldn't find a companion. Foreign wives on Shameen and those pushed onto the island by anti-foreign sentiment in Canton had evacuated to Hong Kong. She was just about the only woman to come the other way in October 1924. There were some French Catholic nuns and a couple of older merchants' wives who refused to leave, but that was the entire female population of Shameen.

With the bombed ballroom still out of action, the Victoria had set up a makeshift dining room for breakfast and also served tea and drinks on its small veranda. Dinner was a problem—food supplies had run out; Chinese porters would not deliver to Shameen.

Meals were brought in from the American consulate, who themselves sourced foodstuffs from the American gunboats (including Win's *Pampanga*), transported up from Hong Kong.* Wallis could sit and observe the crowded houseboats inhabited by entire families, which lay moored close to the Shameen jetty. From her bedroom windows, she could glimpse the busy tide of life surging on the opposite shore, so near and yet so far.

Any documents delivered, Wallis's role on Shameen was essentially over. Once again, just as at the Kowloon Hotel, she spent most of her days alone, in their small room or in the Victoria's "public rooms." Unless there was some other purpose in Wallis coming to Canton (by British warship, no less) it is hard to justify her presence in the troubled city merely to provide some company for Win in his few off-duty hours. Having your wife journey to Canton to join you on deployment seems to be a privilege none of the other officers of the South China Patrol enjoyed.

If Win had engineered Wallis's voyage to Shameen to spend time with her, it hadn't worked out that way. Win was rarely at the Victoria, being either aboard the *Pampanga* or in the consulate working with Office of Naval Intelligence staff who were trying to ascertain which faction had the upper hand, just how much Sun and Chiang were being influenced by Borodin and the Soviet advisers, how far the communist-influenced labor unions would go in their attempt to smash the right-wing Merchants' Volunteer Corps, whether the foreign concessions were a target for invasion and riot, and when—if deemed necessary—to evacuate.

He was still drinking excessively. He couldn't risk drinking aboard the *Pampanga*, so his drinking was done exclusively ashore. Their rooms at the Victoria were cramped—just a bedroom and shared bathroom. When Win was off-duty, he drank heavily in the

* According to Franck in *Roving Through Southern China*, 246–47.

bar at the Victoria—pretty much the only one on Shameen. He then came upstairs, belligerent and looking for a fight. In Hong Kong, Win had been verbally abusive as well as controlling, either forcing Wallis to stay at the hotel while he went out or to accompany him to disreputable bars full of prostitutes, where she had felt uncomfortable. But in Canton, his behavior appears to have escalated, and he became physically abusive.

What actually happened remains unclear, but things came to a violent head one evening. Win maintained that Wallis had some sort of kidney problem—a "severe kidney infection accompanied by a high temperature"—though others have asserted that she received some sort of internal injury from his violent outbursts.[*] It was not something that, later, Wallis cared to comment on in detail. But whatever happened in their room at the Victoria, Wallis became unwell and required evacuation for medical treatment unavailable on Shameen.

Wallis sailed back to Hong Kong on October 28, 1924. It seems she did see a doctor in Hong Kong and may have had a brief stay in the hospital—there are no records, and Wallis never spoke of these events.[†] In *The Heart Has Its Reasons*, Wallis writes, "I came down

---

[*] See Simpson, *The Heart Has Its Reasons*, 105. Other theories suggested by biographers (though none confirmed by Wallis herself) include that she may have drunk contaminated water during her stay in Canton and contracted an infection. This is not an impossible suggestion, and of course, consumption of contaminated water could have led to all manner of ailments requiring Wallis to leave Canton. Contaminated water and poor sanitation are linked to transmission of diseases such as cholera, diarrhea, dysentery, hepatitis A, and typhoid, among others.

[†] If Wallis did actually attend a hospital or stay in one in Hong Kong, there are no apparent records. The unreliable Higham biography claims she had an abortion at Hong Kong's Women's Hospital. The problem here is that the only hospital in Hong Kong to ever be formally known as the Women's Hospital in the colony was the former Lock Hospital. However, that institution closed permanently in 1894. The only other hospital sometimes referred to as the Women's Hospital was the Tsan Yuk Hospital, run by the London Missionary Society. But this was exclusively for Chinese female patients. Of course, Western women had other hospitals in Hong Kong they could attend, though none admitted to performing illegal abortions.

with a severe kidney infection; this was accompanied by a high temperature, and for several days I was almost delirious."[*] The fever and pain apparently vanished, and soon after arriving back in Hong Kong she was able to return to the Kowloon Hotel to rest and recuperate.

TIME FOR A MAJOR DECISION

The situation in Canton stabilized in early November. Despite perhaps over two thousand dead, the Nationalist government had triumphed. The immediate threat to Shameen and foreign interests in Canton receded; the *Pampanga* with Win aboard returned to Hong Kong and shore leave.

Wallis was still recuperating. But it immediately became apparent that Win's drinking was just getting worse—starting before breakfast even. For a while, Wallis continued to try to make the marriage work; her Baltimore upbringing conditioned her to placate him. But the drinking and his behavior were becoming harder to take. There seemed to be no prospect of improvement. The Win of those few idyllic days of their second honeymoon at Repulse Bay was long gone. Not just the repeated humiliations in bars and singsong houses but, it seems, now routine drunken violence toward Wallis.

And so she finally decided enough was enough. Wallis realized that she needed to extricate herself from the situation and to obtain a divorce. It was hard for her to make this decision, knowing what her conservative family in Baltimore would say, knowing they would think she was to blame and that it was the Warfield name being dragged through the mud; that she hadn't worked hard enough in the marriage, had been too strident, too difficult, and of course, there was the little-spoken-of issue of children—whether or not

---

[*] Simpson, *The Heart Has Its Reasons*, 105.

Wallis wanted them or could have them, or whether Win was interested or capable. She knew a separation and divorce would reflect badly on Win in the naval officers' mess. But the reality was that he was a drunk and a bully.

Perhaps Win admitted his drinking and his violence were out of control too. Likewise, his uncontrolled spending—his navy pay was largely going on bar chits and hotel liquor bills. Although Wallis never gives the details (and nor, later, did Win), it seems an arrangement was reached, a financial settlement of sorts arrived at for the time being till the divorce could be secured. Win appears to have accepted the situation.* They would separate; she would seek a divorce. The American couple couldn't obtain a divorce in a British Crown Colony. Of course, Win couldn't just abandon his naval posting in Hong Kong. A solution had to be found.

Then an opportunity arose. A chance for Wallis to take a ship north, to the Shanghai International Settlement—not a colony but not quite China as such. Shanghai was a treaty port, by far the largest and richest of all the treaty ports in China. It was run by a multinational municipal council and subject to the laws of extraterritoriality (whereby foreign nationals were governed by their own home country laws and not those of China). Crucially, it was also home to an American court presided over by an American judge who might be able to grant two Americans a divorce.

How the opportunity to journey the seven hundred miles up to

---

* Charles Higham suggests that after the trawl through the "bordellos" followed by some angry scenes, Win left the Kowloon Hotel and moved in with a "handsome young painter." However, he never suggests who the painter was—male or female, Chinese or European. This appears to be an apocryphal story. This story and the accusation that Win was a "bisexual adventurer" is also made in Ken Bayliss's self-published *Secret Royal History* (2007, Lulu.com) and Christopher Wilson's *Dancing with the Devil: The Windsors and Jimmy Donohue* (London: HarperCollins, 2001). Of course, it has also been suggested that Win's rumored bisexuality was simply another allegation in the supposed China Dossier. He did go on to marry three more times.

Shanghai came about so fortuitously remains unclear. Wallis knew nobody in Shanghai. Though the situation in Canton had calmed down, much of eastern China, around Shanghai, had erupted into warlord factional skirmishing, once again concerning US naval intelligence, and making secure and unfettered communications between Hong Kong and Shanghai at best problematic and in the winter of 1924 quite impossible.

Whether or not Wallis was once again asked to courier documents for the US State Department or Office of Naval Intelligence is unclear. But head to Shanghai she certainly did, leaving Win behind in Hong Kong, and with no apparent intention to return. It appears she traveled on the US Navy's dime and with a fellow China Bird, the wife of another navy officer stationed with America's Asiatic Fleet. A pair heading to Shanghai to see the town or to deliver documents?

And in Shanghai, that legendarily thrilling, moneyed, pulsating modern city at the head of the Yangtze River, Wallis was to be one thing she had not been for a long time. Free, or at least as she said herself, able to "live under the dangerous illusion of quasi-independence."*

---

* Simpson, *The Heart Has Its Reasons*, 107.

The Shanghai Foreign Concessions

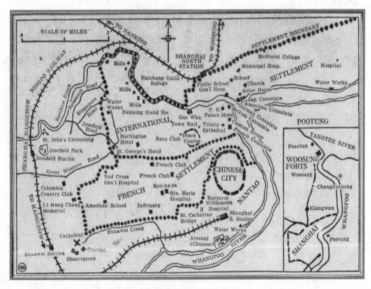

Greater Shanghai

4

THE PEARL
OF THE ORIENT

THE PALACE HOTEL
CORNER OF THE BUND AND NANKING ROAD
SHANGHAI INTERNATIONAL SETTLEMENT
MID-NOVEMBER TO EARLY DECEMBER 1924

I doubt if any city in the world is more amazing than Shanghai, where
the culture of the East and the West has met to turn curiosity into
something different; where the silver and riches of China are hoarded
for safety; where opéra-bouffe Oriental millionaires drive their lim-
ousines along the Bund; where the interests of Europe meet the Orient and clash in a sparkle of uniforms and jewels, where practical
realities of Western industrialism meet the fatality of the East...
Believe me, I repeat, anything can happen in Shanghai, from a sordid
European intrigue to a meeting with a Prince.

—J. P. Marquand, *Your Turn, Mr. Moto*

Nothing more intensely living can be imagined than Shanghai.

—Aldous Huxley, *Jesting Pilate*

It's such a long way and such a strange place—Shanghai. But I've always let Wallis make her own decisions and I'm not going to influence her now.

—Wallis's mother, Alice, on hearing her daughter
had reached Shanghai

NOVEMBER 15, 1924—THE SHANGHAI BUND

How things had changed in just over two months. That November, not long back from revolutionary Canton and just out of the hospital, Wallis, separated from Win, had left Hong Kong for Shanghai. She was accompanied by Mary Sadler, another navy wife.

Most biographies mention Sadler only fleetingly, an incidental traveling companion of Wallis, another China Bird moving around the Far East following her husband's postings. But in fact, Sadler knew both Wallis and Win well, initially from Washington, DC's US Navy circles as well as Hong Kong's small expatriate society. Mary's husband, Frank Sadler, was a navy captain, a US Naval War College graduate, who had been in charge of the US Naval Torpedo Station in Newport, Rhode Island, before being posted to the Far East.* While in Newport, he'd met local girl Mary Brown and married her in 1908. Sadler served in the Great War and was awarded the Navy Cross. In November 1924, Wallis was not yet thirty and Mary was forty-two.

Mary was well aware of Wallis's marital problems, as Win's excessive drinking had become standard US Navy gossip in Hong Kong. Indeed, it is possible that Mary arranged for Wallis to accompany her to Shanghai. Wallis was certainly curious about Shanghai. While the city's reputation preceded it, she also had a very practical reason to visit.

With the KCR and onward train service out of action due to fighting around southern and eastern China, the pair opted for the coastal voyage. They wisely avoided the rather rickety steamers that plowed between Hong Kong and Shanghai, a voyage of a few days

---

* Several biographies of Wallis have Mary Sadler as the wife of Admiral Sadler, the commanding officer of the USS *Saratoga*. Sadler would indeed become a rear admiral, but not until 1935. In 1924, he was still a captain. The USS *Saratoga* would eventually join the US Pacific Fleet, but not until 1928, by which time Mary, Frank, and Wallis had all left China.

that would have meant considerable discomfort; it was the tail end of the typhoon season and could still get blustery. Seasickness, bad food, and the threat of pirate attack were all givens of the coastal steamers.

Instead, they took the Canadian Pacific Steamship liner *Empress of Russia*—better cabins, better food, a smoother voyage, and far too large to be attacked by pirate junks. Shanghai was the ship's first stop after Hong Kong before it headed out across the Pacific, via Kobe in Japan, onward to Vancouver. But this was no luxury cruise. The *Empress of Russia*, while a step up from the ramshackle, overcrowded, and noisy coastal steamers, was still essentially a mail ship stopping repeatedly to off-load and take on the post at small ports, making the full crossing a long and tedious enterprise. Its advantage over the smarter passenger-dedicated liners was a significant fare reduction.

They traveled up from Hong Kong, through the Taiwan Strait, never far from the Fukien (Fujian) and Chekiang (Zhejiang) coasts until the ship entered the wide estuary of the Yangtze River. There they moored in the deep water of the Woosung (Wusong) anchorage at the confluence of the Yangtze and Whangpoo (Huangpu) Rivers. Wallis and Mary transferred to a "lighter," a flat-bottomed barge, and with their luggage were ferried up the Whangpoo, which ran up to and through Shanghai. As they rounded the choppy, muddy river close to the junction with the bustling sampan-filled Soochow (Suzhou) Creek, the mile-long stretch of Western-style waterfront architecture known as the Bund heaved into view.* Shanghai was a distinct contrast to Hong Kong and its verdant Peak and mountains rising up from the harbor. The eastern Chinese city was as flat as a pancake and stretched as far as the eye could see.

---

* *Bund* being simply a word borrowed into English from Hindi, originally referring to a dike or embankment. In the Chinese treaty ports, it was taken to mean an embanked quay that ran along the shore. Shanghai's Bund was not the only one in China, but it was by far the longest and grandest.

The lighter slowed as it approached the Bund Terminal. The river was crowded with the gunboats of half a dozen foreign nations, tacking junks, deserted old opium hulks, fuel storage ships, tramp steamers awaiting cargo, and tenders resupplying larger ships. All were swarmed by an army of sampans hawking food and souvenirs, begging, or collecting night soil for fertilizer. Multigenerational families survived off the rubbish scraps of Shanghai's maritime life, and all in front of the majestic sweep of the Bund. Visiting merchant seamen noted that there were strangely no seagulls in Shanghai. This was believed to be because after the sampans had bustled about salvaging every scrap of rubbish and the night soil boats had carried away all the human waste, there was nothing left for the gulls to feast on.[*] On the opposite side of the river was Pootung (Pudong), a mass of warehouses, petroleum storage facilities, and dry docks, which soon gave way to farmland that stretched inland for miles.

Wallis and Mary disembarked on the Bund waterfront to a crowd of porters, rickshaw pullers, taxi drivers, and awaiting hotel concierges proffering umbrellas. It was pouring rain. That November would indeed be the wettest month on record in Shanghai. It would rain constantly nearly every moment of Wallis's stay. It was the afternoon of Saturday, November 15, 1924.

THE PALACE HOTEL

There is some discrepancy among biographers of Wallis as to exactly where she stayed in Shanghai that winter. Several have her staying

---

[*] There is a tale, told by James Bond creator Ian Fleming in his 1963 book *Thrilling Cities*, that (in the early 1960s) there were no seagulls in Hong Kong's Victoria Harbor due to the remaining number of sampans picking all the trash out of the water. Fleming says that he was told that this was also the case in Shanghai on the Huangpu River until 1949, when sampan families were largely forced to move ashore and settle. Seagulls then appeared in Shanghai where none had been seen for generations.

at the Astor House Hotel, across the Soochow Creek that divided the central business district of the International Settlement from its northern and more working-class environs of Hongkew (Hongkou). This wouldn't be surprising, as the Astor House was a popular hotel, especially with visiting Americans.

However, other biographers, and Wallis herself, maintain that she stayed at the Palace Hotel on the Bund. This was a grander hotel, the location more prestigious, and was popular with well-heeled Americans visiting Shanghai. So the Palace it is.* And once we know she stayed at the Palace, it tells us something more about her trip to Shanghai—the Palace was significantly more expensive than the Astor House, and in mid-November 1924, Wallis was not well-heeled.

Wallis maintained that she opted to stay at the Palace because it was a favorite of American officers' wives. Mary was staying there, and she thought it likely she would bump into someone of her acquaintance. It's a fair argument. The Palace was definitely one of the top two hotels in Shanghai at the time, along with the Majestic nearby. Built in 1907, its terra-cotta-and-white edifice rose six stories high and contained 110 en suite rooms, the most desirable with riverfront views. It boasted one of the first elevators in China, and all the public areas, banqueting spaces, and ballrooms were paneled in teakwood. Five years later, the Palace would be overshadowed by the completion of Sir Victor Sassoon's art deco Cathay Hotel next door, but in 1924, it was the only hotel directly facing onto the famous Bund.

But the principal reason many navy wives stayed there was that it was close to the American consulate, who were often paying their tab. Having left Win in Hong Kong, arriving in Shanghai with

---

* Quite why some biographers have placed Wallis at the Astor I have not ascertained except that, written once, it gets repeated. It seems to me that Wallis might be quite reliable on this question, as she only visited Shanghai briefly and didn't return in later years, so there is unlikely to be any confusion. It is possible that the Astor House story starts with Charles Higham, whose biography is riddled with factual and historical errors regarding Wallis's time in China.

limited and uncertain funds, Wallis would unlikely have been staying at the Palace on her own dime. It was, quite simply, beyond her means. This suggests that Mary and Wallis did indeed courier documents from Hong Kong to Shanghai for the navy and that the navy paid their hotel bill in return.

SEEKING THE PEARL OF THE ORIENT

What would have impressed Wallis on her arrival in Shanghai, as it did most visitors, was its modernity. In 1924, the International Settlement (largely run by the British) and the adjacent French Concession were significantly more developed than Canton, while few would disagree that the laissez-faire society of treaty port Shanghai was more fun than the stuffy and snobbish colonial milieu of Hong Kong. It was a city of vast department stores, neon lights, its traffic jammed with imported American automobiles, and a cacophony of noise blaring from new radio stations, gramophones, and dance halls. The streets were thronged with foreigners and smartly dressed westernized Chinese alongside the city's merchants, rickshaw pullers, and beggars. Aldous Huxley visited at around the same time as Wallis and remarked, "In no city, West or East, have I ever had such an impression of dense, rank richly clotted life."*

A walled town of traders and fishermen, Shanghai had been forcibly opened as a treaty port, or foreign concession, after the First Opium War in the mid-nineteenth century. Its economy and population boomed. By the second decade of the twentieth century, Shanghai had become notorious for its freebooting attitude to capitalism and embrace of the modern in all its forms.

From her initial arrival at the Bund Terminal, looking out of her

---

* Aldous Huxley's diary, published as *Jesting Pilate* (London: Chatto & Windus, 1926), 271.

window at the Palace, exploring just a few blocks around her hotel, Wallis would have encountered the bustling life of the city, teeming with itinerant vendors, Western businessmen, fashionably clad Chinese women, European and Chinese policemen patrolling together, off-duty soldiers and sailors of a dozen nations looking for fun, country bumpkins come to town with big dreams and high hopes. Shanghai's pivotal role as an entrepôt—sending out the products of China's vast hinterlands to the world, receiving imports from every continent—was obvious just looking at the constant stream of barges, junks, and steamers on the Whangpoo. She could see the cotton mills and silk filatures that stretched for miles along the banks of the Whangpoo in Hongkew almost back as far as the Yangtze through the northern semi-industrial areas of Tilanchao (Tilanqiao) and Shanghai's most easterly district, Yangtszepoo (Yangpu).

And along with goods came new technologies and foreign cultures. Western ideas took hold fast in Shanghai. Almost simultaneously, the Shanghai Securities & Commodities Exchange started operations in 1921, and a group of like-minded Chinese met clandestinely in a French Concession school to establish the Chinese Communist Party. Wallis could not possibly have missed the polyglot and multicultural nature of the city—Europeans and Americans, Russian émigrés from Bolshevism and Baghdadi Jewish merchants, Sikh coppers in the settlement and Annamese *flics* in Frenchtown. North of Soochow Creek, a "Little Tokyo" district had emerged as large numbers of Japanese (the largest non-Chinese community in Shanghai) arrived. The European and American foreigners termed themselves "Shanghailanders" and were not shy to show their assumed superiority. The Chinese who settled became Shanghainese, developing their own distinctive dialect, cuisine, and aesthetic—*hai-pai*—a brazen and vibrant East-meets-West culture.

Not everybody took to Shanghai, finding it vulgar and brash. The British writer Harold Acton, resident for many years in Peking, recorded his first visits to Shanghai in his book *Memoirs of an*

Aesthete. Acton, a dedicated Pekingophile, didn't think much of Shanghailander society:

> Thirty years—sometimes more—without troubling to learn the language, and these "Old China Hands" pickled in alcohol considered themselves supreme authorities on the country and the people ... They were inveterate grumblers. A traveler fresh from Europe who, instead of sozzling, went about sober with his eyes open, was plain "green"; his views worthless.[*]

And in among all this cacophony of diverse Shanghai humanity were Americans. The journalist Edgar Snow, fleeing the onset of the Depression in America for what he hoped would be an opportunity to prove himself a talented writer in China, wrote extensively of his fellow countrymen and -women:

> Shanghai, to a noticeable extent, has become Americanized. There, in the most polyglot city in Asia, the roving American finds all the comforts of home: Clara Bow and Buddy Rogers, the radio and jazz bands, cocktails and correspondence schools, night clubs and cabarets, neon lights and skyscrapers, chewing gum and Buicks, wide trousers and long skirts, Methodist evangelists and the Salvation Army. And there, too, he finds such peculiarly American institutions as Navy Wives, shot-gun weddings, Girl Scouts, Spanish-American War veterans, a board of censors, daylight hold-ups, immaculate barbershops, a Short Story Club, wheat cakes, and a Chamber of Commerce ... The fact is that nobody in Shanghai worries himself very much about Sino-American understanding. Both the Chinese and Americans are too busy making money."[†]

---

[*] Harold Acton, *Memoirs of an Aesthete* (London: Methuen, 1948), 291.
[†] Edgar Snow, "The Americans in Shanghai," *American Mercury*, August 1930.

Mary and Wallis thus joined approximately thirty thousand other foreigners in a city of three million Chinese—one of the five largest conurbations in the world and the most densely populated of any major global metropolis. In the International Settlement in 1924, two thousand American citizens were registered as residents, with about another thousand or so in the adjacent French Concession. That compared to nearly six thousand Brits, three thousand Russian émigrés, and fourteen thousand Japanese.

DISAPPOINTMENT

Wallis arrived in Shanghai determined to divorce Win. Win appears to have been apologetic for his behavior. He actually came to see her off on the liner from Hong Kong. She wrote in *The Heart Has Its Reasons*: "As he said good-bye at the gangway, his parting words were: 'Pensacola, Coronado, Washington, and now Hong Kong—we've come a long way, only to lose what we began with.'"* Win had also agreed to provide her with a monthly sum of money, what was called an *allotment*, of (a not ungenerous) $225.†

Despite the abuse and violence in their marriage, in later life, Wallis would reminisce quite fondly of Win. But she had planned her escape and the possible divorce route of the US court in Shanghai. She sailed out of Hong Kong Harbour for Shanghai. She would only ever see Win once more in his lifetime.

Despite her family's continuing distaste for separations, Wallis knew that she had to get a divorce. She had originally tried in Paris,

---

* Wallis Simpson, *The Heart Has Its Reasons* (London: Michael Joseph, 1956), 106.
† An allotment was a fairly common arrangement, whereby a portion of a man's pay could, at his request, be released directly to his wife, his family, or whomever he named. US$225 in 1924 would be equivalent to US$4,100 in 2024, assuming annual inflation over this period at 2.91 percent. Wallis described the sum as "adequate" but allowed for few extras (*The Heart Has Its Reasons*, 97).

but it had proved too difficult and too costly, while her family talked her out of it. A divorce in British Hong Kong was impossible; certainly nothing could be done in Chinese Canton. But rumor had it that she might be able to succeed in Shanghai.

As a treaty port, Shanghai had special exemptions. Shanghailanders were not subject to Chinese law and justice, answering only to their own national courts—the so-called system of extraterritoriality. The Europeans had run their own courts to settle business disputes and contested estates, and to control their errant citizens since the late nineteenth century. But America had only just got its legal act together in Shanghai. In 1906, President Teddy Roosevelt, alarmed at the number of American citizens who'd moved to Shanghai to become casino operators and brothel madams, legislated for the creation of the United States Court for China at Shanghai. It was not before time either. Shanghai, at the turn of the century (and then an influx after the 1906 San Francisco earthquake), had been infested with so many American prostitutes that the term *American girl* had become popular slang across Asia for white women of dubious virtue.

Roosevelt was outraged on behalf of the nation. While the Shanghai International Settlement authorities might not always wish to prosecute an American for running a bordello, an opium den, or a casino, extraterritoriality could go both ways. If it was illegal in America, then they could be prosecuted for it in China. Extrality would become a tool of conviction rather than a way to slip through the grip of the law. And so he acted. The court was presided over by American judges and had the power to send the guilty to the hangman or alternatively to the harsh Bilibid Prison in the Philippines or back home to McNeil Island Corrections Center in Puget Sound. Additionally, the court could deal with all manner of everyday estates, wills, contractual issues, and (so Wallis had been led to believe in Hong Kong) divorce cases.

However, it transpired that the American court could not in fact divorce the Spencers. It could grant divorces for adultery, desertion, cruelty, or nonsupport, but it required two years' residence in China (not counting British Hong Kong). Wallis's plans of making a permanent legal break with Win in Shanghai were dashed.

The Shanghai-based American lawyer Norwood Allman had seen others turn up in the hope of obtaining "quicky" separations. He advised that anyone requiring a "hurry-up" divorce would do better to head home to Nevada, Oklahoma, or Arkansas to make arrangements.* This strange, extraterritorial legal situation in Shanghai has confused many Wallis biographers over the years, leading to some falsehoods. For instance, Joe Bryan and Charles J. V. Murphy's 1979 biography, *The Windsor Story*, claimed that Wallis couldn't afford the cost of the divorce charged by the "International Court." Shanghai had no such institution as the "International Court" for her to be unable to afford, and ultimately, it wasn't a matter of money but regulation.

ON THE TOWN WITH ROBBIE

Wallis sat around in the Palace Hotel for a few days, taking tea with the other navy wives in residence. Not that they were all the most edifying companions. In the suite next to Wallis's was a rather morose, gin-drinking woman who wrote endless letters to her husband, away at sea. According to Wallis, she maintained a state of semi-inebriation and never left the hotel.† Wallis needed to escape the Palace, see the town, and plot her next move.

She had only one personal contact in Shanghai. A friend from her Washington days had given her a letter of introduction to an Englishman working in the Settlement. It was her gin-drinking neighbor who actually urged her to look him up. "What can you

---

* Norwood F. Allman, *Shanghai Lawyer* (New York: Whittlesey House, 1943), 185.
† Simpson, *The Heart Has Its Reasons*, 106.

lose? If he's a bore, you can shed him easily enough."* Wallis sent a note to the address she'd been given.

As it turned out, her sole connection proved to be far from a bore. A day later, a basket of mangoes arrived, followed by a telephone call inviting her to cocktails. Wallis wore a red camellia to be recognized. Her new friend arrived and turned out to be handsome, impeccably dressed, and charming.

In her memoirs, Wallis remembers the man fondly as "Robbie." In fact, his name was Harold Graham Fector Robinson, an architect, originally from Hampstead in London, working in Shanghai and staying in the smart Western district of the settlement in a large villa at the junction of Great Western Road and Tifeng Road.† Robbie was single and very social, and he shared his house with a man Wallis described as "his business partner."‡ Robbie was approximately the same age as Wallis and doing very well for himself. After coming out from England in 1905 to train with the prestigious architectural firm of Scott and Carter (who happened to have built the Palace Hotel), he had qualified in 1911 and was now a successful architect.§

The two hit it off immediately. Wallis admitted that after meeting Robbie, she went from being lonely and depressed, uncertain of

---

* Simpson, *The Heart Has Its Reasons*, 107.

† Yan'an Lu and Wulumuqi Lu now.

‡ Simpson, *The Heart Has Its Reasons*, 109. Wallis never names the "business partner," but it was probably John Mackie Ventors (born 1888), originally from Fife, Scotland, and who had come to Shanghai to work with the large and successful architectural practice Atkinson and Dallas after training in Glasgow, war service in the Great War, and then working a stint with HM Office of Works in London. In 1931, Robbie proposed Ventors to become a fellow of the Royal Institute of British Architects (FRIBA). Robbie had become a FRIBA in 1929.

§ Antonia Brodie, ed., *Directory of British Architecture, 1834–1914*, vol. 2 (London: Bloomsbury Academic, 2001), 489. Robbie's career would continue to rise. He became a founding partner in the Shanghai architectural firm of Messrs. Spence, Robinson & Partners. He is now perhaps best remembered for being an architect on the neoclassical Shanghai Race Club building, with its distinctive ten-story clock tower, completed in 1934, with a 330-foot grandstand attached. It is now a history museum.

what to do after the disappointment of the American court, to de-lightfully distracted; "From knowing nobody I was drawn swiftly into a totally different kind of world—garden parties, race meetings of the Shanghai Race Club, and dinner parties in the lovely old Ma-jestic Hotel on Bubbling Well Road, where in the bower of flowers one danced in a sunken courtyard by the light of coloured lanterns."[*]

Everything changed overnight. The grim Kowloon boarding-house, the snobby exclusionist social world of Hong Kong, the cramped Victoria Hotel, and the bad experiences in Canton with Win were all forgotten, or at least pushed to the back of her mind. Wallis gave herself to Robbie's care and the social whirl of Shanghai. She would refuse to allow the travails of the previous couple of months to bother her any longer while she remained in China: "It was here [at the Majestic Hotel] in the company of Robbie . . . the moonlight, the jasmine, not to mention that Shangri-la illusion of the courtyard, that made me feel that I had really entered the Celestial Kingdom."[†]

Through Robbie, Wallis was introduced to many of Shanghai's legendary "400," the wealthiest and most influential foreigners in the settlement, most of whom were British. W. Somerset Maugham, staying in Shanghai in the early 1920s, recalled mahogany dinner tables that "groaned with silver . . . tall silver vases in which were large chrysanthemums making it possible to catch only glimpses of the person opposite you . . . tall silver candlesticks reared their proud heads two by two down the length of the table." The typical fare was Western, or at least as Western as could be obtained, and always accompanied by alcohol—cocktails or a gin and bitters upon arrival, sherry with the soup to start; hock with the fish entrée. The Shang-hai 400 always insisted on two entrées; a white entrée and a brown entrée—that is, fish and then meat. Sauterne with a flavored ice; port with a cheese imported from Hong Kong.

---

[*] Simpson, *The Heart Has Its Reasons*, 107.
[†] Simpson, *The Heart Has Its Reasons*, 107.

Still, Maugham thought the conversation at Shanghai dinner parties limited—the ponies at the race club, the best spots for duck and snipe hunting in the interior, golf at Hungjao (Hongqiao), the annoying boycotts at Canton spreading toward Shanghai, onerous taxation by the imperial customs, ever-rising freight charges, petty Shanghai municipal politics. Maugham noted, "China bored them all, they did not want to speak of that." The servants were dismissively addressed in China coast pidgin, and anyone who studied the Chinese language was distrusted (unless a missionary or a diplomat). The 400 were the business elite of the city, the number ones and the *taipan* "big bosses" at Jardine Matheson HSBC—the Hongkers and Shankers, Standard Chartered, British American Tobacco, and the other major foreign businesses in the settlement.[*]

So when Robbie, dining in such company almost nightly, met Wallis, it was little surprise that he was immediately taken with this newly arrived and intriguing young American woman in town. Wallis might just have cheered Robbie up as much as he restored her lust for life.

Together, Wallis and Robbie enjoyed the races and the tea dances at the Majestic—where legendarily more *stengahs* (a whiskey and soda in Shanghai) were drunk than cups of tea. As a member of the race club, he was able to secure Wallis a complimentary membership and access to the members' stand on race day.

During the weekday, when Robbie was at work, Wallis explored Shanghai's retail delights with Mary Sadler. Where her limited means allowed, she shopped at the city's Western department stores, silk shops, and curio dealers. Within a stone's throw from the Palace were the giant department stores of the Nanking Road (Nanjing Road) and the antique shops of Peking Road (Beijing Road). The side streets were filled with dressmakers and tailors. Shanghai was

* W. Somerset Maugham, here and above, "Dinner Parties," *On a Chinese Screen* (London: Jonathan Cape, 1928), 26–32.

handily compact and bustling with rickshaws to whisk you cheaply from hotel lobby to garden party to rooftop tea dance to supper club and home again.

The race club members' stand, the Majestic's ballroom, the Palace Hotel tiffin, and dinner, supper, and garden parties at the homes of the 400 were all virtually exclusively white activities where the vast bulk of the guests would have been either European or American. But Robbie also ensured Wallis saw some of the more vital sides of Shanghai life. Wallis could not have ignored the streets' beggars with terrible scars, burns, and amputations, or the gangs of children that roamed the streets seemingly self-supported. The other side of Shanghai life—the clusters of beggar sampans or overcrowded housing for poorly paid factory workers—was on full view.

Robbie also took Wallis to see Chinese Shanghai at play. Just across the boundary from the International Settlement on the French Concession side of the Avenue Edward VII (Yan'an Road) at the junction of the Boulevard de Montigny (Xizang Road), was the vast Great World (Da Shijie) amusement arcade. It was a multistory building with a tall spire that dominated the area, attracting crowds of Chinese, along with some curious foreigners. The Hollywood film director Josef von Sternberg, whose movies *Shanghai Express* (1932) and *The Shanghai Gesture* (1941) would do so much to shape images of Shanghai and China in the popular Western imagination slightly later, visited the Great World:

> On the first floor were gaming tables, singsong girls, magicians, pickpockets, slot machines, fireworks, birdcages, fans, stick incense, acrobats, and ginger. One flight up were the restaurants, a dozen different groups of actors, crickets and cages, pimps, midwives, barbers, and earwax extractors. The third floor had jugglers, herb medicines, ice cream parlors, a new bevy of girls, their high

collared gowns slit to reveal their hips, and, under the heading of novelty, several rows of exposed toilets. The fourth floor was crowded with shooting galleries, fan-tan tables, revolving wheels, massage benches, acupuncture and moxa cabinets, hot towel counters, dried fish and intestines, and dance platforms . . . The fifth floor featured girls with dresses slit to the armpits, a stuffed whale, storytellers, balloons, peep shows, masks, a mirror maze, two love letter booths with scribes who guaranteed results, rubber goods, and a temple filled with ferocious gods and joss sticks. On the top floor and roof of that house of multiple joys a jumble of tightrope walkers slithered back and forth, and there were seesaws, Chinese checkers, mahjong, strings of firecrackers, lottery tickets, and marriage brokers.[*]

Wallis's time in Shanghai was, by her own account, a time of initial disappointment followed by a whirl of social engagements, the races, and shopping. In *The Heart Has Its Reasons*, Wallis reflected on her brief stay in the city: "No doubt about it, life in Shanghai in 1924 was good, very good, and, in fact, almost too good."[†]

The Shanghai of 1924 may not have been quite the wild nightclub-and-jazz-filled town of the 1930s that captured the public imagination as a "sin city" of debauchery and excess, but it had already acquired a ribald reputation. Wallis sojourned in a city already notorious, a notoriety that would only increase over the decade between her few weeks there and the salacious revelations of the supposed China Dossier a dozen years later. It was all too easy for faraway London society to believe anything of a single woman who had spent time in Shanghai.

---

[*] Josef von Sternberg, *Fun in a Chinese Laundry* (London: Macmillan, 1965), 83.
[†] Simpson, *The Heart Has Its Reasons*, 107.

CITY OF RUMOR

Though she couldn't have imagined it at the time, those newly care-free few weeks in Shanghai would come back to haunt Wallis a dozen or so years later when rumors of her behavior were circulated in London at the start of the abdication crisis. By then, Wallis was no longer Mrs. Win Spencer but Mrs. Ernest Simpson, involved in a full-blown affair with King Edward VIII. The China Dossier aimed to destroy her reputation by reviving her Shanghai days and was basically a concoction of falsehoods.

In the 1930s, Shanghai was as often referred to as "the Whore of the Orient" as it was "the Paris of the East" or "the Pearl of the Orient." The city's reputation by 1936 was pretty firmly fixed in people's minds, thanks to a welter of Hollywood B movies, Yellow Peril penny dreadfuls from the likes of Sax Rohmer and his Fu Manchu books, and plays such as John Colton's *The Shanghai Gesture* (1926) that had critics on Broadway and in the West End "shocked by the worst ever penned sex-play," exclaiming that it was "a vile travesty on the morals of English residents in the East and is the acme of indecency."[*] The sensationalist—and bestselling—Dutch writer Hendrik de Leeuw published a book in 1934, *Cities of Sin*, which of course had a long chapter on Shanghai that just happened to focus on one of the city's best known bordellos, run by an American madam and employing exclusively those "American girls" Teddy Roosevelt had been so outraged by.[†] De Leeuw's book confirmed every notion of a Shanghai convulsed by miscegenation, sex for sale, American girls, "white slavers," and opium dens. As one anonymous American missionary in

---

[*] "Critics are Shocked by Sex Play Considered Worst Ever Penned," *Ottawa Journal*, January 30, 1926 (originally reported in the London press and syndicated to the *Ottawa Journal*).

[†] Hendrick de Leeuw, *Cities of Sin* (London: Noel Douglas, 1934), 114–46.

China had famously declared, "If God lets Shanghai endure, then he owes an apology to Sodom and Gomorrah."*

The campaign against Wallis, the accusations about her time in Shanghai, are still regularly circulated today in tabloid news articles, and they still appear in new biographies a century after she left the city. But what is interesting about the China Dossier is that its compilers clearly knew their Shanghai and were familiar with certain events that occurred there in the first decades of the twentieth century. Although it is not known who initially suggested many of the claims made in the supposed dossier (remember no physical copy has ever surfaced), we can perhaps look to the British Special Intelligence Service outpost in Shanghai and China at the time as a strong potential source. And that source would, most probably, be the long-time SIS and Special Branch head of station in Shanghai (including during Wallis's sojourn), Harry Steptoe.

Little concrete is known about Steptoe except that he maintained diplomatic cover as a vice consul in the British consulate. The few who have remembered him describe him as an energetic, colorful, and somewhat odd person controlling a vast number of agents. He was said to be from the Midlands area of England with the distinctive accent of Birmingham, fond of flamboyant uniforms, and had developed a "surreptitious mode of walking"! One contact remembered Steptoe operating in Peking before the Great War: "He loves to weave a veil of mystery over his doings and whisper strange warnings."† Steptoe certainly had the imaginative powers

---

* Attributed to an anonymous source and frequently quoted in the old Shanghai press and various histories, including Stella Dong, *Shanghai: The Rise and Fall of a Decadent City* (New York: HarperCollins, 2001), 1.

† Keith Jeffery, *MI6: The History of the Secret Intelligence Service, 1909–1949* (London: Bloomsbury, 2011). At the start of the Second World War, Steptoe was posted to Iraq and then became the head of the anti-communist MI6 Section IX on its formation in March 1944.

and the intimate knowledge of interwar Shanghai to concoct most of the tales comprising the China Dossier.

Among the rumors that circulated then, and which still resurfaces regularly, is that Wallis spent time in a Shanghai bordello where she learned a sexual technique referred to as the "Shanghai Grip," the skill of tightening and relaxing the vaginal muscles at will. This story was circulated in London society, elaborated upon, and salaciously enjoyed ("Makes a matchstick feel like a cigar," someone infamously said, damning both Wallis and Edward!).[*]

Several of her biographers have repeated it too. Charles Higham suggested Wallis was taught "perverse practises" in Hong Kong rather than Shanghai, and was also taught Chinese erotic massage techniques (*fang chung* or *fang zhong*), though he had no evidence he cared to reveal.[†] Caroline Blackwood has a range of terms for the skills—the Chinese Trick, the Chinese Clasp, the Chinese Grip—and claims that Wallis used her "Oriental powers" on the king. Blackwood also says that Lady Alexandra Metcalfe (née Curzon, third daughter of Lord George Curzon, the former viceroy of India) wanted to ask Wallis about the Shanghai Grip but didn't have the courage.[‡] It seems nobody ever quite had the courage to mention it to her face.

There certainly had been American-run bordellos in Shanghai, employing American prostitutes since the late nineteenth century. But even the most upmarket of these would never have been patronized by respectable women even if they were offering lessons in technique, which is a detail drawn from the realms of prurient fantasy.

---

[*] The rumor has spread far and wide. According to Oxford Reference (an online reference product, spanning twenty-five different subject areas, bringing together two million digitized entries across Oxford University Press's dictionaries, companions, and encyclopedias), the Shanghai Grip is "a sexual technique, allegedly mastered by the American divorcée Wallis Simpson, that 'makes a matchstick feel like a cigar.'"
[†] Charles Higham, "Intrigue Follows Wallis Spencer in Hong Kong," *Courier News* (Bridgewater, NJ), October 17, 1988 (syndicated by the *Los Angeles Times*).
[‡] Caroline Blackwood, *The Last of the Duchess* (London: Vintage, 2012),169.

Similarly so the oft-repeated rumor that while in Shanghai Wallis posed naked (or at least wearing only a life buoy) for saucy, if not pornographic, photographs. None have ever surfaced, and again, this seems highly unlikely. The rumor was that she was desperate for money, but while not overly flush, Wallis was far from broke in Shanghai. Often, this rumor is conflated with the story that it was Sir Victor Sassoon, the heir to the vast Baghdadi-Jewish trading fortune, who took these photos. Sassoon was indeed a keen amateur photographer and serial philanderer. However, he was not in Shanghai in 1924. When Wallis was in Shanghai, and indeed all the time she was in China, Sassoon was in Bombay following his father's death in 1924 and his subsequent elevation to become third baronet of Bombay. Rather than taking pornographic snaps in Shanghai, Sassoon was managing the family textile business and sitting in the Indian Legislative Assembly, making sure his remarks were recorded in the assembly's minutes.[*]

Other rumors more obviously drawn from popular culture at the time have circulated. That Wallis gambled, got into debt, had to work for gangsters to pay off the debt.[†] That she became addicted to opium. Both of these are essentially part of the plot of John Colton's controversial but popular play *The Shanghai Gesture* (later adapted as a movie of the same name by Josef von Sternberg in 1941 with the tagline being "Shanghai—Where Women Are Weak").

And what of her actual acquaintances in Shanghai? It has been asserted in several biographies that Wallis had an affair with Robbie. In her biography, Wallis addresses this possibility but states that the relationship and the time she spent in Shanghai with him was ulti-

---

[*] Any number of books detailing the lives of Sir Victor and the Sassoon clan note his time in Bombay, most recently Joseph Sassoon, *The Global Merchants: The Enterprise and the Extravagance of the Sassoon Dynasty* (London: Allen Lane, 2022).

[†] Asserted by Higham and others, again as above.

mately "purposeless."[*] Biographers, including perhaps Wallis's best, Anne Sebba, take this to mean that Robbie was gay.

Sebba reveals that as well as being her entrée into Shanghailander society, Robbie was useful to Wallis in that he introduced her to Dr. Hugo Rudolph Friedlander, known in society as Freddy Friedlander.[†] Friedlander, according to Robbie's niece, gave Wallis some help with "her problem," indicating that the condition Wallis had been treated for in Hong Kong just the previous month was still troubling her. Some have taken this to suggest Wallis had an abortion while in Shanghai, but again, there is no evidence of that.

CITY OF WAR

We can safely dismiss the allegations of the China Dossier as the Orientalist fever dreams of the intelligence services, Foreign Office, and Downing Street. Still, for all the parties, dances, race meetings, shopping, and fun, the one aspect biographers of Wallis miss when looking at her adventures in Shanghai is that it was a city completely permeated by war. In 1924, it was a potentially very dangerous place. And this was the second time, after her brief visit to Shameen Island in Canton, that Wallis had been in proximity to intense fighting.

Often, the sound of artillery and gunfire just outside the Settlement's boundaries could be heard from the rooftop *thé-dansants* along Nanking Road or the garden of Robbie's villa. The ongoing political vacuum in China caused by the rift between Peking and Sun Yat-sen's Southern Government in Canton was felt nationwide by late 1924. The so-called northern warlords battled for control of Manchuria, the treaty port of Tientsin, while the ancient capital of

---

[*] Simpson, *The Heart Has Its Reasons*, 107.
[†] Anne Sebba, "On the Trail of Wallis and Her Shanghai Surprises," *Daily Telegraph*, March 15, 2012.

Peking was a prize constantly being skirmished over. And across the fertile provinces of eastern China, right on Shanghai's doorstep, the internecine fighting was ongoing too.

Despite the extravagance of colonial life and Shanghai's apparent prosperity and industry, Wallis could not have avoided conversations about the threatened state of the city's economy, now dipping severely after a post–Great War boom that had seen a construction frenzy and seemingly endless investment and profits. And as the fighting disrupted trade up and down the Yangtze hinterland, for the numerous farms and market gardens in Shanghai's surrounding provinces, the city's economy worsened.

Leaving restaurants at night, Wallis would see wounded troops brought in on trains, gangrenous, missing limbs. Robbie would have to escort Wallis back to the Palace, the situation too uncertain to leave her to find a taxi or rickshaw alone. Large and imposing Sikh doormen made sure nobody without authorization entered the hotel. Thieves were rampant. Deserting soldiers roamed the International Settlement's streets, reduced to begging or petty crime. Refugees from the countryside flooded in, starving, their crops destroyed. They slept in back alleys across the Settlement, whole families crowded in doorways along the Bund right outside the Palace, trying to stay warm as Shanghai's chilly and wet winter deepened. Chinese charities were overwhelmed, the Settlement's hospitals and meager social services likewise. There was an outburst of spy mania in the Chinese community, with people denounced for supposedly revealing the Settlement's fortifications to possible warlord invaders. Foreigners were accused of conniving, profiting from, and prolonging the fighting. Photographs emerged in the American press of munitions being delivered to the warlords in crates labeled KRUPPS—MADE IN GERMANY. And indeed, in the winter of 1924, it was not difficult to find a European or American arms dealer in the Settlement's restaurants or hotel lobby coffee shops.

It felt like law and order was collapsing. Bank and post office robberies became common. Pickpocketing, purse snatchings, and petty theft boomed, while kidnappings and home invasions, of both wealthy Chinese and foreigners, reached a record high. Tit-for-tat assassinations between the rival factions occurred regularly on the streets; occasionally, innocent civilians got caught in the cross fire. The Settlement's authorities were rattled at a possible invasion of the foreign concessions, the Shanghai Municipal Police hopelessly overstretched.

Shanghailander nerves were jangled. The Chinese joked that 1924 was certainly the Year of the Rat. It was in the sense of the Chinese zodiac, but also in terms of the overcrowded conditions in the city that led to a plague of the rodents too. Added to war, assassination, and kidnapping, the threat of a plague outbreak caused concern. In Shanghai, just as in Canton, Wallis was once again up close to the scattergun civil wars being fought out across China.

Foreign troops were mobilized to reinforce the Settlement's boundaries. Additional US Marines were redeployed from Manila, a British regiment sent up from Hong Kong. The Whangpoo was home to twenty foreign battle cruisers. Five American destroyers sailed south from their base at Chefoo (Yantai), a similar number from the Royal Navy China Fleet at Weihaiwei. The French battle cruiser *Jules Ferry* had recently arrived from Saigon. The stretch of the river directly opposite the Bund had been nicknamed "Gunboat Alley." Sampans and supply vessels swarmed the battle cruisers, and Wallis watched it all from her hotel window.

At the garden parties and hotel dances Wallis attended, many of the Shanghailander men would have to excuse themselves early for duty. That November, the Shanghai Volunteer Corps (SVC), the local auxiliary militia, had mustered. They moved out to protect railway lines around the city after warlord fighting cut the Shanghai-to-Tientsin railway line completely. Armored trucks patrolled the streets at the Settlement's edges, machine gun posts were set up along Soochow Creek and other strategic positions. The Settlement was ringed with barbed wire to prevent warlord troops infiltrating.

The nasty and brutal Kiangsu-Chekiang (Jiangsu-Zhejiang) War dragged on throughout the winter. A total of 120,000 soldiers in private armies battled away to gain a few villages only to lose them the following week. And all that November, it rained continuously in eastern China. The soldiers on both sides were constantly drenched, their weapons misfiring, ammunition damp and useless, morale low. Food supplies rotted in the damp, tents leaked, waterproof clothing was scant to nonexistent. The week Wallis arrived in Shanghai, a reporter for the *Syracuse Journal and Republican-News* visited Nansiang (Nanxiang), a railway depot about five miles from the International Settlement, to report that "the wounded are not cared for but left lying where they fall."[*]

The armies bunkered down between Soochow and the Chinese suburbs of Shanghai. Provincial governors, army generals, and self-appointed warlords came and went with alarming frequency. Quite who was in control was never clear. And occasionally the fighting came close to the Settlement's borders. Very close, indeed, on occasion—the Shanghai Golf Club in Hungjao, on the western edge of the Settlement, closed in 1924 due to the danger posed by shrapnel on the greens.

America was watching the situation closely. To Washington's mind, the uncertainty around who controlled Kiangsu, Chekiang, and the hinterlands around Shanghai was as potentially destabilizing as the strikes and boycotts in Canton or the constant skirmishing across northern China. It was another powder keg indicating the possibility of a full-on civil war in China. America was backing Sun Yat-sen in the hope that, despite being sick with the cancer that would eventually kill him the following year, he was still the only man who could possibly bring all the myriad factions together. There was talk

---

[*] "Chekiang Troops Back of the Fighting Line," *Syracuse Journal and Republican-News*, November 14, 1924.

of a major peace conference to be held in Tientsin. It would be partly brokered by the US and chaired by Dr. Sun. But how to coordinate the efforts?

Canton, Shanghai, Tientsin, and Peking were now all surrounded by warlord troops, with faction constantly fighting faction across the region, adding to the general outbreak of banditry, kidnapping, and lawless chaos. Crop yields collapsed, disease outbreaks were common; the unprecedentedly heavy rains of late 1924 saw rivers burst their banks, dams break, and more fields and villages flooded.

The confusion meant that transport and communications between the four major cities of the country, each with a sizable US diplomatic presence, were massively disrupted. The KCR was cut, isolating Canton from Hong Kong; the Shanghai-Tientsin line likewise, meaning no rail connections northward. Telephone conversations were impossible, radio telegraph transmissions intermittent at best, postal services essentially defunct. Just to add to the problems in Tientsin, the city and surrounding countryside were in the grip of a severe and deadly typhoid outbreak. Human couriers were the only form of reliable transmission between diplomatic outposts, and with manpower short, that meant using navy wives as document couriers. At some point in this chaotic situation, it was decided that Wallis and Mary would travel to Tientsin.

Wallis claimed in her memoirs that Mary suggested a "shopping trip to Peking," an odd notion given the circumstances.[*] She also noted in her memoirs that her aunt Bessie and cousin Leila had traveled widely and visited Peking some years previous, being appreciative of the city's ancient charms.[†] But these again are unconvincing reasons to travel in such obviously dangerous times. Neither Mary nor Wallis could have failed to read in the newspapers of the dire situation regarding warlords, bandits, and typhoid in Tientsin in late

---

[*] Simpson, *The Heart Has Its Reasons*, 108.
[†] Simpson, *The Heart Has Its Reasons*, 108.

1924, of the hazardous traveling conditions. Knowing she needed to return home to obtain a divorce, Wallis could have left directly for the United States. There were regular, almost weekly, liner sailings to America from Shanghai. To head north, to Tientsin, and then onward to Peking in late 1924 for shopping and sightseeing is by any measure a very strange decision.

Was Wallis once again asked by the US Navy or the American consulate in Shanghai to make the trip carrying documents? Or did she volunteer herself to them? She does not say in her memoirs; the official records in the public domain do not mention who couriered what at this hectic time for American shuttle diplomacy around China. The arrangements appear ad hoc. Whatever the truth, Wallis was now headed into a China in an even more hopelessly tumultuous state than either Canton or Shanghai, a China beset by vicious fratricidal fighting, political intrigue, rampant banditry, and a major deadly epidemic.

In hindsight, Hong Kong, Canton, and Shanghai were just initial experiences for Wallis, small tastes of China. It was to be northern China and the ancient capital of Peking that would be where she would discover an aesthetic that formed her lifelong style, an abiding love of the alleyways and lanes of the city and reveal to her much about her own character and potential.

She gathered her belongings, packed her trunks, said goodbye to Robbie, and headed with Mary back to the Bund Terminal, the lighter, making their journey in reverse down the Whangpoo to Woosung and the waiting passenger steamers. But this time, Wallis was heading north toward even more intense warlord fighting, disease, and bandit-infested countryside. She cannot but have been a little apprehensive at what awaited her in northern China.

5

TWENTY-FOUR HOURS IN TYPHOID TOWN

TIENTSIN EAST RAILWAY STATION
NORTH BANK OF THE PEIHO RIVER, TIENTSIN
DECEMBER 10-12, 1924

Eighty miles to the west lies the Celestial City of Peking where the emperor, the Son of Heaven, reigned. Because the old port at the meeting of the waters gave travellers a way across them to the Celestial City, it was called Tientsin, the Ford of Heaven.

—Brian Power, *The Ford of Heaven*

A local war was in progress, trains were being raided daily . . . a mere civil war.

—Wallis on Tientsin in December 1924

DECEMBER 10, 1924—THE TAKU FORTS

Wallis's only commentary on her brief stop in Tientsin was to casually remark that "a local war was in progress, trains were being raided daily."* After Canton and Shanghai, it seemed war was simply

---

* Wallis Simpson, *The Heart Has Its Reasons* (London: Michael Joseph, 1956), 109.

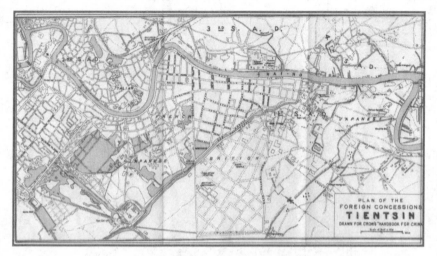

The Tientsin Foreign Concessions

following Wallis; it was everywhere she went from the borders of Hong Kong and mainland China to here in northern China. Wallis didn't tarry long in the treaty port city, but it was an eventful stopover. As she recalled, "a mere civil war" was not going to stop her reaching Peking.[*]

Normally in winter, the Shanghai-Tientsin train was the easiest way north. The train went from Shanghai's North Station in the city's Chinese Chapei (Zhabei) district, via the town of Pukow (Pukou), near Nanking. With no bridge across the Yangtze until the 1960s, passengers left the Shanghai train and took a launch across the river before joining another train to continue to Tientsin. Convoluted, perhaps, but this was the preferred route given the winter ice floes and blockages around Tientsin's port, Tanggu. But in December 1924, train services were suspended due to the continual warlord battles and rampant banditry that saw the track torn up,

_____

* Simpson, *The Heart Has Its Reasons*, 109.

trains attacked, and stations burned. The coastal steamers plowed on regardless, hoping to avoid pirate raids, and hoped the Tanggu port would stay ice-free.

Wallis and Mary Sadler took the Butterfield and Swire coastal steamer SS *Shuntien* from Shanghai north to Tientsin. There was a brief stop to load and off-load cargo and passengers at the port of Chefoo, before arriving at Tientsin. But that didn't always guarantee you'd be able to land at the port of Tientsin, considerably farther north than the subtropical climes of Hong Kong and Shanghai. The biggest worry was ice. Tanggu often completely iced up in the winter months, closing access to Tientsin up the Peiho (Baihe) River. If that happened, then vessels would have to steam even farther north to either Newchwang (Yingkou), a small treaty port on the Bohai Gulf, or even farther to the naval city of Dairen (Dalian), the only guaranteed ice-free port for northern China and with a strong Japanese presence.

Wallis and Mary left Shanghai on December 4. The dropping temperatures as they pushed north meant their cabin remained constantly cold even though, by virtue of being white, they were automatically allocated first-class tickets and cabins. But first class on a coastal steamer was a relative concept. Wallis described the steamer as "a creaky, leaky, rusting tub."* The pair spent most of the voyage in the dining room hesitantly expecting the ship to spring a leak and sink at any moment.

Six days later, on the tenth, they reached the Peiho River, entering between the two imposing Taku Forts, a couple of Ming-era (1520s) strongholds, thirty-seven miles downriver from the treaty port. A wait for high tide to allow the liner to traverse the two-mile sandbar, known as the Taku bar, and then they headed upriver to the foreign concessions. On the Peiho (or often the White River, as the Chinese

---

* Simpson, *The Heart Has Its Reasons*, 108.

believed it looked like a dragon with white scales), they passed wind-
mills and salt farms until they came to the junction with the Grand
Canal, the incredible thousand-mile-long network of man-made canals connecting northern and southern China. Tientsin was technically a port but, like Shanghai, some thirty-five miles inland of
the sea, though the Peiho was capable of accepting passenger and
cargo vessels with larger drafts. Wallis would have been aware of how
the landscape and climate had changed from southern and eastern
China—gray skies, black clouds, the drabness of the northern China
plains, the vast largely deserted kaoliang (sorghum) fields contrast-
ing gloomily with the verdant hills, paddy fields, and market gardens
of southern China.

They finally docked after almost a week at sea, forty-eight hours
longer than the scheduled voyage duration. The captain had sailed
out in a wide arc from Shanghai, farther from the coast, keen to
avoid the common coastal pirate raids and ship-jackings.

THE NORTHERN WARLORDS

Dr. Sun Yat-sen's revolution of 1911 had seen the 267-year-old Qing,
or Manchu, dynasty replaced by the first Chinese Republic. The long,
snaking queues of plaited hair Han Chinese men were forced to wear
had been defiantly cut off, the Manchu elite removed from power,
the imperial system, along with the royal family, dismantled and dispersed. Modernity was in—clothing, railways, and automobiles, as
well as a new, improved, and better-trained army. Sun's government
evolved a concerted carrot-and-stick plan of co-option or coercion
to quell the scourge of warlordism. The self-appointed generals were
entrenched in strongholds across the region from Dairen and the
Korean border near Mukden (Shenyang) to the Russo-Mongolian
borderlands. Unsurprisingly, given the geography, both the Soviets
and the Japanese were interfering while the European "Great Powers"

sat back, waiting to see who would ultimately come to dominate the region. The United States was a far-from-disinterested party in all this. America's embassy and consulates in China were deeply enmeshed in the machinations between the various warlords, the Southern Government, and the competing foreign powers.

As Wallis had witnessed for herself in Canton, the new Chinese Republic was a shaky and divided edifice. Central and southern China had most energetically rallied to the new republic and Dr. Sun. But his administration was divided with splits and schisms amid accusations of Soviet influence, cronyism, and corruption. The Northern Government, based in Peking, had splintered and dissolved at the end of the previous decade and was now constantly up for grabs for any warlord strong enough to take it. China was effectively cleaved down the middle, and in the northern Chinese power vacuum, a plethora of warlords rampaged constantly with Peking as the ultimate prize in their internecine struggles. Meanwhile, that same vacuum was allowing the predatory Japanese to encroach yet further on northern China. During the Great War, Japan had seized the coastal city of Tsingtao (Qingdao) from Germany and then occupied the province of Shantung (Shandong). Sensing weakness in disunity, Tokyo had attempted to force yet more territorial concessions from China using both diplomatic means and through backing various bandit and breakaway warlord factions. In protest at the continued occupation of Shantung by Japan, China had been the only nation not to sign the post–Great War Versailles Peace Treaty.

By the early 1920s, China was more divided than ever between south and north. Attempts were made to restore the pre-1911 monarchy by the warlord Chang Hsun (Zhang Xun), the Pigtailed General (who had stubbornly retained his Manchu-era queue) and his five-thousand-strong private army. Zhang was eventually driven from Peking, but this was only the beginning of a decade of revolving warlord occupations of the city. Battles raged across the vast plains of northern China—Peking to Tientsin, up into Manchuria, from

Dairen on the coast to Harbin toward the Sino-Soviet border. These skirmishes took place throughout Wallis's sojourn. From the time she landed at Tientsin until she left China half a year later, she was never more than a few miles from a warlord encampment.

The northern warlords formed, broke, and re-formed in countless temporary and often disingenuous alliances and cliques. The foreign powers, including America, sent some of their smartest diplomats to try to work out what they termed the "centrifugalism" of the warlord disputes—who had the upper hand, which clique or faction might emerge as dominant, whether Dr. Sun and his military commander, Chiang Kai-shek, brought unity. But nobody could keep track of it all.

In 1922, the Mukden-based warlord Chang Tso-lin (Zhang Zuolin), known by many sobriquets—including the Old Marshal, the Tiger of Mukden, and the Rain General, to name a few—attempted to seize power in Peking. He was repelled and forced to retreat to his base in Manchuria, where he regrouped before marching once again on Peking. But a rival warlord Feng Yu-hsiang (Feng Yuxiang), with 170,000 men under arms, occupied the city before Chang could get there. Feng, aka the Christian General (and sometimes the Betrayal General, as he regularly made alliances and then violently broke them) meant business. In November 1924, Feng finally stripped the last emperor, Puyi (not yet twenty years old), of his title, evicting him and his entourage from the Forbidden City to go into exile. Puyi had been given sanctuary by Tokyo, ever playing a game of divide and conquer in northern China, in Tientsin's Japanese concession.

Looking to calm the situation in northern China, and vociferously supported by America, Sun was invited to Peking to attend a National Conference for the Chinese People to discuss the possibility of peace and reunification. Wallis arrived in Tientsin the same day that Sun gave an incendiary speech calling for an end to warlord-ism, something all the foreign powers could support, and then the abolition of all the unequal treaties with the foreign powers. This latter call was not a popular line in London or Paris. The Europeans, adamant at retaining their treaty port powers, accused Sun of being under the sway of Moscow. But he found a more receptive audience in Washington, where the State Department could see potential advantages for America in weakening the traditional power of the Europeans.

Tientsin, like Shanghai, was a treaty port of foreign concessions with an adjacent Chinese city. Not quite as big with just a million inhabit-ants (approximately ten thousand of whom were foreigners in 1924) or quite as rich but arguably as developed and modern as Shanghai. Tientsin was a city of traffic jams, trams, foreign clubs, a tennis club, a racetrack, restaurants, and a varied range of architecture, from British Gothic to Italianate neo-Renaissance. The city's wealth largely derived from being landlocked Peking's port, its nearest gateway to the sea— hence it was known as the "Ford of Heaven," historically providing travelers with access to the Celestial City of Peking and the Emperor of Heaven. Though nowadays Tientsin is often overlooked in rela-tion to Beijing and Shanghai, it was a wealthy, dynamic, and prosper-ous trading port during the interwar years.

For Wallis and Mary, Tientsin should have been safe. The city was a posting for foreign troops of some half dozen nations—American, British, French, Belgian, Japanese, Italian—stationed permanently in the treaty port and with the support of foreign-led concession po-lice forces, again similar to Shanghai. But just outside the city's con-fines, things became decidedly chaotic and lawless. The continued factional fighting of the northern warlords was accentuated by the myriad bandit gangs and traditional criminal secret societies who roamed the countryside, taking advantage of the constant power vacuum and the impotence of the peasants to resist them.

That early December, Tientsin was typically icy cold with below-freezing temperatures accentuated by the biting winds in which the north China coast specializes. Wallis's steamer had had to push past rapidly forming ice floes in the Peiho. The winds whipped down from the Gobi Desert, hundreds of miles to the north, depositing yellow dust on the redbrick buildings of the foreign concessions. The former emperor as well as several warlords were all living in the foreign concessions, with their rivals threatening to storm the city. Skirmishing on the city's outskirts had led to a critical rice shortage in Tientsin with the consequent rampant inflation that happened whenever the most staple food in China was in short supply. And just to add to the chaos, in late 1924, there was a serious and deadly outbreak of typhoid fever.

The typhoid epidemic had followed disastrous flooding in northern China the previous summer that had penetrated Tientsin. For most of the winter, the Old Marshal, Chang Tso-lin, had been camped just outside the city with a reported forty thousand troops mustered and waiting to be transported to Peking to fight rival warlord Feng Yu-hsiang. Typhoid ravaged Chang's men. It was no respecter of boundaries, appearing in the foreign concessions, making all Tientsin a deadly place. That December, if the warlords or the bandits didn't get you, then there was the typhoid. And if you managed to avoid that, there was the freezing cold and widespread food shortages to contend with.

The breakdown in local governance just outside the concessions meant that controlling the epidemic was impossible. The situation was desperate. Various American physicians in the city were involved in trying to coordinate a response but were low on everything from medicines to nurses to blankets. The Asiatic Fleet's USS *Asheville* was dispatched from Manila to Tientsin to evacuate US citizens if necessary but would not arrive until Christmas.

THE ASTOR HOUSE HOTEL, VICTORIA ROAD, BRITISH CONCESSION, TIENTSIN

Wallis and Mary stepped off their lighter at the docks into Tientsin to a sea of hassling beggars, exhausted soldiers, insistent peddlers, and beckoning rickshaw pullers. Amid the crowd was one stiff-backed senior official from the US Foreign Service, Clarence E. Gauss, the American consul general for Tsinan (Jinan) in Shantung Province. Gauss informed Wallis and Mary that the situation in northern China was moving fast, but confusingly—"a local war was in progress" as Wallis casually commented.[*]

Gauss took Wallis and Mary to the Astor House Hotel, a haven of warmth, luxury, and peace in the British Concession, and ordered hot tea from the blue-gowned waiters. For those supporting the argument that Wallis was a courier of important documents on behalf of US naval intelligence, her arrival at Tientsin came at a key moment in Chinese politics.

Dr. Sun's presence in Tientsin had led to scuffles among his supporters and the local Chinese police. Students, supportive of the Southern Government, tried to raise a red flag. After his incendiary speech, the general supposition was that Sun and the Old Marshal would jointly meet with the potential local deal broker Li Yuan-hong, a corpulent ex-president of China who had taken up residence in the relative safety of Tientsin's British Concession.[†] Li, who in 1911 (and in his slightly less corpulent days) had commanded Sun's revolutionary army, had maintained good relations with all factions and was generally liked and trusted by just about everyone.

---

[*] Simpson, *The Heart Has Its Reasons*, 108.
[†] Li was president of the Chinese Republic between 1916 and 1917, and then again between 1922 and 1923. He had been chased out of Peking by the Tientsin-based northern warlord Tsao Kun (Cao Kun). Li fled to Japan for medical treatment, then returned to the Tientsin foreign concessions where he died in 1928.

However, both Sun and Li were terminally ill men. Tientsin's freezing-cold weather and the typhoid outbreak were hardly beneficial to their ailments. Still, the hope was that Sun, with Li's help, could calm the constant bickering and fighting of the northern warlords that was causing so much displacement and economic chaos.

Now here was Wallis, who, although separated from her husband, still had official US Navy permission to travel. She was accompanied by Mary Sadler, whose husband, like Wallis's, was also an officer with naval intelligence connections.

As all telegraph communication between Tientsin and Peking had been severed, there was no effective way to triangulate coordinated policy responses between the three major US diplomatic outposts in China. The American consulate in Shanghai could not communicate with Tientsin, and neither city could communicate directly with the American embassy in Peking. Navy wife couriers were just about the only way to communicate large documents across China.

There was certainly nothing else of interest in Tientsin for Wallis—no friends, no shopping, no particular sights of interest, and nobody who could help her with her desired divorce. The city was frozen, diseased, and a potential powder keg of Chinese warlord violence. Onward travel to Peking was disrupted. Quite simply, nobody went to Tientsin in December 1924 who didn't absolutely have to!

And despite being estranged from her mid-ranking US Navy husband, Wallis was met in Tientsin by Clarence Gauss, a man who in other biographies of Wallis has received at best scant attention. Yet Gauss (who had never met Wallis before and didn't know "her people" back home or her husband in a work capacity) found time to journey to a typhoid-ridden city surrounded by warlord armies to meet with her. Gauss would not, in the normal course of events, have had any reason to be in Tientsin. He lived over two hundred miles away in Tsinan. Yet here he was, on the dockside at Tientsin, welcoming Wallis and Mary to the city. Why?

As noted before, the only way to move important documents was by hand—via trusted couriers. And the immediate reason communication with Tientsin was so crucial in December 1924 was that America's State Department, largely through the work of Gauss, had in part brokered the national peace conference Sun had arrived to attend. So if Wallis and Mary had been recruited once more as couriers, this would explain why Gauss, one of the most experienced and informed American "China Hands," was waiting dockside to meet them.

Originally from Bridgeport, Connecticut, but largely raised in Washington, DC, in a Republican family, Clarence Edward Gauss was just thirty-seven in 1924. He had a noticeably large head accentuated by his thin lips and small eyes covered by his round wire spectacles. Though still under forty, Gauss had risen through the ranks to become a consul general, having started his career as a vice consul in Shanghai in 1912. He had been rapidly promoted to consul in Shanghai in 1916 before moving to be consul in the treaty port of Amoy (Xiamen) and then Tsinan. More promotions followed, and he became consul general (the highest post possible outside of a full ambassadorship) in the northern town of Mukden, near the Korean border and a stronghold of the northern warlords. Having served in Tsinan and Mukden, traveling regularly to other northern Chinese cities—Peking to Dairen, Tientsin to Harbin—he had become the State Department's specialist on the northern warlord scourge.

Though not a city that attracts much attention outside China today, Tsinan in the 1920s was largely controlled by the larger-than-life northern warlord Chang Tsung-chan (Zhang Zongchang), alternatively known as the Dogmeat General (due to a fondness for the gambling game *pai gow*, known colloquially as "eating dog meat"), Seventy-Two-Cannon Chang (as he actually had seventy-two cannons), and alternatively the Three-Don't-Knows General (since he could never keep count of how much money, how many soldiers, or how many concubines he had). Tsinan was crucially a major trading post for the Japanese into China (via the Shantung ports) as well as (always helpful to the Dogmeat General's strained coffers) a shipment center for Korean-produced opium into China. Narcotics, warlord politics, and the ever-ongoing Japanese machinations in China all met in Tsinan and were all of interest to the State Department in Washington and to Clarence Gauss. Tsinan in the 1920s was truly that most overworked of espionage novel phrases, a "nest of spies."

The American diplomatic presence in the city at that point required an experienced and knowledgeable representative. Gauss was charged with monitoring an area of potential major conflict with some seriously combustible characters, likely to switch sides at the drop of a hat, mixing warlord politics with criminal gain, and quite possibly, through the financial inducements of Tokyo, traitorous intent. Any Japanese wins in the region were perceived as automatic losses for the United States.

Gauss was a busy man. So it would not be in his normal routine to take the trouble to travel a couple of hundred problematic miles to a typhoid-ridden port to meet an estranged navy wife simply to offer her tiffin at the Astor House Hotel. Gauss had a reason for the trip, and it seems most likely to have been that Wallis and/or Mary were carrying documents pertaining to the potential US-sponsored peace negotiations between Sun and the northern warlords.

Gauss also had a proposition to make. Would the women be prepared to take the train from Tientsin across bandit country to the Chinese capital of Peking?

TIENTSIN EAST STATION, TERMINUS OF THE JINGFENG (PEKING-HARBIN) RAILWAY

Mary Sadler had taken one look at the chaotic state of the Tientsin docks and not liked what she saw. She had stomach trouble, probably from the food on the SS *Shuntien* up from Shanghai. Crowds of feverish-looking Chinese, typhoid leaving them weakened, clutching their stomachs in pain, or seeking privacy to cope with the diarrhea that was often a symptom of the fever, did not allay her concerns. Dangerous-looking men—warlord soldiers, bandits, army deserters—stood about with guns openly displayed while nervous foreigners queued to board the lighter back to the steamer to sail to Shanghai, hoping to escape the fever outbreak and possible invasion of the city by the Old Marshal.

Time was running out. The ice that could block the port completely was closing in—the next steamer out would probably be the last for the next couple of months. Mary, like everyone, had heard the rumors that every train carriage between Tientsin and Peking was full of opium smugglers with pig bladders full of dope strapped to their stomachs, or tales of desperate bandits holding up the trains and robbing the passengers. The bandit tales at least were true. Gauss personally confirmed the situation was deteriorating as the winter cold bit into bandit finances and food reserves. The number of marauding thieves was swelled by deserting troops and desperate villagers scavenging for food.

Wallis weighed up Gauss's offer and also his frank account of the state of the countryside between the two cities. She opted to continue on to the capital. Mary decided this was as far as she wished to go; she was not willing to continue on to Peking. Wallis recalled that Mary, adamant that her husband would never forgive her if she carried onward in such circumstances, boarded the steamer for the return voyage to Shanghai, leaving Wallis alone in Tientsin.[*]

The rail line to Peking was taking up to two days or possibly more of stop-start to complete the eighty miles to Peking in what would normally have been a journey of no more than six hours. The line was subject to derailings, bandit attacks, and endless delays for water,

---

* Simpson, *The Heart Has Its Reasons*, 109.

coal, and track obstructions. None of this appears to have deterred Wallis. She secured from Gauss the necessary travel permits and tickets to proceed to Peking in return for, it seems valid to speculate, agreeing to carry yet more documents to the city.

She could have refused. If Wallis wanted to return to Shanghai, she could easily have done so with Mary. It was also the case that ocean liners destined for North America departed from Tientsin, as well as Shanghai, regularly. She knew only that she might have one or two very casual acquaintances in Peking. Heading to the capital was to head inland, not just potentially into bandit country but also away from any straightforward method of return to the United States.

All that year, American diplomats had been dealing with kidnapping cases across northern China of American citizens, mostly missionaries. The kidnappings were usually by desperate bandits faced with an urgent need to pay their potentially mutinous men, the alternative to being strung up by them. These often did not end well, and several missionaries at remote mission stations had perished before being rescued or their ransoms paid.

After breakfast, Gauss escorted Wallis to Tientsin's East Railway Station to board the Peking train. Charles Higham asserts that no travel was permitted by American women to Peking at the time, unless on official business, due to the warlord menace. This was not strictly true, though travel was officially discouraged. Higham, who believes Wallis was carrying "very important documents," also says that Wallis required a "special military authorization" to travel to Peking and had a "special intelligence-authorised naval passport."*

---

* It does not seem that any such special military authorization was required for American citizens to travel between Tientsin and Peking, though it does seem that Wallis may have been issued a special US Navy pass in order to travel from Hong Kong to Shameen with the Royal Navy (see chapter 4).

Such authorizations were not actually required, and Wallis was traveling on the passport issued in the US prior to her voyage to Hong Kong (which later had to be renewed before she departed China).* Still, Gauss ensured she got the train.

The platforms were crowded. Passengers mingled with hawkers, beggars, railway employees, the inevitable pickpockets, and the "wonks," or stray mongrel dogs, that infested Tientsin that winter. They had no idea when the train would actually leave the station or how long it would take to reach the capital. Gauss told Wallis he would try to cable the American Embassy in Peking, if at all possible, and have her met at the other end. His final words to her were, "Well, if it should be your bad luck to run into trouble, I fancy the bandits will be the ones to regret it. You'll not be a comfortable hostage, that's for sure."†

It was another freezing-cold day, and Wallis was left sitting on her luggage on the platform, as all the Chinese porters had vanished, afraid of approaching warlord armies and the outbreak of typhoid, and in support of yet another citywide labor strike. Once she was finally aboard, an American living in Peking and working for the salt gabelle agency, Eddie Mills, helped her with her bags.‡ Wallis confessed her concerns to Mills about warlords, bandits, holdups on the line, and being robbed. He gave her a useful piece of advice gleaned from his years living in China: "The trick about living in China is to recognise the inconvenient as the normal. But I am inclined to believe that we'll get there all right, after the usual nonsense." Relieved to hear this, Wallis asked, "No bandits, then?" and Mills replied, "Of

---

* Charles Higham, *Wallis: Secret Lives of the Duchess of Windsor* (London: Sidgwick & Jackson, 1988), 40–1.

† Simpson, *The Heart Has Its Reasons*, 109.

‡ As with the customs and posts, the Chinese government employed foreigners to run the national salt gabelle (taxation) agency, which was a major revenue earner and open to corruption.

course. But, as bandits go, the Chinese are the most courteous in the world."[*]

Eventually, the train pulled out of the station and started its long, slow crawl across the gray plains of northern China to Peking. One biographer of Wallis, Ralph G. Martin, claimed she told him the train was stopped by bandits, "but they were very polite bandits, and they let us go on. It was really very exciting."[†] A slight embellishment by Wallis, perhaps, as no mention was made by her again of such adventures and there are no newspaper reports of bandits holding up trains on the line at the time she traveled. But Martin wanted a good story, Wallis wanted to give him one, and by then, everyone had seen Marlene Dietrich in *Shanghai Express*!

Wallis was now headed to a city under the control of an unelected, undeniably bloodthirsty, and anti-foreign warlord who might be usurped in a burst of renewed factional fighting at any moment and replaced by someone even worse, bloodthirstier, and more anti-foreign. Wallis claimed that, following Eddie Mills's advice, she "assumed an air of utter indifference" to sudden jerking halts, rifle-bearing soldiers rushing through the carriages, and the intense cold.[‡] Still, it was disconcerting not knowing until she arrived whether anyone would be at the station to meet her, what sort of lodgings would be provided, or if indeed anybody had any idea she was even on her way.

There was little to see out the windows but endless drab sorghum fields, cold, hard ground, and the occasional poverty-stricken village in the distance. There were frequent stops and starts to check

---

* Simpson, *The Heart Has Its Reasons*, 109–10. Edwin Mills, then living in Peking, was a Harvard graduate and engineer who'd spent time in Korea and Japan as well as China.

† Ralph G. Martin, *The Woman He Loved: The Story of the Duke and Duchess of Windsor* (New York: Simon & Schuster, 1974), 70.

‡ Simpson, *The Heart Has Its Reasons*, 110.

for broken track and a prolonged nervous stop at the heavily guarded Fengtai Railway Station to the southwest of Peking, where passengers could theoretically bypass the capital and catch trains heading south to Canton or north to China's coal capital of Taiyuan (hence the guards aboard ostensibly to protect the vital coal shipments to the capital). The train's heating was off, the complimentary green tea was thinner than usual, the buffet car closed. Wallis would have undoubtedly agreed with the French diplomat Alexis Leger, traveling the line shortly before Wallis had, that "presently China is no longer a country where one can travel in any kind of style."*

Peking would be nothing like colonial Hong Kong, densely packed Canton, or modern Western-style Shanghai. It would be a completely different and much more immersive experience of China from what Wallis had experienced so far. And she would respond positively to the ancient city. Peking was where she would spend the majority of her sojourn in China—not in up-to-date, jazz-age Shanghai as is so often assumed but in the ancient walled city of hutong alleyways, temples, and former imperial splendor. Wallis would stay in Peking for the next six months, eventually to leave a very different woman from the one who arrived on the train from Tientsin that December day.

After Fengtai, the train skirted the Western Hills that dominated the horizon to the west of the city before passing through a tunnel cut through the thick, imposing Tartar Wall that ringed and protected the old imperial city of Peking. And it was to be in Peking that Wallis's Lotus Year really began.

---

* Alexis Leger was also known by his pen name as a poet, Saint-John Perse. Saint-John Perse, *Letters* (Princeton, NJ: Princeton University Press, 1979), 371.

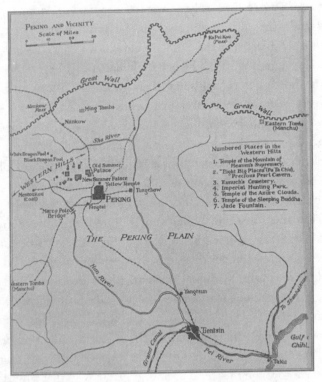

Peking & Environs—From the Great Wall to Tientsin

6

CHANCE ENCOUNTERS
IN PEKING

THE GRAND HÔTEL DE PÉKIN
CHANG'AN AVENUE–ETERNAL PEACE STREET
CENTRAL PEKING
DECEMBER 13–31, 1924

It's difficult for anyone today to think of Peking as the romantic place it seemed (and was) in the early 1920s. Dragons, lacquer and jade, age-old palaces, the Forbidden City, the Temple of Heaven, the Mysterious East, this was the dream, and it was very nearly true.

—Cecil Lewis, *All My Yesterdays*

In a community as small as the Foreign Colony of Peking everybody meets, and a stranger is always welcome.

—J. P. Marquand, *Thank You, Mr. Moto*

SATURDAY, DECEMBER 13, 1924–
CHIENMEN STATION, PEKING

The vast gray mass of the Tartar Wall ran parallel to the train tracks as the Express from Tientsin crawled alongside the concrete platforms of Peking's Chienmen Station. It had taken thirty-eight hours of stops and starts to cover the eighty miles between the two cities.

Signals had been broken here and there, while the driver, worried about track damage, was forced to maintain a slow speed. The train stopped repeatedly, seemingly in the middle of nowhere, often for no explicable reason. Fortunately, on this run at least, the Express had not been attacked. Perhaps the presence on board of armed Chinese soldiers had deterred the rebels; perhaps it was too cold, maybe they all had typhoid, or other people to fight? Still, bandit attacks had become so routine along the line that Chinese, French, and British soldiers regularly accompanied the train. If the Express needed to stop at night to take on additional water or coal, it would be straightaway surrounded by armed sentries, their rifles pointing out into the pitch-blackness, fingers on the triggers. The troubles on the line had been reported excitedly in the American newspapers even before Wallis had left for Hong Kong:

ATTACK ON THE PEKIN EXPRESS

The troops routed the gang of several hundred bandits who attempted to rout the Peking-Hankow express. The driver backed the train out of danger under fire. Bullets struck the locomotive, but no passengers were injured. Traffic on the railway has been temporarily suspended.[*]

A long and potentially dangerous journey. Although, when times were good, the Express was not the worst place to spend a day and a half. Wallis could have stocked up on cigarettes and snacks of candied hawthorns on sticks or boiled sweet potatoes from the peddlers who moved past the train's windows before it departed Tientsin. There was a plush dining car where first-class passengers might order beer, a *stengah* (whiskey and soda), brandy, or a pot of coffee. There were tables for informal games of poker with other passengers or

---

[*] "Attack on the Pekin Express," *Age* (Kansas City), October 26, 1923.

solitaire by oneself. Cigars were available from an onboard humidor. The dining car stewards in their impeccable white uniforms ensured that nobody's ashtray ever overflowed or teacup was ever completely empty. The small dishes of *dianxin* (dim sum)—Chinese snacks—were constantly refilled.

These, however, were not good times. In December 1924, when the Express did manage to run, it was without its usual sleeping cars coupled, and only second- and third-class carriages remained in use. One traveler on the train that month, Gertrude Bass Warner, wrote that the second-class seats had no springs, which made for an exceedingly rough journey, especially hard on her spine and posterior, as the padding had all been removed from behind the seat leather (and "recycled" as insulation in the train staff's winter coats). Due to coal shortages, the train's heating wasn't functioning; the carriages felt as cold inside as out. In first class, men and women kept their furs and gloves on for warmth. Those in the know brought along woolen travel rugs. Passengers could see one another's breath as though everyone was constantly smoking—which they actually were, adding to the hazy atmosphere. Opening a window would have caused a riot of the frozen. Those unfortunate enough to be in the third-class carriages, all Chinese, had only slatted wooden seats to sit on, with no cushioning whatsoever. The electric lighting in the train was broken, and so candles had to be used.

In Peking, the enormous Chienmen Gate (Zhengyangmen) towered over the train, instilling awe in any new visitor. In a sense, Wallis's arrival at Peking was her first journey into a wholly Chinese city, somewhere completely Chinese—no treaty port, no foreign concession, no colony. Peking was technically the capital of China, though Dr. Sun's Southern Government in Canton now existed as an alternative center of power. As Wallis would find throughout her stay, Peking remained seriously contested territory.

If Hong Kong was a tropical England, Shameen a tiny speck of Europe surrounded by a vast Chinese conurbation, and Shanghai one of the most modern cities in the world, then Peking was Wallis's first encounter with what was often termed the *timelessness of China*. Later, the American Graham Peck, who made his first trip to China in 1935, published a memoir, *Two Kinds of Time* (1950).* Peck's account puts into perspective how much had changed in China and how much had remained exactly the same for at least several centuries. This idea of two kinds of Chinese time, the contrast of old and new, was most obvious in Peking.

Wallis was about to encounter the most up-to-date hotel in Asia, where she would be kept awake by the ungreased wheels of electric trolley cars running on the newly laid track down the center of the broad thoroughfare outside her suite. And she would rise at dawn to ride ponies on the ancient Tartar Wall that surrounded the imperial city and watch the camel trains, sometimes up to half a mile long when strung out, stagger to their feet and depart Peking through the Chienmen Gate for the Gobi Desert and the ancient Silk Road. Youthful Chinese flappers, with marceled hair and bright lipstick, contrasted with their elders, hobbled by bound feet. New cinemas played Hollywood movies—"electric shadows"—while Peking opera was performed on street corners and in teahouses nearby.

Wallis disembarked at Chienmen Station into a throng of people. Passengers foreign and Chinese, rich and poor, were instantly accosted by beggars and bootblacks, itinerant vendors of sweetmeats, candied fruits, and hot green tea. Country bumpkins, lost and bewildered, forced off their land and into the capital by marauding warlord troops, mingled wide-eyed with European and American sojourners on the Oriental grand tour fending off or trying to find station porters.

The latter were met by taxis, rickshaws, or liveried hotel buses,

---

* Graham Peck, *Two Kinds of Time: Life in Provincial China* (New York: Houghton Mifflin, 1950).

their welcoming greeters holding signboards. The former were accosted by pushy touts jostling for the more down-market by-the-night hotel and lodging house trade. Station staff and patrolling cops monitored pickpockets and bag-snatchers.

Snow was on the ground. Vicious cold winds swept down from the Gobi and far Siberia beyond, chilling the alighting passengers to the bone. Peking was a bitterly cold city in December 1924, one of the coldest winters on record and probably the most extreme cold Wallis had ever experienced. Fortunately, it seems Clarence Gauss had managed to get a message through to the American legation (as embassies were called in Peking), warning them of her arrival.* As Wallis stepped down from the Express, she was met by Colonel Louis McCarty Little, broad-shouldered in an army greatcoat offering some protection against the cold. Little was the commander of the Marine Corps Guard at the US legation. Wallis had had a vague idea Little was in Peking with the leathernecks (the universal moniker for the US Marines) but had not been sure. It must have been a relief to see him there, his "unmistakable Leatherneck grimness underlying the surface heartiness of his greeting."

"Oh, Louis," she said, "have I really done a terrible thing in coming here?"

Wallis recalled that Little replied with practical Marine logic: "Well, maybe you shouldn't have done it. But you're here, and what might have happened is no longer important."†

---

* It is perhaps a minor point but worth noting that the term *legation* was used in Peking, although at the time, the legations in Peking were essentially embassies. The technical difference between a legation and an embassy is that a legation is headed by an envoy while an embassy is headed by an ambassador. An ambassador was considered the personal representative of the head of state, while an envoy was considered the representative of the government (but not the head of state). Though usually referred to as *ambassadors*, the senior national diplomatic personages in China were invariably formally titled as *envoy extraordinary* and *minister plenipotentiary*. Such distinctions are perhaps arcane but were deemed incredibly important by the diplomatic corps.

† Wallis Simpson, *The Heart Has Its Reasons* (London: Michael Joseph, 1956), 110.

Again, it is worth remembering that Wallis had left a Tientsin mired in political chaos and raging typhoid for another city also surrounded and menaced by competing warlords. She had ventured deeper into China's war-racked interior at the suggestion of an American diplomat she had never met before. The onward journey is further suggestive of the notion that Wallis did work as a courier for the US Office of Naval Intelligence. Tasked by Gauss, having journeyed to Tientsin with documents for him, she then traveled to Peking, where she was met at the railway station by none other than the most senior military official at the American legation, who, apart from presumably a cable from Gauss, had only heard some hours before about the arrival of Wallis Spencer, whom he had met briefly some years earlier in Paris when he had been stationed with the marine guard at the US embassy. He was acquainted with Wallis's cousin Corrine. Charles Higham, in his biography of Wallis, suggests that being met personally by Little indicated that she "must have been carrying some very important documents; it was a rule that a commanding officer was never to leave a major military post in a civil war without some hugely pressing reason, such as contacting a courier."* That Colonel Little should take the time to leave his post to meet Wallis from her train is unlikely had she not been bringing with her from Tientsin something he wanted very badly.

Perhaps further evidence is that Little appears to have pulled a few strings for Wallis—above and beyond those one might reasonably expect a slight acquaintance to proffer an unexpected visitor. If she wasn't couriering something of importance to Colonel Little, then, notwithstanding that they had met fleetingly before in Europe, his considerate treatment of her and the American legation's assistance in securing her accommodation seems beyond what any ordinary visiting American might expect.

---

* Charles Higham, *Wallis: Secret Lives of the Duchess of Windsor* (London: Sidgwick & Jackson, 1988), 41.

THE GRAND HÔTEL DE PÉKIN, CHANG'AN AVENUE

From Chienmen Station, Little escorted Wallis in his car across the city's Legation Quarter, the gated cluster of embassies where most of the city's foreign residents lived, to the nearby Grand Hôtel de Pékin. The white stone building lay off the main thoroughfare of Chang'an, Eternal Peace Street, that formed the northern boundary of the Legation Quarter. It was approached by a grand brick entryway lined at all hours of the day and night with waiting rickshaws, the pullers sitting on their shafts, smoking, chatting, laughing, waiting for fares.

Wallis waited in the ground-floor cocktail lounge crowded with stuffed leather chesterfields and small bamboo tables while Little checked her in. It seems that Little and the American legation had arranged an expensive and, in December 1924, extremely hard-to-secure suite for Wallis. It is questionable whether this could have been achieved without some official pull.

In her autobiography, Wallis accounts for her presence in the city: "My intention then was to stay in Peking perhaps a fortnight, seeing the sights, and shopping around for silks and porcelain."* Her nonchalance belies the facts. A single woman who began traveling in China to seek a divorce, then ventured on to a typhoid-ridden port, and afterward to China's warlord-racked northern provinces, simply in town for a brief sightseeing trip and some shopping?

Wallis was not a woman of independent means. She had no trust fund or monthly stipend beyond a small inheritance from her grandmother and the $225 per month from Win.† Wallis never mentions Win ever augmenting that amount, and it seems unlikely

---

* Simpson, *The Heart Has Its Reasons*, 110.
† According to Wallis in *The Heart Has Its Reasons* and, among others, Ralph G. Martin, *The Woman He Loved: The Story of the Duke and Duchess of Windsor* (New York: Simon & Schuster, 1974), 221.

that a mid-ranking officer with a taste for the bottle would have agreed to foot the bill for his estranged wife to stay in the luxury of the Grand Hôtel de Pékin, by far the city's most expensive establishment. Perhaps Wallis had some money of her own saved, though Shanghai was an expensive city, and she had just stayed at one of the International Settlement's best (and dearest) hotels for a fortnight.

Quite frankly, the Grand Hôtel de Pékin was not an establishment within her budget. Many biographies of Wallis note her arriving in Peking and staying at the Grand Hôtel. However, none seem to have asked the question of how, at a time of immense disruption with many foreigners crowding into Peking to escape the dangerous Chinese hinterlands and city suburbs, she managed to secure a room or how she could afford it.

Wallis's phrasing in her autobiography that she simply "established" herself at the Grand Hôtel ignores the frantic accommodation crunch in warlord-surrounded Peking at the time.* Getting a room in any half-decent hotel in the city in December 1924, not least one as luxurious as the Grand Hôtel in walking distance of the safety of the Legation Quarter, the American legation, and its marine guard, was problematic. Gertrude Bass Warner, the wealthy art collector and indomitable traveler in difficult terrains, arrived in Peking at about the same time in 1924.† In her early sixties, Warner had faced similar challenges as Wallis regarding travel and endured

---

* Simpson, *The Heart Has Its Reasons*, 110.
† Gertrude Bass Warner (1863–1951) was the daughter of Clara Foster and Perkins Bass, who had been Abraham Lincoln's US district attorney. The Foster family had purchased real estate early in the development of Chicago and become immensely wealthy from their investments. She traveled widely in Asia, particularly Japan and China, acquiring artworks. Much of her collection became the foundation of the Murray Warner Collection of Asian Art housed at the University of Oregon's Jordan Schnitzer Museum of Art.

the same much-delayed, chilly, and spartan Express from Tientsin, though with considerably more funds at her disposal to ease the journey and smooth out any problems. In her letters home, Warner recalls December 1924, the freezing and disrupted journey from Tientsin, and observing the Old Marshal's troops camped out by the train lines along the way.[*] Another visitor around the same time was the much-traveled French journalist and writer Albert Londres, who watched the internecine warlord struggles from Peking and declared, "China has gone mad."[†]

Warner had managed, at some cost and argument, to secure rooms at the Grand Hôtel des Wagons-Lits, Peking's second-best hotel after the Grand Hôtel de Pékin and just a short walk to the railway station via the old Water Gate. Known by the wealthy Chinese, who favored the hotel's Palm Court over the snobbier and racially exclusive Grand Hôtel, as the Liu Kuo Fan Tien (Hotel of the Six Empires), the rooms were, according to Ellen Newbold La Motte (an American anti-opium campaigner regularly in China in the 1920s), "dark and shabby," while the large dining room was "big, shabby and gilded."[‡]

Warner recalled Peking in those last weeks of December 1924 in her extensive correspondence. Foreigners traveling across Peking in rickshaws flew the flag of their nation to warn off potential attackers; automobiles were impossible to procure, as they had all been commandeered by General Feng's troops. Warner wrote that looting and the possible sacking of the city by warlord troops was considered highly likely, and shopkeepers slept the night on the floors of their stores. She lamented that the best (by which she meant the

---

[*] Warner's travel diaries are part of the Gertrude Bass Warner papers (AX701) held at the University of Oregon Library.

[†] Albert Londres, *La Chine en folie* (Paris: Albin Michel, 1925).

[‡] Ellen Newbold La Motte, *Peking Dust* (New York: Century, 1919), 14.

Western-run) hotels of Peking were full to bursting with wealthy foreigners and privileged Chinese, such as the Princess Der Ling.* Rooms were simply not to be had even if one was willing and able to pay a substantial premium. Warner thought that the Legation Quarter was probably the only safe part of the city due to the presence of foreign troops. Shocked by the chaos of Peking, she was eager to get herself, and the priceless curios she had purchased for her collection, back to Tientsin, out of the country, and home to the United States. However, with the trains so problematic, she worried that if she checked out of the Wagons-Lits to go to the station only to find services canceled, it would be impossible to get a room again when she returned.

Into this same frenzy stepped a considerably less well-funded Wallis. However, she was met at the station by a marine colonel and escorted by car to the best hotel in the city where a suite had been made ready for her. Clearly, Wallis Spencer was no ordinary arrival to the beleaguered capital.

The city of Peking itself—that is to say, the once imperial city contained within the Tartar Wall—rarely saw actual warlord fighting up close. The presence of the foreign legations and their guards kept the northern warlords off the streets of the Legation Quarter and outside the Tartar City wall. However, on the other side of that looming wall, in the tumultuous decade between 1920 and 1930, no less than six full-scale wars—featuring cavalry, armored vehicles and trains,

---

* Warner is mistaken here and actually means "Nellie" Yu Rongling, the younger sister of Der Ling, who had served as a lady-in-waiting to the empress dowager Cixi in the final years of the Qing dynasty. Yu Rongling is perhaps best remembered now for having studied dance with Sarah Bernhardt in Paris and effectively introducing the concept of modern dance to China. Der Ling was married and living in America in 1924.

heavy artillery, low-flying aircraft, and thousands of troops—took place across the North China plains. Warlord armies roamed the nearby Western Hills that overlooked the city and often encamped right up against the city wall itself in full view of anyone strolling along the top. Deserters, posing as refugees from the countryside, entered the city, stealing from shops and robbing houses, becoming a constant problem for the police.

As the man ultimately in charge of the security of all Americans in northern China, Louis Little had enough pull to get Wallis a room at the Grand Hôtel de Pékin. He also had the budget, through legation funds, to pay for the room. It was no doubt the commanding presence of Little, the highest representative of the American military in the city, that assuaged any fears the management may have harbored toward checking in an unchaperoned young woman for an indeterminate stay. Wallis had next to no luggage and offered no forwarding or permanent address, simply signing that she had arrived from the Palace Hotel, Shanghai.

Without Little to vouch for her, Wallis had "Coaster" written all over her! Harry Hervey, traveling much the same route from Hong Kong to Canton to Shanghai to Peking at the same time Wallis did, described a Coaster as "a woman of somewhat easy virtue who makes her living off men up and down the China coast." Hervey went on to fictionalize the China Coaster, a variation on the American girls of Shanghai legend, in the person of Madeline, aka Shanghai Lily, immortalized by Marlene Dietrich in Josef von Sternberg's hit movie *Shanghai Express* (1932):

> "Shanghai Lily is aboard, the Coaster . . ."
>
> "What in the name of Confucius is a 'Coaster'?"
>
> "You're hopeless. It's a woman who lives by her wits on the China Coast."

And Dietrich was given the immortal line:

"It took more than one man to change my name to Shanghai Lily."*

Chaos reigned a couple of miles away, but the Beaux-Arts-style, seven-story hotel, opened in 1915 with two hundred luxury rooms, still liked to think it maintained the highest of standards—no Coasters at the *Grand Hôtel*!

Wallis got to her room and collapsed. She had been on the road for the best part of a week, and it had been a rough ride. But all that could be forgotten in a heated room with clean sheets and thick pillows, an en suite bathroom with hot running water, and twenty-four-hour room service provided by French chefs. Heaven.†

That first morning, flinging back the curtains, Wallis saw ancient Peking for the first time in daylight. French windows led out onto little balconies from where one could see the rose-colored walls and yellow-tiled roofs of the Forbidden City close by and, in December, ice in its surrounding moats.

The narrow and ancient hutong lanes between the hotel and the former Chinese imperial palace awoke early as old men walked their pet birds, flutes attached to their tails, the music a sort of whirring

---

* Harry Hervey, treatment for *Shanghai Express*, Joseph Freeman Papers (Collection Number: 80159), folder 11, Hoover Institution Archives, Stanford, California. The Dietrich character Madeline is named Laura Mason in Hervey's original treatment. The dialogue is from Jules Furthman's script for *Shanghai Express* (Los Angeles: Paramount Pictures, 1932).

† The Grand Hôtel was, at the time, considered to be smarter than either the Palace or the Astor House in Shanghai. The Majestic in Shanghai had only been opened a few months before in 1924. Rivals such as the Peninsula in Hong Kong and the Cathay on Shanghai's Bund came later, in 1928 and 1929, respectively. Arguably, the only two establishments in Asia to compete with the Grand Hôtel were Raffles in Singapore and the Imperial in Tokyo, designed by Frank Lloyd Wright and newly opened in 1923 after the first hotel was destroyed by fire a year earlier (incidentally while Edward, Prince of Wales, was staying there on a state visit).

aeolian harp sound. From the higher rooms, one could see above the uniform gray Peking dust as far as the Western Hills, so hopefully avoiding the infamous *ganmao*, or hacking "Peking cough," with a blocked nose and other flu-like symptoms, or just the commonplace sore throats and bronchial colds of the winter months.*

For the next week or so, Wallis appears to have stayed at the Grand Hôtel de Pékin on the American government's largesse, supplemented by her stipend from Win. The former would not last forever; the latter was a limited amount. And so the question of what Wallis was to do next gradually became more urgent as her funds ran low and Christmas approached.

Then by pure serendipity, in the fortnight between her arrival and Christmas 1924, Wallis was the fortunate recipient of three chance encounters. These would decide her stay in the city for an extended sojourn and make her self-proclaimed Lotus Year possible.

CHANCE ENCOUNTERS

Wallis's first chance encounter had been Louis Little. While some have seen her arrival in Peking and meeting with him as an example of her ability to milk even the most minor acquaintance to her advantage, there really is no evidence that she knew it would be Colonel Little who would meet her from the incoming Tientsin train and even less evidence that, were that the case, he could have suddenly magicked up a room at the Grand Hôtel. Still, Little did prove to be

---

* A young L. Ron Hubbard, whose father was based at the US Navy station at Guam, visited Peking a few years after Wallis and wrote in his journal, "Peking is not a very pleasant place to live. Every year, about October their winter sets in and remains seated until May, without any moisture at all. The dust becomes ankle deep in the roads and gets into everything. It causes a 'Peking sore throat' which lasts all winter." L. Ron Hubbard, *Early Years of Adventure: Letters and Journals* (Copenhagen: New Era Cap, 2012).

useful in the early days of her stay, and their meeting does seem to have led to a renewed and deeper friendship.

Wallis immediately began to explore Peking, partly in the company of Little, partly on her own. Louis Little appears to have provided her an introduction to the American colony around the Legation Quarter, particularly the officers of the Marine Corps Legation Guard, some of whom she seems to have known slightly from Coronado, Paris, Washington, Hong Kong, Canton, and Shanghai. It was to be this crowd that initially formed her social nucleus for the Christmas period of 1924.

Little was a good-looking, blond-haired man, a career soldier with family ties to the navy. He was born in 1878 in New York, though was educated in France and then Rhode Island before graduating as a civil engineer. After joining the Marine Corps in 1899, he became part of the American forces that joined the so-called Eight-Nation Alliance to suppress the Boxer Uprising in 1900 and relieve the besieged foreign legations in Peking in the dying years of the Qing dynasty. After China, he served in the American-administered Philippines, Panama, and Cuba. He then returned to China in the summer of 1913 as a language student. Though it perhaps sounds a humble position, it was not uncommon for a Marine Corps officer selected to head the Legation Guard to study Chinese in order to be better able to do his job.

Little was based at the newly rebuilt American legation on the western end of the Legation Quarter's main throughfare and directly opposite the former Russian, now Soviet, legation. The original American embassy had been destroyed by the Boxers in 1900, and a new expanded legation compound in Colonial-Renaissance style was completed by 1905. New embassy buildings and marine barracks were all constructed, a grand entrance arch erected, as well as a central parade ground with a large Marconi radio tower (the tallest structure in Peking) that allowed the city's foreign diplomatic community quarter to maintain at least basic short telegram

contact with the outside world independently of the Chinese telegram system.[*]

Little had spent a spell detached to the US Navy's Asiatic Fleet
before the Great War intervened and he was posted to London. Then
he was moved around a bit—Haiti, Rhode Island, DC—before
somebody must have remembered his time as a language student in
Peking, and after a refresher course, he assumed the post of commander of the American Legation Guard.

Little was in his mid-forties when Wallis arrived on his doorstep.
He enjoyed northern China and Peking life and kept a small stable
of ponies. She was a fellow American citizen in northern China at
a tricky time, and a relation of his old friend Corrine. The pair had
acquaintances in common. However, despite rumors that swirled for
years, it does not seem that Wallis and Little ever became lovers. Little was regarded as a good and serious soldier and a fair commander
by his troops. Some commented that he cared more for his ponies
than his men, though he was invariably described as charming.

Wallis also came to know Little's wife, Elsie, and refers to them
collectively, and fondly, as "the Littles." They had only recently married. But she may well have been familiar with her work, as Elsie was
well known to many Americans with an interest in fashion and décor. As Elsie Cobb Wilson (her maiden name and the moniker by
which, professionally, she was always known), she had been a society
decorator in New York and Washington. Born in South Carolina,
she had started to make her name in DC as an interior decorator
shortly before the Great War. Elsie had worked for the Red Cross
in Europe for a time but always retained her business, receiving

---

[*] The US Congress had agreed to an appropriation of US$60,000 (approximately
US$2,000,000 today) to rebuild the legation compound, though the extremely low
cost of labor in China meant that in purchasing power parity (PPP) terms, this sum
was significant in 1905. Michael J. Moser and Yeone Wei-Chih Moser, *Foreigners
Within the Gates: The Legations at Peking* (Hong Kong: Oxford University Press,
1993), 102.

commissions to decorate private Washington residences as well as hotel suites in Manhattan. Her brother was a marine and introduced her to Louis Little. She found him charming and well-mannered. They married, and she followed him to his new post in Peking.

Elsie was stylish, accomplished, and American—a good friend for the newly arrived Wallis. But watching the couples at the late-afternoon/early-evening *thé-dansants* (tea dances) and the rooftop dances at the Grand Hôtel, Wallis may have been thinking that what she really would have liked was a dance partner.

In the course of an average week, probably at least half of the Foreign Colony of Peking, as the foreigners referred to themselves in the city, passed through the lobby of the Grand Hôtel. If you wanted to know who was who in the Chinese capital's foreign world, at least the upper end of its social scale, then the "GHP" was the place to stay, shop, drink, dance, or take the legendary tiffin.*

Christmas was coming, and it wasn't necessary to leave the hotel or venture far beyond its environs to source all one's holiday requirements. The busy commercial thoroughfare of Morrison Street close by specialized in stores much favored by the Foreign Colony and known by the Chinese as "one price" shops because, to their frequent amazement, there was no haggling on price! Morrison Street was Wanfuting (Wangfujing) to the Chinese, with department stores, jewelers, furriers, dentists, and banks. The adjacent Tung An Shih Chang, known to the Foreign Colony as the Morrison Street Bazaar, was full of perfect stocking stuffers and open virtually all night.† So

---

* The China coast pidgin English pseudonymous poet Shamus A'Rabbitt once described a Peking tiffin as "a midday meal of such proportions as to induce sleep." Shamus A'Rabbitt, *China Coast Ballads* (Shanghai: A. R. Hager, 1938).

† In 1924–25, the only areas of Peking with electric streetlights were the Legation Quarter and Morrison Street.

popular was it with foreigners and curious Chinese that a Salvation Army band gathered there to perform at Christmastime.

But if the cold or snow was too much, the lobby of the Grand Hô-tel could provide just about everything. Antiques, curios, artworks, fur coats, and silk dresses were for sale at the Camel's Bell, an emporium of everything the foreign visitor could want, and run by a stylish and very social American woman of long residence in the city, Helen Burton. If you wanted the latest novels from Europe or the United States, you could acquire them along with an original calligraphic scroll for your wall back home from another Peking veteran, the Frenchman Henri Vetch, who ran the hotel bookshop. Handily, there was an American Express kiosk for liner, train, or onward hotel booking and tickets, and a currency exchange.

One day, as Christmas approached and Wallis loitered in the Grand Hôtel's lobby, perhaps sampling the complimentary eggnog Helen Burton offered to customers at the Camel's Bell at this festive time, she ran into Gerry Greene, another former acquaintance.

Wallis had been introduced to Greene a couple of times in Paris, where he had been stationed as a minor American diplomat. At least he had been "minor" back then. Now, in Peking, he was something far grander—first secretary to the United States legation to the Republic of China. To be fair, there were several first secretaries at the legation, but it was still a high position and awarded Greene an automatic leading role in the Foreign Colony. It was also the case that, being the Chinese capital and the center for all foreign embassies, diplomats were considered the top of the social tree in the city. The social swirl of Peking revolved around the diplomacy business and the Legation Quarter rather than commerce or finance, as in Shanghai and Tientsin. Peking had far fewer rich foreign businessmen, bullion dealers, or bankers. If you wanted to be noticed and invited to all the right parties and receptions in Peking, then being squired around town by a senior diplomat was the most effective way.

Wallis would claim that a mutual acquaintance in Shanghai had told her Greene was now stationed in Peking. Indeed, he had only been posted to the city the previous July so was relatively new to Peking and its Foreign Colony. Greene appears to have been keen to renew their slight acquaintance and liked Wallis. She seems to have genuinely liked him too. Like Robbie in Shanghai, he was a most suitable bachelor companion about town.

Elbridge Gerry Greene (who may have been a descendant of Elbridge Gerry, the founding father and vice president to America's fifth president, James Madison) was born in 1888 in Dresden, Germany, to Bostonian parents. After Harvard, he had spent most of the Great War posted to London as third secretary at the US embassy, responsible for communications using wartime codes. When the war ended, Greene stayed with the State Department but moved about a lot, spending time in Paris at the Versailles peace treaty negotiations, the Bulgarian capital of Sofia, Paris again (when he briefly met a visiting Mrs. Spencer once again through her cousin Corrine), and then Peking. He was eight years older than Wallis, single, and loved to dance.

And the Grand Hôtel was a great place to dance. The extremely well-traveled (and coincidentally Baltimore-born) artist Helen Wells Seymour checked into the Grand Hôtel slightly earlier in 1924, having experienced many of the same discomforts as Wallis while traveling up from Shanghai. She was put out that nobody in the Foreign Colony ever dined before 8:30 p.m. and complained of being constantly hungry in the afternoons and early evenings. In order to eat earlier, Helen Wells Seymour would meet with friends on the roof of the Grand Hôtel arriving for the *thé-dansant*. She thought the orchestra marvelous, and observed that many Chinese came to the *thé-dansant* and that "there were many lovely Chinese girls dancing."*

Greene began escorting Wallis to the same *thé-dansants*. They

---

* Helen Wells Seymour, *A Japanese Diary* (New Haven, CT: self-pub., 1956), 136.

were held daily, and Wallis loved them. The orchestra that winter was led by a popular Italian bandleader of long standing in Peking, Signor d'Alessio, and featured a new Russian émigré musician, Monsieur Dobrinsky. Despite the cold weather, Peking is a largely dry city that sees little rainfall, hence the tradition of rooftop dances. You reached the roof garden by one of two American-made Otis elevators. The doors opened onto a large space, exposed to the sky and stars above. It was crisp but beautiful, magical even with the constantly flitting birds and bats, the looming darkness of the now-deserted Forbidden City to the west, and the Legation Quarter's electric streetlamps glimmering opposite.

There was a bar, a bandstand, and a dance floor strung with colored Chinese paper lanterns. There were rattan tables and chairs and charcoal braziers to keep the patrons warm on chilly December nights. Hot toddies were served, and the women offered Mongolian cashmere blankets to wrap around themselves between dances. The Western men wore tails, white silk scarves, or uniforms. The wealthy Chinese men wore Western suits or traditional robes, accompanied by their female partners in tailored silk gowns with Siberian fur wraps, hats, and muffs.

AMONG THE FOREIGN COLONY

If Louis Little had introduced Wallis to the American Legation Quarter clique, Gerry Greene was Wallis's entrée into Peking's Foreign Colony set. He took her to the old temples close to the Forbidden City, down Peking's traditional ancient alleyways, the hutongs, of rose-red walls and roof tiles of imperial yellow denoting their having once been the households of high officials. Near the Grand Hôtel, several disused temples had been turned into restaurants or small supper clubs; others had been colonized by artists, including American women like Bertha Lum, who had studied in Tokyo before moving to China. Lucy Calhoun, the wife of a former American ambassador, had remained in Peking after being widowed and lived in these hutong alleyways too. They had each taken over temples—Lum to create a studio where she worked on her painting, stained glass, and wood-block printing, "Aunt Lucy" running a small boutique pension for a few guests to provide companionship. The temples were beautiful with green roof tiles, raftered ceilings with faded gold dragons on red beams. Hard to heat, but elegant to live in.

There was a tradition at the Grand Hôtel that, after supper, a moonlight rickshaw ride could be arranged. The novelist and long-term China sojourner Stella Benson described these excursions: "Out along the soft dusty roads, in the filigree shadows of the carvings above the shopfronts, in the soft light of paper lanterns, to the sound of cymbals and flutes from the theatres."* The rides ended with visits to the Temple of Heaven, the Temple of Agriculture, the Yellow Temple, or the gray and slightly foreboding Yonghegong Lama Temple. A Great Wall expedition was a must and required rather more planning but could be done within a day. Bus tours were available from the Grand Hôtel, but many preferred to ride the small railway to the Nankow Pass (Juyongguan), the Southern Entry, and then take the so-called camel roads up to the wall, a three-hour trek by donkey.

By day, the Foreign Colony took advantage of the freezing weather to sleigh, skate, and picnic on the frozen canals and lakes. These were often highly organized and quite large affairs, with any number of rented sleighs that could hold six to eight people each. The sleighs were pulled along the canals by hired Chinese, while the guests snuggled down under warm fur blankets with hot water bottles and the inevitable flasks of something alcoholic and warming. Occasionally, the pullers would stop to allow the parties to get out of the sleighs and skate on the ice. Later, they would pause somewhere scenic, the shore of a frozen lake or at a canal-side temple, where it had been prearranged for

---

* Stella Benson, *The Little World* (New York: Macmillan, 1925), 76.

Chinese servants to set up tables covered in white linen with full silver service, a hot buffet, and, of course, ice-cold buckets of champagne.

In her memoirs, Wallis mentions Greene fondly.* He was the first bachelor she was close to in Peking, a charming dancing partner, and a man who could provide her with a social entrée to the Foreign Colony. And so the question arises of whether or not she had an affair with him. Of course, the rumor mill of the China Dossier period suggests she did, but she maintains not. What she does admit was that as Christmas came, her funds had run perilously low. She maintained that she had intended to stay a fortnight at most in Peking, and the impending Christmas marked that deadline.† Delightful as this short interlude in Greene's company had been, Wallis needed to think about her immediate future. But once again, fate intervened.

Christmas arrived, and it seemed the American legation's gratitude for Wallis's document couriering and her own limited funds were fast running out. Fortunately, in her next serendipitous encounter— her third such in Peking—she met another old friend.

Accompanying the Littles and Gerry Greene to the regular late-afternoon *thé-dansant* at the Grand Hôtel, Wallis looked across the ballroom and was surprised to see a familiar face. She couldn't place her at first; the woman was wearing an expensive dress and jewels. But then she remembered—Katherine "Kitty" Bigelow, her friend, former bridge companion, dinner guest, and, just before the Great War, fellow navy wife in Coronado. She described Kitty as "strikingly handsome with a slim figure, shining golden hair, and slate blue eyes."‡

* In her memoirs, Wallis remembers Greene, though repeatedly misspells his surname as *Green*.
† Simpson, *The Heart Has Its Reasons*, 110.
‡ Simpson, *The Heart Has Its Reasons*, 111.

Kitty had been married to a navy pilot, Ernest Bigelow, who had been friends with Win. Unlike Win, Ernest had been deployed to France in 1917. Kitty had followed her husband to Europe, signing up as a nurse with the American Red Cross. The Bigelows left California, leaving Wallis with few friends in Coronado and with the aggrieved Win, feeling left out of the war, drinking heavily. Wallis had not seen her since. But Kitty had decidedly moved on and up in the world. In *The Heart Has Its Reasons*, Wallis admits she had heard the Littles were in Peking and, while in Shanghai, had heard Gerry Greene had been posted to the city, but she had absolutely no idea Kitty was in China at all.

Widowed in the war, Kitty had subsequently remarried a US army intelligence officer in France and was now Mrs. Herman Rogers. Herman Livingston Rogers, born in 1891, was a handsome and erudite man, an athlete and well educated, a graduate of Yale and then the Massachusetts Institute of Technology. He was also extremely wealthy and the son of an American millionaire railroad tycoon. Home was the Gothic Crumwold estate, adjacent to the Hyde Park property of the Roosevelt family in upstate New York. Crumwold was said to be a happy home and always open to friends and family. Herman was said to have acquired his habit of generous hospitality from his father.

After their marriage in 1920, the Rogerses decided to explore the world. Herman determined to devote himself to a life of travel and self-cultivation. He had the vague idea of writing a book about China. As had so many on the post–Great War grand tour, they visited Peking. They decided they liked the city and its narrow, charming hutongs. They discovered a beautiful courtyard dwelling to rent and settled down to a prolonged sojourn in the city. Herman was struggling to write a book. Kitty, despite being the wife of the wealthiest American expatriate in Peking at the time, was finding the days long and empty.

So Kitty was thrilled to meet Wallis again. They caught up on each other's gossip. Kitty was shocked at the circumstances that had brought Wallis to Peking, but not overly surprised. She was eager to have a close friend. The Rogerses' marriage was good, the couple very much in love, but Herman's literary efforts were stalled, and he was frustratingly blocked. He often spent long hours out riding his ponies or sat at his writing desk, willing himself, unsuccessfully, to put pen to paper. It suited Herman too for Kitty to have a companion, and their courtyard hutong house had plenty of room to spare for guests. They made a well-suited trio; Herman was thirty-three, Kitty thirty, and Wallis twenty-eight.   ·

Herman readily agreed that Kitty's old Coronado friend should come live with them. Thus, after a series of seemingly completely serendipitous encounters, Wallis's Peking fortnight became an extended and open-ended stay.

Wallis's 1936 biographer, Edwina H. Wilson, asserts, without any evidence, that Kitty, hearing Wallis was in Shanghai (though how she would have known this is not specified), invited her to Peking. She also suggests that perhaps Wallis took advantage of Kitty's newfound wealth and generosity. If Kitty did know Wallis was in Peking, then she didn't meet Wallis when she arrived and left her to her own devices for at least a fortnight before making contact, which seems unlikely. There is absolutely no evidence that Wallis had any notion that Kitty was in Peking, and she probably had no knowledge of the change in Kitty's personal circumstances.

Other darker voices have alleged that Wallis was somehow aware of Kitty's good fortune in the marriage stakes (which is possible via newspapers, etc.), knew she was resident in Peking (which I can find no records of having been publicly reported), and traveled to the Chinese capital on a rusty coastal steamer via Tientsin in the middle of a typhoid epidemic and raging warlord battles to engineer herself a place in Kitty's home and her husband's affections and bed—having avoided contact with her for a fortnight until her finances were on the verge of running out. This again seems far-fetched.

So many rumors would swirl around the true nature of the friendship between Wallis, Kitty, and Herman that it proves difficult to discern the original relationship. Most of the later allegations—that they formed a passionate ménage à trois; that Wallis tried to separate Kitty from her millionaire husband and catch him for herself; that she borrowed money from them without ever intending to repay it; that Wallis stirred up trouble, causing horrible arguments between the Rogerses that almost led to their divorce—are all unverifiable. As is the suggestion that Wallis became pregnant by Herman and had an abortion in Peking. These are further examples, with no evidence, of the contents of the China Dossier concerning Wallis.

If anything of this nature did occur, then how does one reconcile this with the fact that the Rogerses were to be regular guests of Mrs. Wallis Simpson ten years later at Fort Belvedere (the Windsor home of the Prince of Wales) and that, in December 1936, it was to Herman and Kitty's villa on the French Riviera that Wallis, by then the recently divorced Mrs. Simpson, escaped to hide from the British press when the abdication crisis struck? Herman then gave her away at her wedding to the abdicated king. She remained friends with the couple for the rest of their lives. Herman helped the duke and duchess house hunt in Paris after their marriage.[*] None of this indicates that she did anything to disturb the equilibrium of the Rogerses' marriage, nor of Herman's remarriage after Kitty's death in 1949.

Shortly after their reacquaintance, it was agreed that Wallis should move in with the couple. Rickshaws were dispatched to col-

---

[*] According to an article by Wallis biographer Andrew Morton, who alleges there was some relationship. Andrew Morton, "Demented with Jealousy, Wallis Tried to Sabotage the Wedding of the Woman Who Stole the Love of Her Life," *Scottish Daily Mail*, February 5, 2018, and Andrew Morton, *Wallis in Love: The Untold Life of the Duchess of Windsor, the Woman Who Changed the Monarchy* (New York: Grand Central, 2018).

lect her luggage. She checked out of the Grand Hôtel and moved less than a mile away to #4 Shih-Chia Hutong, the Rogerses' courtyard home.*

Wallis must have been mightily relieved at this third chance encounter, this piece of luck in meeting Kitty again and in such different personal circumstances. Any American legation largesse could not be expected to last much longer. Staying at the Grand Hôtel on her limited resources would have been impossible.

It is difficult to estimate given currency fluctuations and the vast differences in purchasing power parity between the United States and China in the 1920s, but the poet, author, and wife of a Peking hotel manager at the time, Margaret Mackprang Mackay, estimated that in the mid-1920s, US$250 might keep a woman in basic needs for at most three months in Peking if she ate local food, avoided alcohol, and lived in a small wing of a hutong property.† Wallis was getting a far better offer from Kitty.

She attended the western New Year's Eve celebrations on the roof of the Grand Hôtel with Kitty and Herman. Most of the Foreign Colony gathered to watch fireworks arc and explode over the pavilions of the Forbidden City. The last day of 1924 was one of great relief for Mrs. Wallis Spencer and the start of a great adventure in Peking.

---

* Again, it is unclear who settled the bill at the Grand Hôtel—Wallis, the US authorities in Peking, the Rogerses, a mix of all three?

† Margaret Mackprang Mackay, *The Lady with Jade* (New York: John Day, 1939).

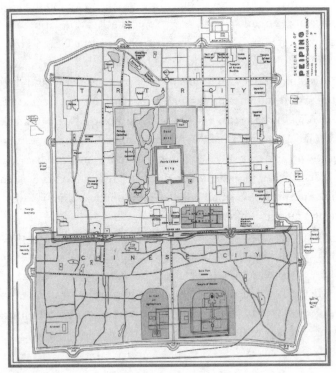

The City of Peking

7

A HUTONG HEAVEN

SHIH-CHIA HUTONG
TARTAR CITY
PEKING
JANUARY 1–JANUARY 24, 1925

Peking is like Paris. It's a city of great antiquity. . . . It's a culture that is so embedded in the place that it has a life of its own.

—Isamu Noguchi

I came to love Peking as I have loved only one other city—Paris.

—Wallis, *The Heart Has Its Reasons*

I pride myself that I know the city of Peking rather better than most Europeans, although no one can be wholly familiar with its infinite complexities or can ever know all the secrets which lie between the blank gray walls of its narrow hutongs.

—J. P. Marquand

NEW YEAR'S DAY 1925
SHIH-CHIA HUTONG, TARTAR CITY

Ancient Peking was composed of three concentric walls, one inside the other, the Forbidden City being the inner and most secret enclave, the Great Within. The Tartar Wall enclosed the imperial Manchu city, lane after lane of quiet hutongs, courtyard homes, and temples, bisected by wide thoroughfares, as well as the foreign-dominated and separate Legation Quarter. Outside the Tartar Wall was the Chinese city and the Great Beyond of the Yellow Winds, the dust storms (or to be more precise, loess storms) that regularly swept in to smother the city.

Since her teenage years, after leaving her wealthy uncle Sol's house, Wallis had missed living in tasteful surroundings. She had endured Aunt Bessie's crowded Baltimore guesthouse, the utilitarian bland functionality of US Navy married quarters in Coronado, long-stay hotels in Washington, and latterly, the basic and dimly lit suites of the Kowloon Hotel. Shih-Chia Hutong was something entirely different. Its aesthetic appealed to Wallis, for here was the chic oriental fashion of contemporary Anglo-European taste she had encountered in Hong Kong and Shanghai's International Settlement in its natural setting. The Rogerses' home was well situated, beautifully decorated, and extremely spacious. Herman and Kitty, with their money-is-no-object ability to furnish the courtyard property, had attended to every detail, from the ashtrays to the stables. Their home was heaven and a refuge to Wallis. As she said in her memoirs, she would come to love Peking as she had only previously loved Paris, and the core of that affection was located at #4 Shih-Chia Hutong.[*]

The lanes that proliferated throughout Peking and came to define its uniqueness for the capital's residents and visitors were (and are what is left of them) known as *hutongs*, the defining structures of Peking, the ancient arteries and veins of the city, a unique Peking form of architecture. The seemingly endless mazes of narrow streets were lined with gated and walled *siheyuan* (or, literally, "four-sided dwellings"), courtyard houses separated from their neighbors and

---

[*] Wallis Simpson, *The Heart Has Its Reasons* (London: Michael Joseph, 1956), 117.

the street by high walls lined with broken glass to deter thieves.* The courtyards were at once both very social dwellings while also very private from the outside world. Many dated back to the Mongol Yuan dynasty (1271–1368) and were extremely practical for Peking life, affording privacy and shade in the hot summers and an effective barrier against the chill winds of winter, as well as space for multi-generational homes.

Robert William Swallow, a *mishkid* (the common slang for the offspring of missionaries) born in Ningpo (Ningbo), wrote in his 1927 book, *Sidelights on Peking Life*:

> A hutong may mean anything from a miserable blind alley, containing a few dilapidated hovels, to a broad side street full of beautiful houses and official buildings. . . . The hutongs are filled with cries and noises of various vendors. These calls are all kinds and descriptions: Some are long and drawn-out wails, ending with a crescendo cadence: a few are short and sharp, but not sweet, whilst others seem to come from the very bowels of the criers.†

While generally calm and peaceful most of the day, there was a constant parade of itinerant tradesmen offering essential services—the world came to the hutongs. That first morning on Shih-Chia Hutong, Wallis would have been woken by the cries of the tradesmen with their large barrows pulled by Mongolian ponies selling water—regular or "sweet water" brought from the springs of the Western Hills—coal, or sesame oil. There were menders of plates, grinders of knives, cobblers, letter writers, and fortune tellers, peddlers of wooden toys, bunches of cut flowers, and embroideries. And

---

* *Siheyuan* simply refers to a courtyard surrounded by buildings and/or walls on all four (*si*) sides. Hutong are invariably lined with *siheyuan* courtyard residences.
† Robert William Swallow, *Sidelights on Peking Life* (Peking: French Bookstore, 1927), 13.

a constant stream of food and beverage vendors with almond tea, rice flour cakes, melon seeds, and all manner of dried fruits on offer. On occasion, everything from an almanac seller to jugglers and acrobats, magicians, impromptu marionette shows to amuse children, and possibly even a dancing bear or a trained mice show. Barbers temporarily set up their stools for customers outside courtyard gates, as did earwax removers, back masseurs, and hair braiders.

The evening might bring a Peking opera troupe who would erect a small stage at the intersection of two hutongs and put on a performance for the residents. Throughout the night could be heard the regular clack-clack of the night watchmen with their pieces of wood banging together to drive away thieves, and a rattle or gong (or both) every two hours—two Western hours being one traditional Chinese hour, a practice still adhered to in the 1920s in the timeless hutongs. Harold Acton wrote that the rattles and gongs always woke up foreigners, while the Chinese woke up if the watchman forgot to bang the gong.* It was a very different Peking from the modern sophistication, elevators, and hot running water of the Grand Hôtel, where Wallis's sleep was disturbed by the honks of taxi horns or screech of trolleybus wheels outside. This was Graham Peck's two kinds of time in action within barely a quarter of a mile of each other.

Western sojourners and aesthetes had long enjoyed living in the hutongs. Before the Great War, this had largely been a practical necessity, as the city had very limited stock of Western-style housing. By the mid-1920s, many foreigners had moved into the confines of the Legation Quarter, where quite a few modern apartment blocks had sprung up. Additionally, some American-style housing had been built for the doctors at the Rockefeller family–funded Peking Union Medical College (PUMC), at the better-funded Christian missions, and for foreign academics employed at Peking's universities.

---

* Harold Acton, *Peonies and Ponies* (London: Chatto & Windus, 1941), 7.

The Repulse Bay Hotel luggage label, Hong Kong, 1920s *(Courtesy of Paul French)*

TOP LEFT: Wallis at Coronado, California, c. 1918

TOP MIDDLE: Wallis with Win just south of San Diego, 1918

RIGHT: The Repulse Bay Hotel, Hong Kong, 1920s *(Courtesy of Paul French)*

BELOW: Hong Kong's Central District *(Courtesy of the University of Bristol, Historical Photographs of China)*

A flower market in Hong Kong *(Courtesy of the University of Bristol, Historical Photographs of China)*

The USS *Pampanga (Courtesy of the US Navy)*

LEFT: The Victoria Hotel, Shameen Island *(Courtesy of the Library of Congress)*

BELOW: Shameen Island, Canton *(Courtesy of Paul French)*

Canton, 1920s *(Courtesy of the University of Bristol, Historical Photographs of China)*

BELOW: The Palace Hotel, Shanghai, 1920s *(Courtesy of Paul French)*

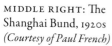

MIDDLE RIGHT: The Shanghai Bund, 1920s *(Courtesy of Paul French)*

BOTTOM RIGHT: The Shanghai Race Club, 1920s *(Courtesy of the University of Bristol, Historical Photographs of China)*

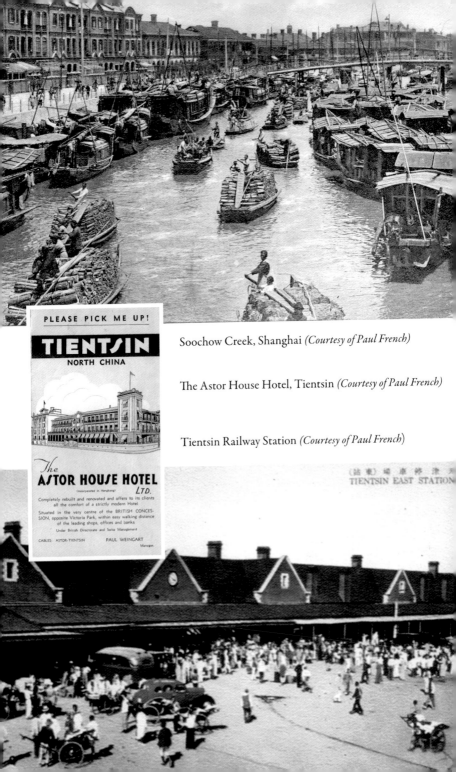

Soochow Creek, Shanghai *(Courtesy of Paul French)*

The Astor House Hotel, Tientsin *(Courtesy of Paul French)*

Tientsin Railway Station *(Courtesy of Paul French)*

PLEASE PICK ME UP!

TIENTSIN
NORTH CHINA

The
ASTOR HOUSE HOTEL
LTD.
(Incorporated in Hongkong)

Completely rebuilt and renovated and offers to its clients
all the comfort of a strictly modern Hotel.

Situated in the very centre of the BRITISH CONCES-
SION, opposite Victoria Park, within easy walking distance
of the leading shops, offices and banks

Under British Directorate and Swiss Management

CABLES: ASTOR-TIENTSIN   PAUL WEINGART
Manager

(法東) 站車停津天
TIENTSIN EAST STATION

TOP: Peking Railway Station *(Courtesy of Paul French)*

MIDDLE: The Grand Hôtel de Pékin, Chang'an Avenue *(Courtesy of Paul French)*

RIGHT: Peking shopfronts *(Courtesy of Special Collections, University of Bristol Library)*

A camel train by the Tartar Wall, 1922
(Photograph by Donald Mennie, courtesy of
Special Collections, University of Bristol Library)

RIGHT: A typical temple in the Western
Hills, 1920s (Photograph by Donald Mennie,
courtesy of Special Collections, University of
Bristol Library)

An aerial view of
the Peking Legation
Quarter (Courtesy of
Paul French)

Wallis and Alberto de Zara at the
Peking Races, Poamachang, 1925

RIGHT: Herman Rogers in 1936 *(Courtesy of* The Illustrated London News*)*

FAR RIGHT: Kitty Rogers *(Courtesy of* The Illustrated London News*)*

RIGHT: Colonel Louis M. Little, Commander of the Marine Corps Guard at the US Legation, Peking

FAR RIGHT: Clarence E. Gauss, US consul-general for Tsinan

The Chienmen Gate, 1922 *(Photograph by Donald Mennie)*

The Villa Lou Viei, French Riviera, 1936, during the abdication crisis. LEFT TO RIGHT: Herman and Kitty Rogers, Wallis, and Lord Perry Brownlow

Graffiti in Peking: "God Damn Britishers! Get out this Road," June 1925 *(Courtesy of Special Collections, University of Bristol Library)*

Still, for those who enjoyed the traditional romance of the city, the hutongs remained the preferred place to live. Among the approximately three thousand hutongs, Shih-Chia, Nan-Chi Tze, and Kuei Chia-Chang were the most popular with the Foreign Colony. Nan-Chi Tze, and the many hutongs close by, ran parallel to the eastern wall of the old Ancestral Temple, north from Chang'an Avenue where the Grand Hôtel was, to Donghuamen (East Flowery Gate), the imposing eastern gate of the Forbidden City. It was well situated for access to the Legation Quarter, which enhanced its popularity among foreigners. Kuei Chia-Chang Hutong (or Armour Factory Alley) was made up of slightly smaller *siheyuan* on average than those on Shih-Chia or Nan-Chi Tze but was close to the Tartar Wall and the looming sixteenth-century watchtower, which the foreigners, hearing the rumors it was haunted by fox spirits, dubbed the Fox Tower (and the Chinese, more prosaically knew as the Dongbianmen, or Eastern Gate). Kuei Chia-Chang afforded easy access to both the Legation Quarter and the retail, restaurant, and socializing district along Hatamen Street (Chongwenmen, and the eastern edge of the Legation Quarter) with its distinctive large red Tung Ssu Pailou (or gateway arch).

Today, the hutongs are mostly destroyed, the remainder truncated with multilane ring roads driven through them. In the 1920s, however, it was possible to walk entirely across the city without leaving the traditional lanes.* Foreign aesthetes thrilled at imagining lives

---

* According to the last survey of Peking by the Nationalist government in 1949, there were over 3,000 largely pristine hutongs. Since then, there has been a drastic decline in their numbers. In 1990, the number fell to 2,250 as large-scale demolition commenced. By 2004, just 1,300 remained, with many of those condemned, the ubiquitous character for demolition (chai, or 拆) chalked on whole hutong lanes due to be eradicated before the city's showcase 2008 Olympics. In 2012, just 900 remained. And today? Best estimate is now fewer than 300, with virtually all those remaining being changed significantly with the addition of new and out-of-character buildings or truncated by demolition.

lived timelessly behind the gates, while flocks of swallows and swifts soared and banked, whistles attached to their tails, their melody adding to the gentle cacophony of peddler cries.

In the 1930s, the English aesthetes Harold Acton and Desmond Parsons both lived on hutongs in large, rented courtyard homes. Parsons's home on Tsui-Hua Hutong was relatively close to Shih-Chia Hutong at the other end of Morrison Street, while Acton lived on the western side of the Forbidden City in his beautifully maintained courtyard home on Gong-Jian Hutong, near Jingshan Park and close to the famous Peking opera performer Mei Lanfang.[*]

Of course, not everyone warmed to this claustrophobic world. The English travel writer Robert Byron visited Peking and stayed with his friend Desmond Parsons on Tsui-Hua Hutong, where he found solitude to write his book *The Road to Oxiana*. But the hutongs were not for him: "Apart from the temples and palaces—all [Peking] is grey, the most positive and emphatic grey you ever saw— all the brick is grey—the landscape is as grey as an engraving—the tiles are grey, so is the air."[†] Byron disliked the icy winds and initially had little interest in Chinese art.[‡] Peking was clearly not for everyone, but Wallis loved Peking's hutongs.

The quiet and leafy Shih-Chia Hutong, which contained several dozen well-built and large courtyard houses, was desirable to both the more aesthetic of the Foreign Colony and the wealthy and cul-

---

[*] Tsui-Hua Hutong is now the truncated Cui-Hua Hutong. Gong-Jian Hutong is now more commonly Gongjian Hutong and remains in reasonable condition.

[†] Robert Byron, *Letters Home*, ed. Lucy Butler (London: John Murray, 1991), 272.

[‡] To be fair, Byron arrived to dreadful weather after coming from the warmth and vividness of Persia and Afghanistan. He also found out that his friend Parsons was dying. Not overly propitious circumstances to forge a relationship with the city. He did eventually come to appreciate Peking's charms more and to acquire a small collection of Chinese paintings.

tured Chinese. Long favored by high officials of the Qing dynasty, Shih-Chia Hutong would continue to be popular with the senior officials of the new Republican government. The hutong was close to Morrison Street, not far from the Legation Quarter, and near the Grand Hôtel de Pékin.

At #4 Shih-Chia Hutong, the Rogerses had the best of both worlds. While the lane was narrow and ancient, with a few small shops and the daily round of itinerant vendors and salesmen, once the Rogerses were in their courtyard, the sounds of the street outside, heard over high walls, through thin embrasures, or the occasionally opening front door, seemed distant.

In Shih-Chia Hutong, little changed since the thirteenth century, just about wide enough to accommodate rickshaws and carts but not motorized taxis—cars deposited their occupants at either end of the lane rather than venture down. Rickshaws came and went, of course, and the occasional sleek mule pulling a Peking cart, wheels studded with nails, polished wooden seats, blue linen blinds pulled down to deliver their anonymous passengers at courtyard gates. Like all the best homes in Peking, it faced south. Robert Byron described Tsui-Hua Hutong:

> The street, like all hutongs, is about 12–15 feet wide—just grey walls of one storey, with trees peeking over the top. The front door is scarlet—and there are large inscriptions over it. No.8 inside is a little court for the rickshaw and the servants' bicycle. Turn left, through a door, into a little vestibule, which is the spirit gateway . . . turn right again, then to the left once more and you are in the main courtyard. Behind is another whole row of rooms and two more courtyards—in one of which, in a main line with the first spirit gate and the axis of the big room is a tall wooden screen, covered with ducks and lotuses, to impede the spirits from reaching the concubine's quarters. The back court has a big tree in it, and the small court beside it . . . a clump of bamboos. Round the walls are various beds which have tree-peonies in them now done

up in straw. The great pot in the middle of the main court is filled with lotuses in summer. The whole is of grey brick, bright grey, but the fronts of every pavilion consist of wooden lattices covered with paper. The courts are brick paved.[*]

The Rogerses had rented their Peking courtyard on a long lease, intending to spend at least several years in China. Quite what they paid for it is not known exactly, though the popular, artistically inclined two-time Italian ambassador to China Daniele Varè wrote in his novel of early-twentieth-century Peking, *The Maker of Heavenly Trousers*, that the annual rent on a fashionable hutong courtyard property was two hundred silver dollars, payable in advance a year ahead.[†]

The Boston novelist J. P. Marquand first visited Peking a few years after Wallis. He swiftly fell in love with the imperial city and particularly the area immediately adjacent to the eastern side of the Forbidden City.[‡] Marquand's description of a well-appointed hutong from one of his Mr. Moto books is similar to where Wallis stayed on Shih-Chia Hutong:

It was one of the most beautiful rooms that I have seen in any country. There was not a trace of Europe in that room. Pillars of

---

[*] Letter from Byron to his sister Anne, February 29, 1936, c/o Tsui-Hua Hutong 8, East City, Peiping. Byron, *Letters Home*, 271–72.

[†] Daniele Varè, *The Maker of Heavenly Trousers* (London: Methuen, 1941), 4. Foreigners were not allowed to purchase property in Peking at the time.

[‡] Marquand came to Peking charged by *The Saturday Evening Post* with finding a replacement for the popular Hawaiian-Chinese detective Charlie Chan after the death of his creator, Earl Derr Biggers. Visiting Japan and China, Marquand came up with the concept of the Japanese secret policeman Mr. Moto. Though Marquand's six Moto books are rarely read today and have been overshadowed by the numerous (and very different) films starring Peter Lorre, they mostly took place in China, were far subtler than the subsequent B movies, and described Peking and the complicated politics of 1930s China particularly well.

camphor wood supported carved roof beams. The trim around the door and windows was sandalwood, carved into a design of herons and lotus flowers. Poetry scrolls were hanging on the walls in bold black Chinese characters. . . . Stiff-backed chairs and tables of black and gold lacquer stood along the walls.[*]

Herman and Kitty had the entire courtyard to themselves. The front entrance was behind a step and then a stone spirit screen (Chinese ghosts cannot navigate sharp turns or steps) and then a moon gate before you entered the main courtyard. Kitty had furnished the rooms with deep-piled Chinese rugs to soften the hard brick floors. The walls were hung with Chinese brocades found on excursions to Tung Chu Shih Kou, known to the Foreign Colony as Embroidery Street due to the cluster of shops all specializing in decorated fabrics and brocades. The dining and living rooms were furnished with a mix of traditional Chinese straight-backed chairs and blackwood tables alongside more comfortable Western armchairs and divans with yellow silk–brocaded cushions. Around the walls were Shansi (Shanxi) cupboards in red or black lacquer, topped with ceramic vases and statuary. Spittoons, for decorative effect rather than use, were interspersed alongside ashtrays on stands. Dining tables were covered with delicate, elaborately patterned Swatow lace tablecloths from southern China; dinner was served on plates patterned with green dragons, and champagne in flutes of Venetian glass the Rogerses had carefully packed and brought with them to China. The painted ceilings were replete with dragons and other symbols of the Chinese astral world, supported by wooden pillars painted in intermingled greens, blues, and reds.

Servants moved about the house silently in white uniforms and

---

[*] J. P. Marquand, *Thank You, Mr. Moto* (London: Fontana, 1937), 98.

soft slippers, with long blue coats for outside. The cook had to learn to use an imported American charcoal stove.* The interior courtyards featured stone flagged pathways running around planted flower beds and lilac bushes. Trees—gingko (or maidenhair trees), persimmon, and jujube—offered some shade while water features suggested coolness in the hot summers. Indigo-clad gardeners tended the flower beds of oleanders and myrtles, pink tree peonies in tubs, miniature red rose trees, and blue and purple wisteria amid small stone bridges and fake streams. They trimmed fruit trees to domestic size. At night, candles were lit in scarlet lanterns in the gardens.

Chinese property owners on Shih-Chia Hutong had long been keen to secure the higher rents foreigners were willing and able to pay. So, though ancient, the property had been upgraded with glass in the windows (rather than the traditional thick translucent paper), a trunk room for luggage storage, a boiler for hot water (and all water, even for drinking, was boiled not only to prevent diseases but because Peking's water was hard and alkaline), an American-made anthracite stove, steam heating, flush toilets, and all the mod cons of the mid-1920s, including electricity and a telephone (though you could only call within Peking). It was a perfect retreat in the center of the city. Herman was able to concentrate on his writing efforts in a study that contained his sizable library.

Wallis was given her own bedroom, a small adjacent study furnished with comfortable Western-style armchairs covered in chintz, and an en suite bathroom. Herman provided Wallis with her own maidservant, known as an *amah*, an older woman dressed in a uni-

---

* Considered essential by Westerners in Peking but potentially lethal. Osbert Sitwell, when a houseguest of Harold Acton, recalled that his friend had had one imported and installed in his hutong home and that he nearly suffocated to death from carbon monoxide poisoning. Philip Ziegler, *Osbert Sitwell* (London: Chatto & Windus, 1998), 208.

form of black trousers, black tunic, black cloth slippers, and with her hair drawn up in a tight bun. She engaged her own dedicated rickshaw boy; a "top class" rickshaw boy, she claimed, who washed his all-white uniform nightly to erase the dust of Peking. For approximately twenty dollars "Mexican" a month, he transported her around town in a modern rubber-tired rickshaw that made trundling along the rather rutted hutongs of Peking a relatively comfortable experience.*

It was perhaps the best digs anyone could hope for in Peking, combining the traditional culture of the East with the modern conveniences of the West, all thanks to the favorable exchange rate with the American silver dollar and the plentiful supply of cheap labor.

HUTONG LIFE

Shih-Chia Hutong had a mix of foreign and Chinese residents; Wallis's new neighbors were all wealthy and well connected. Among the Rogerses' prominent foreign neighbors were Maggiore (Major) Ambrogis Chirieleison, an Italian veteran of the Great War who had come to Peking to manage the Compagnia Italiana d'Estremo Oriente, Italy's largest Far East trading company. Next door to the major was the dapper, mustachioed, and always monocle-wearing

---

* Description mostly from *The Heart Has Its Reasons*, 112, and other accounts of Shih-Chia Hutong from the time. Wallis says in her memoir that her amah and her rickshaw puller were $15 a month. If that is $15 in 1925, then that would be approximately $269 in 2024, but if she is thinking in 1956 prices (when her memoir was published), then it is $168. Both sums actually seem rather high for the time she is talking of. The eagle-headed Mexican dollar, aka the "Dollar Mex," was frequently used by foreigners in China. According to the American Carl Crow, who spent the interwar years in China, the Dollar Mex was introduced "to avoid carrying around five-to-ten-pound lumps of silver [taels] as spending money . . . prices at hotels and stores are quoted in them." The value of the Dollar Mex varied in the 1920s and 1930s from slightly more than a US silver dollar to about 50 percent of the US dollar's value.

Norwegian ambassador Johan Michelet, his Prussian wife, and their daughters. Michelet, who loved traditional Chinese architecture and décor, had designated his courtyard (previously occupied by a high Manchu dignitary before the fall of the Qing) as the Norwegian legation in Peking.* He had covered the walkways between wings of the courtyard to make internal corridors, installed glass windows throughout (though he retained the ornate carvings on the window lattices), and restored the large and impressive lacquered doors to the compound. Opposite Ambassador Michelet and his family was the home of Hans Henning Schroder, the first secretary to the Danish legation in Peking.†

Other foreigners combined sumptuous Shih-Chia Hutong homes with their places of business. Ohioan Forrest M. Titus, his wife, Mabel, and their children lived in a courtyard that was listed as the Peking branch of the American Locomotive Company of New York, while farther along the hutong, the Peking representatives of the massive German import-export company Carlowitz rented a courtyard as both their living quarters and offices. The staff of the Japanese Railway Administration did the same a few doors down. The mid-1920s was the height of railway mania in China (greatly encouraged by train enthusiast Sun Yat-sen), with numerous foreign companies looking

---

* Michelet (1877–1964) had been posted to Paris and London during the Great War and then Peking in 1919. The life of Michelet in Peking is partially recorded in Laila Embleton's *Dancing on a Volcano: The Michelet Sisters from 1914–1945* (self-pub., Lulu .com, 2011).

† Scandinavians were particularly fond of Shih-Chia Hutong. This was due to the early offices of the Great Northern Telegraph Company, run by Danes, being headquartered nearby on Ta Yuan-fu Hutong (now Da Yuanfu and largely demolished in 2010), just off nearby Morrison Street. In 1880, the Qing authorities had decided to establish telegraph service from Peking to Shanghai and then to the outside world. The Danish engineers had stayed in the area at the Hotel de la Paix, known commonly as the Telegraph Hotel, and the hutongs nearby had over time become a gathering location for various Scandinavians as well as the Danish legation on Ta Yuan-fu Hutong.

to lend money to construct railways, sell engines and rolling stock, and become involved in new projects. One of the largest courtyards on the hutong (larger even than the Rogerses') was occupied by the Belgian baron Edmond de Gaffier, the director of the Banque Belge pour l'Étranger, founded by King Leopold in 1882 to specialize in lending China money to construct railways (in return for a significant level of control over them once completed).

Boris Pavlovich Torgasheff and his wife also lived on Shih-Chia Hutong. Torgasheff had been a member of the Mission of the Far East Republic in China, the last holdout of "White" Russia against the "Red" Bolsheviks after the 1917 revolution. They had maintained a short-lived capital at Chita, near the Mongolian border. In 1922, the Far East Republic collapsed as the Bolsheviks consolidated control of the entire country, and Torgasheff was left, like so many other Russian émigrés, both rich and poor, stranded and stateless in China. He had lived in Shanghai for a while before moving to Peking, where he wrote studies on China's mineral wealth and tea cultivation for the Chinese government. Torgasheff's neighbor was Mongton Chih-hsu, a high-ranking Chinese civil servant who advised the Republican government on railway development.

The hutong was also home to a number of culturally influential Chinese families. Sung Fa-hsiang, known in English usually as Fartsan Sung, had studied at Wesleyan University in Connecticut and then at Chicago University. He was well connected to the Republican government and had a brother-in-law high up at the Chinese embassy in London. He'd parlayed his connections to become the managing director of the Sino-Scandinavian Bank in Peking, a job with a salary that allowed for the comforts of a courtyard home. Dr. Philip K. C. Tyau (aka Tiao Tso-chien, or more commonly now Diao Zuoqian) also lived on the hutong. Tyau, a graduate of both Cambridge and St. John's University in Shanghai, as well as having qualified as a barrister at the Middle Temple in London, was a former Chinese minister to Cuba.

In 1900 (or perhaps 1904, the records conflict), Ling Ruitang was born on Shih-Chia Hutong. Ling was the daughter of the fourth wife of a high-ranking Qing official who later served as the mayor of Peking and had occupied a courtyard on the hutong for many years. As a student at the city's Yenching University, Ling met the writer Chen Yuan. They married in 1924, after which she took the name Ling Shuhua. The couple resided initially at the spacious Ling family residence on Shih-Chia Hutong.* Chen was a university lecturer specializing in literature and editing the journal *Contemporary Review*, which reflected a young and modern outlook valuing individualism and freedom of style, mixing short stories with literary criticism. Ling had recently graduated. Petite and bespectacled, she was an admirer of foreign literature and beginning to explore writing in the vernacular style of everyday Chinese, as opposed to the classical style of more formal Chinese. Everything stopped on the hutong when the Bengali poet and social activist Rabindranath Tagore visited the Ling courtyard for tea. Later, the couple would move to Wuhan, where Chen took a teaching post and, a decade later, Ling would meet and have a scandalous affair with a temporary English teacher who had arrived from Britain called Julian Bell—the son of Clive and Vanessa Bell and nephew of Virginia Woolf. Worlds and networks yet to come collided briefly on Shih-Chia Hutong.

In her memoirs, Ling gives an idea of how spacious the *siheyuan* on Shih-Chia Hutong were. She recalled that their courtyard home amply housed "my father, mother, father's two concubines [Ling's mother was the fourth and the third had died] . . . four children, all girls, the families of my father's private secretary, the head steward, the [live-in] tailor, and the gardener . . . and each had their own ser-

---

* #24, which is now the Shijia Hutong Museum.

vants. It was divided into large and small courtyards, all of the same square shape."*

The Rogerses could afford unparalleled luxuries, even in comparison to the rest of the generally well-to-do Foreign Colony. And despite Peking's relative remoteness—Shanghai was 670 miles away; Vladivostok 830—the city was well stocked with luxury and imported foods, from coffee served with tinned condensed milk to cocktails served with genuine French brut Champagne from the Italian wine shop on Hatamen Street that also sold anchovies and Spanish olives. Sugary pastries from the French *confiserie* next door and small gifts of Japanese-made fancy goods were available for guests from Tai's novelty store. Black Siberian caviar was shipped across the Russian border from Lake Baikal, decorated with yellow chrysanthemums in season. There were imported Italian and French liqueurs, Egyptian and American Lucky Strike cigarettes, Colgate toothpaste and shaving soap along with decent razor blades, and even, when refrigerated supplies turned up at Culty's grocery store on Legation Street, French cheeses. New arrivals of stocks of Gervais, Roquefort, and Brie were eagerly awaited and advertised as either "on their way" or "expected soon," although prices could be prohibitive for all but the wealthiest. Just about everything imaginable was shipped to Peking—except for beer, which apparently didn't travel well east of Suez, though the old German-founded (and by 1924 largely Japanese-run) breweries in Tsingtao could supply any foreigner craving a pilsner.†

---

* Ling Su Hua (more commonly now Ling Shuhua), *Ancient Melodies*, with an introduction by Vita Sackville-West (London: Hogarth Press, 1953), 64.

† Carl Crow, *Four Hundred Million Customers: The Experiences, Some Happy, Some Sad, of an American in China and What They Taught Him* (New York: Harper & Brothers, 1937), 162.

Peking was a long way from home, but with money, life wasn't too bad at all. The Rogerses' library was extensive—Herman had the latest fiction and nonfiction sent directly from a New York bookstore, and he bought his scholarly China works at Henri Vetch's French Bookstore in the lobby of the Grand Hôtel. Gramophone records arrived monthly by boat and from the new recording studios in Shanghai. English and American newspapers and illustrated weeklies—*The Saturday Evening Post*, *The Literary Digest*, and *The New York Times*—were perhaps a month or more old but did arrive eventually. More urgent news and stock prices were received by wire at the Peking Club in the Legation Quarter, while local news and gossip was disseminated via several English-language newspapers printed in Peking and Tientsin.

MORNINGS ON THE TARTAR WALL

After the hectic time she had experienced since fleeing Hong Kong, Wallis was content to sink into the Rogerses' calm hutong lifestyle. She quickly became close to Herman. Herman's university studies had left him with a deep interest in China, and he was planning a book on Chinese mythology. This obviously necessitated a great deal of research, and new packages of books, journals, and documents arrived daily from Henri Vetch. Herman would lock himself away for hours in his study at his rolltop desk imported from America, though he constantly complained of being horribly blocked.*

Wallis would rise early to find her maid had laid out slippers and a kimono along with a porcelain cup of flower tea. Before breakfast was served, Wallis would join Herman and sometimes Kitty for appetite-heightening early-morning rides on their ponies stabled

---

* A case of writer's block that appears to have been permanent, as no book on Chinese mythology, or anything else, ever appeared to my knowledge.

close by. Since her days at Baltimore's Oldfields School, where she had learned to ride, Wallis had been afforded little opportunity to get out for a canter. She was soon kitted out in jodhpurs, riding jacket, and gloves from Kierluff's general store in the Legation Quarter and leather boots from the boot maker on Hatamen Street.

The January sunrise was just after 7:00 a.m., and in the brisk and invigorating chill of Peking winter mornings, Wallis, Kitty, and Herman would ride their ponies along the top of the city wall nearby. Morning rides on the Tartar Wall were as much of an institution in Peking as an early canter was on London's Rotten Row, in Paris's Bois de Boulogne, or Berlin's Tiergarten. Norwood Allman, who had studied Chinese in Peking before becoming the American consul in Shanghai in the early 1920s, recalled in his memoirs that a morning ride on the Tartar Wall "was the thing to do!"[*]

Herman was easily wealthy enough to maintain a stable containing several ponies and employ a Chinese *mafoo* (groom). The ponies were all of the stout and squat Mongolian variety, nurtured on the vast grassland steppes to the north of Peking and brought down annually in herds for auction by horse dealers. Alexis Leger, a French diplomat in China at the time (and noted poet under the pseudonym Saint-John Perse) wrote in his journal that a good Mongolian pony cost less in Peking than did the European saddle ordered from Paris or London required to ride it.[†] It was the convention among the Foreign Colony that a lady should never saddle her horse, take it from the stable, or fix its reins—*mafoos* in their black sateen jackets did all that.

The Mongolian pony was a perfect animal for Peking and was also

[*] Norwood F. Allman, *Shanghai Lawyer* (New York: McGraw-Hill, 1943).

[†] Saint-John Perse, *Letters* (Princeton, NJ: Princeton University Press, 1979), 301. Perse deemed a good saddle essential, as the Mongolian pony had a particularly rigid back. Some foreigners in Peking insisted the best style was a more high-arched "Cossack saddle."

the mount of choice in Shanghai and other Chinese cities. They could endure relatively humid summers and severely cold winters. Stocky, with large heads, sledgehammer noses, long manes and tails, as well as short, strong legs, they are usually only between twelve and four-teen hands tall. They gallop with their heads to the ground (trained to watch for ankle-breaking marmot holes on the Mongolian plains, so Leger believed) and tended to bolt, but were excellent jumpers. In Peking, Mongolian ponies pulled carts and traps, raced at the Pao-machang racetrack laid out on a semidesert space just northwest of the city, bore members of the foreign hunt club (to the bemusement and sometimes anger of Chinese farmers whose land and fences got torn up) on paper chases, and provided excellent polo ponies. They had even become the choice of the US Horse Marines, an elite unit of mounted marines based in the American legation and able to move rapidly by pony in the countryside surrounding the city.

The top section of the thirty- to forty-foot-high Tartar Wall was effectively a bridle path in the mornings, and though a poorly main-tained one, it had to be admitted. W. Somerset Maugham walked along the same section of wall a couple of years before Wallis and de-scribed it as "crumbling, old and crenelated."[*] A stone slope allowed access to the emerald-roofed Fox Tower (an abandoned guardhouse of thick walls built at approximately the same time as Shakespeare's wooden Globe Theatre in London), from where the Tartar Wall ran west looking over the Legation Quarter to the north and with the Temple of Heaven off in the distance to the south. Police boxes were situated at the various ramps up to the wall's parapet. It was a racially discriminatory zone. Chinese, with the exception of some old men who walked their songbirds on strings along the parapet and were deemed harmless, were largely barred from this portion of the wall, indicating foreign exclusiveness as well as lingering fears of a renewed

---

[*] W. Somerset Maugham, *On a Chinese Screen* (London: Jonathan Cape, 1928), 9.

Boxer-like anti-foreign insurrection. Possible warlord troop incursions were perceived a problem—that year, US Marines put up barbed wire entanglements from the Fox Tower to the US legation to prevent anyone clambering over the wall and into the Legation Quarter.

Approximately twenty feet wide on top, the wall allowed enough space to canter and trot before it became a gently inclined ramp close to the American legation and Chienmen—essentially the entire east-west length of the Legation Quarter. At the base of the slope, an enterprising businessman had established a farrier's shop, shoeing ponies.

On these morning rides, Wallis enjoyed listening to Herman discourse on Chinese mythology, history, and culture. If it rained, riders could take shelter in the long-abandoned Manchu guardhouses along the wall. The views were amazing. Kestrels could be seen wheeling in the skies above; there was nothing to block the vista. Looking back across the Tartar City toward Shih-Chia Hutong from the top of the wall at around the same time, Osbert Sitwell wrote that you gazed across "a sea of grey roofs surrounding the tall, vivid islands of the Forbidden and Imperial cities, square and rectangular, one within the other."* Daniele Varè noted you could see the old Jesuit observatory at the southeast corner of the wall.†

---

* Osbert Sitwell, *Escape with Me! An Oriental Sketch-book* (London: Macmillan, 1939), 177. Sitwell wrote a poem titled "Rat Week." Describing the work, he said, "The best feature of the Abdication, I reflected as in my mind I surveyed the scene, had been the eventual rout of these people; the worst, the manner in which they had ratted on the King and his friend, who had done so much for them; even those few who in this particular had not so conducted themselves had shown strongly other qualities connected with this objectionable animal, having burrowed and undermined . . . This was the mood in which I wrote Rat Week." One verse refers specifically to the Establishment turning on Wallis—"They found Her conversation good / They called Him 'Majesty Divine' / (Consuming all the drink and food, / 'they burrow and they undermine')." And slightly later, "Where are they now, where are they now." *Rat Week: An Essay on the Abdication* (London: Michael Joseph, 1986).

† Daniele Varè, *The Temple of Costly Experience* (London: Black Swan, 1939), 57.

Camel trains entered the city along the Tartar Wall outside the Legation Quarter and then through the Chienmen Gate. One of the most thorough chroniclers of Peking just prior to Wallis's arrival was Juliet Bredon (her detailed guide to the city, *Peking*, was published in 1920). She described the view from the wall by the Legation Quarter out to the south and the Temple of Heaven in the distance:

> The Chinese city stretches away. In summer when all the trees—of which every little courtyard contains one or two—are in leaf, we get the impression not of a town but of a huge park dominated by the blue dome of the Temple of Heaven which rises like a graceful stone flower above the foliage.*

On a clear winter's morning, it was easy from the vantage point of the top of the Tartar Wall to see a range of mountains, about twenty miles outside the city and ringing it to the north and west like a giant natural amphitheater. This was the start of the vast range of mountains that separated the northeast of China—and Peking—from the distant Mongolian plateau stretching back over a hundred miles to the Gobi Desert. The range protected Peking from the worst of the icy winds blowing down from the north. With a good pair of binoculars and a clear day, it was possible to glimpse the Great Wall.

Looking back on those days of her Lotus Year, a half century later after she had become the Duchess of Windsor, Wallis told one of her biographers, Ralph G. Martin, "We were young, we were gay."†

---

* Juliet Bredon, *Peking: A Historical and Intimate Description of Its Chief Places of Interest* (Shanghai: Kelly & Walsh, 1920), 26.
† Ralph G. Martin, *The Woman He Loved: The Story of the Duke and Duchess of Windsor* (New York: Simon & Schuster, 1974), 89.

And most people she encountered were indeed young and gaily enjoying Foreign Colony life. Around her, the majority of the ordinary Chinese of Peking were struggling with the reality of life under the warlords, unstable and ever-changing governments, rampant inflation, and crops ruined by flood, drought, or bandit skirmishing. But for the foreigners in Peking, these were generally good times. Times of automatic and universally granted privilege, of extremely favorable exchange rates between the Chinese dollar and the currencies of Europe and North America, and, despite the ongoing skirmishes outside the city, of few serious threats to foreigners. Certainly not to Shih-Chia Hutong.

It truly was a hutong heaven. Looking back, Wallis would remember

> the intricate cries of the street hawkers; the tinkle of bells; the clack of wooden rattles; the blowing of reed flutes and trumpets; the banging of the iron pot vendors; the strange reed-like notes of the pigeons as they circled over our garden in the morning turning the air to music with bamboo whistles ingeniously fastened to their tail feathers; and the rhythmic slap-slap of the rickshaw boy's slippers against the pavement as he trotted me home in the evening through the dim streets.[*]

There was one unpleasant incident Wallis recalled. During a day out with Gerry Greene, his chauffeur left the car on Shih-Chia Hutong. Kitty's rickshaw puller, fascinated by the car's engine, turned the crank. The car was in gear, jumped forward, and pinned another watching puller, a young man, to the wall, crushing him. A doctor was called, and the puller taken home on a stretcher. The next

---

[*] Simpson, *The Heart Has Its Reasons*, 118.

day, Wallis and Kitty visited the family, but gangrene had set in, the doctor only prescribing herbs. Kitty tried to persuade the family to take the puller to the nearby Western-run Peking Union Medical College, but the family refused. The boy died that week.

CHINESE NEW YEAR 1925

The lunar Chinese New Year in early 1925 ran from Saturday, January 24, to Thursday, February 12, a long fortnight of rest from work for the citizens of Peking. Out with the wood rat, symbolizing hard work, but also anxiety. In with the wood ox—decisive, straightforward, and always ready to defend the weak and helpless. With the ongoing warlord battles on the outskirts of the city and ever-changing power structures, 1924 had certainly been a year of anxiety. Ordinary Pekingers could but pray the ox would indeed defend the weak and protect their city.

There was the usual nonstop racket of firecrackers, rockets, banged gongs, and clashed symbols to chase bad spirits away and welcome in auspicious ones. Countinghouses, banks, pawnshops, and money lenders stayed open all day and night before the start of the holidays to allow for the rush to ensure that all debts were settled with merchants and landlords and that employees received their Lunar New Year bonuses. Temple fairs saw crowds surge to burn joss sticks, leave offerings, buy children's toys, and consume the countless tasty snacks on offer. Police patrols were doubled to keep order; pickpockets were out in force looking for carelessly guarded wallets or purses. Despite the continuing fighting and banditry in the countryside, the train station was packed as people tried to return to their home provinces to visit family and fulfill filial duties. The city was a crazy mélange of noise and tumult for a week or more. Even the warlords ceased their bickering and celebrated.

Everyone dined out for the festival. Wallis claimed she soon came to love Chinese food. She enjoyed the obligatory full Chinese imperial banquets, attending one reportedly prepared by a prized eunuch cook who had served the former empress dowager Cixi herself. Wallis maintained that she tried everything and never shied away from a dish, no matter how strange or seemingly off-putting. It was a point of pride to taste everything, and to try to appreciate the Chinese sense of what the mouth feels in terms of taste and texture, a sense that often eluded Westerners when faced with sea slugs, birds' nests, or sharks' fins. She appreciated bamboo shoots and shredded ham with sea slug à la Szechuan, fried fish lips, ducks' tongues, white fungus cooked in Shaohsing (Shaoxing) wine, roast turtle, even (so she claimed) fried bears' paws and a dish called the "pudding of seven heavenly flavours."[*]

Across the city, crowds gathered on street corners and along the hutongs to watch impromptu Peking opera singers, acrobats, jugglers, magicians, strongmen, and tellers of fortunes, ancient tales, and mythic legends. Long queues formed at letter writers as illiterate laborers gathered to send greetings to families across the country. A crescendo of fireworks and firecrackers was reached on the fifth day of the celebration when thoughts turned to the God of Wealth and hopes of good fortune for the year to come. On Shih-Chia Hutong, New Year handmade papier-mâché lanterns in the shape of fish with scaly red backs, popping eyes, and open mouths lined the lane on willow frames in purples, oranges, reds, and greens, costing a few cents each at the temple fairs.

The Foreign Colony gathered to watch the fireworks arc over the roof of the Grand Hôtel de Pekin, where the chefs set up an impromptu

---

[*] Osbert Sitwell, visiting China a few years later, also refers to fried bears' paws and a "pudding of seven heavenly flavours" (Philip Ziegler, *Osbert Sitwell* [London: Chatto & Windus, 1998], 208–9). Both authors were being a little sensationalist, as bears' paws, while possibly available in some form, are never listed on any English-language menus from the time or recommended in any local guides. Perhaps an oft-repeated urban legend of Peking among foreigners.

barbecue. They enjoyed the traditional sumptuous buffet and danced to the orchestra at the Grand Hôtel des Wagons-Lits. The more curious visited the packed Chinese theaters around Chienmen, bought goldfish at the sprawling Long Fu Ssu temple fair, or tried local snacks at the Tung An Shih Chang night markets. As businesses shuttered and embassies took a break, many Foreign Colony members sent invites to "at-homes," where friends could drop by, encouraged to bring along any new arrivals to vary the guest list. Cherry brandy, whiskey sodas, and Asti Spumante were served, lacquerware bowls of bonbons placed on small cloth coasters, small pastries from the Russian bakery on Hatamen Street offered round.

A few years later, Osbert Sitwell was visiting his friend Harold Acton in his Peking hutong home. He arrived around the Lunar New Year and noted "azure skies, everyone in blue, every door with a hanging of red, the symbols for double happiness." He feasted on food from the street hawkers—crab apples in sugar, persimmons, bowls of soup, melon seeds, rice wrapped in leaves. From his lodgings on Kan Yu Hutong (Alley of Sweet Rain), Sitwell watched kites flutter and fill the skies over the legion of lanes throughout the Tartar City from dawn till dusk.[*]

Wallis had spent an idyllic month with Herman and Kitty, their hospitality boundless. But she wanted to make her own way in the city. If Wallis was paid a stipend by the US Navy for couriering documents, she never admitted to it, and no paper trail survives. Her accommodation settled for the moment at least, she was still just about able to survive on Win's agreed allowance and the small funds that came from Aunt Bessie in Baltimore.

Now Wallis set about finding ways to make a little more money and to educate herself about China and things Chinese along the way.

---

[*] Sitwell, *Escape with Me!*, 179.

8

JADE HUNTING AT THE THIEVES' MARKET

LIU LI CHANG DISTRICT

CHIENMEN

PEKING

FEBRUARY–MARCH 1925

Life in Peking in the mid-1920s, before the great Chiang Kai-shek upheaval, before China became a modern nation, before the name of Mao Tse-tung was even a whisper in that age-old land, was for foreigners like me a special experience.

—Wallis, *The Heart Has Its Reasons*

In Peking it [time] was a prodigal substance to be lavished on the whims of the moment; and the whims, now that I reassess them in the perspective of a more complicated life, were by and large as mild and stylised as episodes on a Chinese screen.

—Wallis, *The Heart Has Its Reasons*

JADE STREET, THE WESTERN LANES, CHIENMEN

It is not entirely clear what the state of Wallis's finances were in early 1925, but it's safe to say that they were probably stretched. She had the

Lantern Street, Peking

small income from her grandmother's inheritance and the US$225-a-month stipend from Win in Hong Kong.[*]

She no doubt had some payment from the navy or State Department for carrying documents for them, but we can't be sure whether

---

[*] Wallis Simpson, *The Heart Has Its Reasons* (London: Michael Joseph, 1956), 113.

she was ever paid anything more than expenses for what would most likely have been an informal arrangement. In Peking, the generous offer from the Rogerses meant she could stay on in the city she had come to enjoy.

But even with her accommodation gratis, courtesy of Herman and Kitty, her evening jaunts to dances, soirées, and dinner parties covered by the ever-generous Gerry Greene or invites from the Littles, Wallis still required funds. She needed money for her amah and her rickshaw puller, the dresses she ordered from the tailors, as well as the curios, lacquerwares, and screens that caught her eye and couldn't be resisted. All ate deeply into Wallis's purse.

Employment and money-making options for foreign women in Peking ranged from limited to nonexistent. The wives of diplomatic staff sometimes found they could help out with some secretarial work at their husbands' legations. There were a few stores, like Helen Burton's emporium or Henri Vetch's bookshop in the Grand Hôtel de Pékin, that offered jobs, and a few women survived as artists, selling their work to tourists and the Foreign Colony, but not much else.

However, one possible stream of income was from curio dealing. A number of foreign women in the city were making reasonable livings buying and selling antiques, jewelry, and works of art. They would scour the shops and markets, getting to know the dealers, purchasing antiques, handicrafts, or items of jade. They would then sell them on to other members of the Colony or tourists for a markup. Wallis had a potential market, being connected into the networks of the Foreign Colony, the "at-homes" and dinner parties that formed the core of foreign social life in Peking. But before she could start, she needed cash with which to buy the items. Wallis started building a stake in one of the only other ways a solo American woman in Peking's Foreign Colony could—at poker and bridge.

* * *

Bridge was popular with the British, poker the Americans. Wallis, socializing mostly with her fellow American members of the Colony, tended toward poker. Poker was more fashionable in Peking—"Poker for the smart set; bridge for the others," wrote the authors Damien de Martel and Léon de Hoyer (the former a French diplomat and the latter a Russian émigré banker) in their gossipy novel of the 1920s Foreign Colony, *Silhouettes of Peking.*

Shortly after moving in with the Rogerses, Wallis joined their after-dinner poker games, usually held before the weekend dances on the roof of the Grand Hôtel de Pékin, the lobby of the Wagons-Lits, or the Palm Court at the Hotel du Nord. The dances didn't start till ten or eleven at night and regularly went on till perhaps three or four in the morning. So dinner followed by poker or bridge before setting out for the dances was something of a Colony ritual. Visits to other homes often meant after-dinner poker games there too. Herman Rogers recalled Wallis playing long into the night one evening soon after she moved into Shih-Chia Hutong. She counted her final winnings once the other guests had departed and was delighted when they totaled to the equivalent of US$225, the same as her monthly stipend from Win.

Eventually, Herman began to stake Wallis the odd $50 in the pretty-sure knowledge that she'd pay it back out of her winnings that same evening, leaving her the remainder to fund her lifestyle. He claimed that he was never left out of pocket for more than a couple of days. Wallis had honed her poker skills in the long nights with little else to do back in Coronado.[†] They would stand her in good stead—a dozen years later, the Duke of Windsor, a lover of all things American, would thrill at her poker prowess, learned in California and perfected in Peking.

---

[*] Damien de Martel and Léon de Hoyer, *Silhouettes of Peking* (Peking: Henri Vetch, 1926).

[†] Suzy Menkes, *The Windsor Style* (London: Grafton, 1987), 68.

Ann Bridge recalled that in 1920s Peking, women might play poker or bridge virtually all day long—starting before tiffin through to a break for dinner when their husbands returned home from work, and then resuming once more with new partners, playing late into the night, often for more than ten-hour stretches at the small green table. Poker hands became much analyzed and postmortem discussions assumed ridiculous importance in the Colony.* For many, Wallis's skills at poker were matched only by her ability to remain indefinitely in a room filled with cigarette smoke for hours at a time (a fug she undoubtedly contributed to being a heavy smoker, having started back in school at Oldfields). She could start playing as early as 5:00 p.m. and last till the early hours without the least complaint.†

Once she had built a stake, Wallis went shopping...

Where Hong Kong had been a colony of Western shops and the occasional night market, Shanghai again a cosmopolitan city of department stores and modern retailers, Peking was the real deal when it came to hunting down rare, unusual, or intriguing objets. Initially, she would visit shops such as Helen Burton's Camel's Bell, or Burton's rival dealer, the Golden Dragon, in the lobby of the Grand Hôtel des Wagons-Lits, which sold jade and pearls, its shelves stocked with horn lanterns, embroideries, and Chinese and Manchu curios, as well as antiques from Mongolia.

Later, Wallis began trawling the warrens of antique shops clustered around the Liu Li Chang district close to the Chienmen Gate—Jade Street, Silk Street, Lantern Street, Embroidery Street, Blackwood Street, Bookseller's Street, and Pewter Lane (sometimes known collectively as *the Western Lanes*). Prices were lower at these

---

* Ann Bridge, *The Ginger Griffin* (New York: Little, Brown, 1934), 280.
† Edwina H. Wilson, *Her Name Was Wallis Warfield* (New York: E. P. Dutton, 1936), 18.

local dealers than the likes of the Camel's Bell or the Golden Dragon. But the dealers all knew how to tell a *malalo* (slang for a tourist) from a more seasoned Colony member, or a newly arrived Griffin from an Old China Hand, and fixed their prices accordingly.*

The Western Lanes were full of shops to entice the Foreign Colony. So many to choose from—Flower Street on Ssu Tiao Hutong (Huashi Hutong) near Hatamen Street was lined with little shops that sold either plants (cut flowers themselves were considered dead and only really sold by street vendors in the hutongs) or handmade artificial silk flowers. Lantern Street on Chienmen's Lang Fang Tou Tiao Hutong was filled with shopkeepers selling candles and lampshades, fans, scrolls, and all manner of cards (place cards, menu cards, scorecards, *cartes de visite*), as well as lanterns. On Pewter Lane (Xila Hutong), merchants sold both pewter and silverware from workshops in Shanghai and Canton. The stores of Silk Street were all packed with rolls of silk rising to the ceiling, each store trying to outdo the other with more colorful rolls and brocades. On Embroidery Street (which spread across both Tung Chu Shih Kou and Hsi Hu Ying Hutongs) clustered tailors, as well as Peking knot specialists, brocade manufacturers, and sellers of furs and Mandarin coats. Beside them, shops that specialized in batiks patterned with butterflies and songbirds, bolts of heavy "tribute silk" once brought to the capital from far provinces—Kansu (Gansu), Sinkiang—as offerings to the emperor and left stored, forgotten, in imperial godowns for decades.

The storekeepers of Jade Street—little more than a narrow lane, really—were particularly used to dealing with foreigners, having shop signs in both Chinese and English. They would keep their

---

* "The newcomer, the Griffin, as China-side folks call the young fellow who comes out to the Far East," wrote the 1920s Foreign Colony member Genevieve Wimsatt in her memoirs; Genevieve B. Wimsatt, *A Griffin in China* (New York: Funk & Wagnalls, 1927), ix. Wimsatt was from a politically connected Georgetown family, who, after working for the Red Cross in World War I, traveled the world before sojourning in Peking in the 1920s.

treasures inside for the cognoscenti and display worthless bric-a-brac outside for which unknowing tourists would overpay. Inside, sandalwood chests were piled from floor to ceiling, rows of elegant latticework shutters with elaborate carvings might be acquired, and there were cloisonné enamel objects, porcelain snuff bottles, ropes of pearls, the then popular brownish-red gemstone carnelian alongside the ubiquitous jade.

The curio stores were pleasant places to pass an afternoon browsing and haggling. Genevieve Wimsatt spent many afternoons in the shops of Jade Street and around Liu Li Chang, describing them as "snuggeries," they were so warm and welcoming with tea and snacks.*

CURIO FEVER

The ever-observant commentator on Peking life Harold Acton detected that there was a "curio fever" among the Foreign Colony, a mass outbreak of "collecting measles." He declared that "all the foreigners in Peking collected something."† Collecting was the fad of the 1920s and '30s, and many collections would become highly valuable. Calligraphic scrolls, hand-painted fans and lanterns, archer's thumb rings and amulets, ornate carved cricket's cages, camel's hair blankets and throws, Chinese "mud toy" clay sculptures of gods and sages, or everyday peasant scenes. American mishkid Anne Swann was born in Peking to a New Jersey missionary family. She became a great collector of paper gods and created one of the finest collections in the West, mostly purchased from the famous Peking curio store Renhezhidian (Unity Among Men Paper Shop) situated in the traditional papermakers' district adjacent to Kuei Chia-Chang Hutong.

---

* Wimsatt, *A Griffin in China*, 2.
† Harold Acton, *Memoirs of an Aesthete* (London: Methuen, 1948), 277.

There was an associated "textiles fever," with Colony members seeking out brocades, tribute silks, lace tatting, beadwork, filet lace, crochet, and appliqué in either the Peking, Swatow, Canton, or Soochow styles. Around the same time as Anne Swann, another American, the young art historian Carl Schuster from Milwaukee, was in Peking collecting examples of southwestern Chinese folk textile pieces with blue-and-white cross-stitching. He would become America's foremost authority on Chinese folklore and symbolism.[*]

Others hankered after cloisonné decorated metalware, brassware, Shanghai and Canton silversmithing (the silversmiths clustered on Pei Hsiao-Shun Hutong behind Chienmen), and of course the ever-popular Chinese ceramics from the ancient "dragon kilns" of Jingdezhen in Kiangse (Jiangxi) Province. Tientsin and Peking rugs were sought out with traditional Chinese as well as Western-designed/Chinese-weaved in the new art deco motifs specifically manufactured to appeal to the foreign taste. Furniture was of course popular for those moving into their new hutong homes—rattan, blackwood, kosso (Chinese rosewood), or lacquerware with mother-of-pearl inlay.

Nothing was too obscure. Everything sought out and often repurposed. Old stirrups were made into ashtrays, gilt idols became standard lamps, opium-smoking paraphernalia was displayed on mantelpieces, framed lotus shoes (the slippers worn by women with bound feet) as ornaments. Harold Acton's fondly ridiculous character, but a nonetheless accurate rendering of a Foreign Colony type, Mrs. Mascot in his novel *Peonies and Ponies* declares: "In Peking we

---

* Anne Swann's paper gods collection is now part of the C. V. Starr East Asian Library at Columbia University. See also *Peking's Paper Gods* (Sankt Augustin, Germany: Steyler Verlag, 1991). The two major collections of Schuster's are the Schuster Chinese textile collection in the Field Museum, Chicago, and a collection of Chinese prints, including some important early Buddhist woodcuts and some 250 Chinese popular prints, held at the New York Public Library.

all have collections. One simply has to collect, you know . . . it's in the air, an epidemic that catches everyone sooner or later."[*]

Curio hunting was de rigueur, a game played by all the Colony. Joy Packer, a China Bird who followed her Royal Navy China Station officer husband to Hong Kong and various ports in China between the wars, recalled that people brought along curios when invited to dinner parties. "Each guest arrived with some treasure. One had a little music box of exquisite workmanship; another had brought a small bronze horse. A good-looking Frenchman carried a jade Buddha, another guest unwrapped a crystal ball on a black velvet hassock."[†]

EARLY MORNINGS IN THE THIEVES' MARKET

Wallis swiftly proved adept at spotting a bargain. She built a rapport with the dealers in the streets around Liu Li Chang and the Western Lanes. The dealers competed with one another—erecting great carved wooden façades to catch the eye, with large lacquered "beckoning boards" showing gilded Chinese characters on vermillion backgrounds. Outside were arranged displays of ceramic pots and trays of knickknacks. They employed barkers who spoke missionary-school English to stand outside and attempt to lure in *malalo* tourists. The dealers traditionally wore long gowns and had round steel spectacles and gray wispy beards. They sipped jasmine tea and smoked cigarettes all day long. They sold what they called "top-quality jade" in red silk bags with drawstrings. But looks could be deceiving, the robes and tea an elaborate charade to convey a sense of great learning and aesthetic appreciation. It was a well-rehearsed

---

[*] Acton, *Peonies and Ponies*, 45.
[†] Joy Packer, *Pack and Follow: The Adventures of a Naval Wife in Four Parts of the World* (London: Eyre & Spottiswoode, 1945), 195.

sales narrative, as Wallis soon learned and the author of the 1920 *Peking* guide, Juliet Bredon, recounts:

> Do not imagine that the finest shops necessarily sell the best things, often the merchant hidden away in a blind alley has the handsomest ornaments. . . . We may search and search for days and weeks and months and find nothing worth buying, but the hope of drawing a prize in the artistic lottery keeps us interested.[*]

The dealers soon spotted who their regular customers were and would approach them directly, at home, with the best, supposedly choice, pieces. Thus, #4 Shih-Chia Hutong soon became a prime destination for dealers, pitching up in the afternoon, knowing that foreigners were more liable to spend freely after a lengthy, quite probably liquid, lunch. They would arrive with huge bundles of textiles and antiques, lay them out in the living room or on the outdoor patio, and proceed to unwrap them from protective blue cotton wraps for inspection. They would hold delicate cloisonné bowls to the sunlight, proffer Kanghsi (Kangxi) cups, unroll colorful calligraphy scrolls.[†] Juliet Bredon noted that the only Chinese required at these interactions was *to shao* (how much) and *t'ai kuei* (too much).[‡]

Joy Packer explained how the system worked: "The merchant lends you anything you show a tendency to buy. He knows that if you keep it in your house, you will get attached to it and eventually give him his price."[§] Of course, during the lending period, Wallis

---

[*] Juliet Bredon, *Peking: A Historical and Intimate Description of Its Chief Places of Interest* (Shanghai: Kelly & Walsh, 1920), 379.

[†] Kanghsi cups, "supposedly" from the era of the Kangxi emperor's reign (1661–1722), were made of porcelain and painted with polychrome enamels over glaze and invariably produced in the great dragon kilns of Jingdezhen.

[‡] Bredon, *Peking*, 375. And now, for the twenty-first-century curio hunter, *duoshao* and *tai duole*.

[§] Packer, *Pack and Follow*, 195.

could always find someone willing to pay over the stated price, reimburse the merchant, and pocket the difference. But the merchants had ridiculously high markups—at least double or triple the local market stalls—while those shops that catered largely to the higher end of the Colony and the tourist trade—such as the Camel's Bell, the Golden Dragon, or the well-known Japanese dealer Yamanaka, who had a beautiful courtyard home-cum-showroom on Ma Hsien Hutong (Maxian Hutong)—charged at least quadruple or more. If Wallis could befriend the local dealers, be trusted with items she liked, keep margins low, and manage to sell them on to her *malalo* or fellow Foreign Colony customers, then both Wallis and the shopkeeper could do well.

So Wallis, with her rickshaw puller, became more adventurous. She began venturing out to the markets on the edge of the city where, potentially, real bargains were to be had.

Peking had dozens of markets. Some early morning, some night markets, some all day, every day, some just once a week or once a month. Some had a wide range of handicrafts and curios; others were little more than flea markets of desperate ragpickers. The Lung Fu Ssu (Longfu Temple) People's Fair, also known as the Morrison Street Bazaar, welcomed foreigners with stalls designed to appeal to them, with English-speaking merchants selling Chinese furniture, jewelry, silk, and jade. It was also a snacking feast, with vendors proffering sweetmeats, sesame candies, sugared fruits, walnuts, and plums. The market offered an exotic experience for foreign tourists with earwax removers; pavement dentists; dragon-themed rides; bonesetters' tents; fortune tellers; letter writers; face diviners; almanac sellers; retailers of dubious pills and potions to enhance *chi,* fertility, or intellect; various games of chance; acrobats, jugglers, and sword swallowers; as well as a host of pickpockets and beggars. It was an amusement center—a fair, essentially—but not a place to find bargains. For that, Wallis had to get up much earlier and go to the little-known (at least to the average Foreign Colony member) outer reaches of the city.

The Morning Market (Hsiao Shih) was more commonly known to everyone as the Thieves' Market, and according to common lore, the provenance of many of the items on sale was indeed questionable. Sidney Gamble, a researcher with the joint Sino-American universities' Princeton-Yenching Foundation, visited regularly in the 1920s: "The Thieves' Market held outside of Chienmen by flaring torches very early in the morning is one of the sights of the city and people who have 'lost' goods are often able to find them offered for sale there. Through watching the pawn shops and the market, the police are wonderfully successful in tracing stolen goods."[*]

Lit by pitch torches or naphtha flares, traders spread their wares out on the paving stones—often pretty worthless broken doorknobs, old bottles, and bent nails alongside stringless tennis rackets and soleless shoes. But just possibly, a valuable bargain waited to be unearthed by the keen-eyed—purloined or legitimate. As Wallis moved through the market in the semidarkness, she also had to circumnavigate the lazing camels newly arrived at Chienmen around midnight after carrying coal from the Mentoukou mines west of the city. Among the stalls strolled entertainers, storytellers, exhibition boxers, magicians, singers, and sometimes even lecturers from the Board of Education extolling the joint virtues of literacy and republicanism. But not so many members of the Foreign Colony, who either found it all too dirty, too criminal, or too early. The market operated during the hours of early-morning darkness, and then shortly after dawn, stallholders gathered their stock, rolled up their blankets, doused their torches, and disappeared as if the market had never existed.

No less disreputable was the Ghost Market (sometimes called the

---

[*] Sidney D. Gamble, *Peking: A Social Survey* (New York: George H. Doran, 1921), 82. Gamble's work was conducted under the auspices of the Princeton University Center in China and the Peking Young Men's Christian Association.

Dirt Market) at Panjiayuan to the southeast of the city. That market dated back to the late days of the declining Qing dynasty when many officials, realizing their time was almost up and a new republic inevitable, brought their curios (or their purloined Manchu masters' curios) to sell at very low prices, no questions asked. Starting around dawn, the Ghost Market also entailed an early start, as the market was a good half hour's rickshaw ride from Shih-Chia Hutong.

When she began visiting the markets to search for treasures, Wallis inadvertently had perfect timing. In 1924, knowing that expulsion from the Forbidden City was imminent by one warlord or another, many of those around the last emperor, Puyi—the servants, guards, concubines, and palace eunuchs—had been pilfering and selling treasures from the vast collections of the royal family on a grand scale. Many of these items ended up in the Thieves' or Ghost Markets. It was (unfortunately for the conservation of the Forbidden City's heritage and collections) a "golden age" for the private collector.

And Wallis did begin to collect. Rather randomly at first, though many of these items—lacquerware, jade, trinkets, Chinese-style clothes, and furs—would be cherished by Wallis for the rest of her life. In later homes in America, London, Lisbon, Nassau, and France, her lacquerware Chinese boxes, brocades, silks screens, and jade and ivory ornaments accompanied her and took pride of place on coffee tables and mantelpieces. Her early mornings traipsing around Peking's markets, the afternoons sipping jasmine tea and smoking with the dealers in the antiques stores of Liu Li Chang, her rickshaw puller waiting patiently outside, would establish Wallis's aesthetic taste for life.

JADE HUNTER

Above all other collecting obsessions, jade had been the first and would be the longest-lasting passion for Wallis. She developed a "fever" for jade, and she became quite the expert in it.

Oriental jade objets and jewelry had a worldwide vogue in the 1920s, and Wallis found herself at one of the great hearts of the global jade trade. She initially began to collect affordable small jade elephants (also carved in ivory and turquoise) that although not particularly valuable became of enormous sentimental and nostalgic value, accompanying her around the world on her peripatetic travels ever after. After a short spell rummaging through everything the dealers and markets offered, Wallis soon began to seek out jade almost exclusively, both to sell to visitors to Peking and to keep for herself.

Jade (*yu*) was, according to the British expert Una Pope-Hennessy's comprehensive 1923 study, *Early Chinese Jades*, "the purest and most divine of China's national treasures."* Collectors sought nephrite from Turkestan and Yarkand (modern-day Xinjiang) in China's far west, dark green stones from as far north as Lake Baikal in Siberia, and the reputedly best-quality gemstones to be found in the jadeite mines of Burma. Much of the carving, valuation, and trade in jade occurred in Peking, and prices of the most exquisite samples could exceed those of gold.

Jade attracted many foreigners in China—at least those who could afford it. Victor Sassoon, scion of the phenomenally wealthy Baghdadi-Jewish trading family, Cambridge alumna, Great War pilot, and keen amateur photographer, arrived in China from Bombay to learn the family business. He was wildly successful, moving from trading into real estate and creating any number of iconic buildings (from the Bund-front Cathay Hotel to modern apartment and office blocks) that did much to define Shanghai's interwar architectural modernity. Sassoon spent his free time seeking out exquisite pieces of jade and Chinese ivory along Shanghai's Bubbling Well

---

* Una Pope-Hennessy, *Early Chinese Jades* (New York: Frederick A. Stokes, 1923), 17.

Road and the antique stores that clustered along nearby Peking Road.* But Sassoon had grown up in a world of enormous wealth and appreciation for Asian arts and crafts. For Wallis, the complex world of jade was new—jade seals, ceremonial ornaments, girdle clasps, sword hilts, bracelets, incense burners, pen rests, altarpieces. How to grade quality, to tell fake from genuine, price appropriately? Wallis would need a teacher to help her spot the best pieces at the best prices.

Wallis's guide to the world of jade and Peking's jade market was the cosmopolitan aesthete Georges Sebastian. It is often thought that the later trips by the Duke and Duchess of Windsor to see Sebastian in the postwar period were made because he was a friend of Ernest Simpson, or possibly the Duke of Windsor. Sebastian had settled in Hammamet, a coastal resort outside Tunis, Tunisia, where he had built himself a sumptuous villa that housed his extensive jade, art, and antiques collection. Several biographers have noted the unlikely friendship between the aesthete Sebastian and Edward VIII, while Wallis's biographer Michael Bloch considered that Sebastian was an odd sort of friend for Ernest.† This confusion is because he was originally Wallis's friend while he too was sojourning in Peking, and it

---

* Sassoon's vast collection of jade and ivories was eventually bequeathed to the British Museum in 2018.

† Michael Bloch, ed., *Wallis and Edward: Letters, 1931–1937* (London: Weidenfeld & Nicolson, 1986). Wallis does write to Edward that she was going to Tunis to visit Sebastian ("E's friend"—i.e., Ernest), though Bloch thinks him an unlikely friend of Simpson's, and it may be Wallis avoiding telling Edward how she originally knew Sebastian. Charles Higham, Diana Mosley and, later, Andrew Lownie note that Sebastian was primarily Wallis's friend. Sebastian's exact dates in Peking are hard to establish. Had he sailed, we would have shipping records, but coming from Bucharest, it is most likely that Sebastian took the Trans-Siberian Express from Moscow to Peking, of which no passenger records have survived for the time.

was she, later, who introduced her second husband, Ernest Simpson, as well as the former king to the aesthete.

Georges Sebastian was a polyglot Romanian born in Bucharest and brought up in France, universally acknowledged as a man of great aesthetic discernment and social influence, a noted tastemaker. In the early 1920s, he was considered handsome, with crystal-blue eyes and raven-black, brilliantined hair. Rumor and gossip constantly swirled around his origins. Most probably, his father was a Russian living in Romania and his mother a Moldovan aristocrat, though rumors that he was the illegitimate son of a member of the Romanian royal family or that he was the son of a wealthy gypsy king both persisted.

He was in his late twenties when he met Wallis—that is to say, approximately the same age as she but far more worldly-wise. Sebastian was independently wealthy, though how much of this money came from his family or his own investments is unclear. It seems he spent some time as a private secretary to the Romanian politician and diplomat Radu Irimescu. He then lived in Paris's select residential suburb of Neuilly-sur-Seine for some years just after the Great War. There he made friends with other wealthy, and gay, aesthetes, including the older society photographer Baron Adolph de Meyer as well as Jean-Michel Frank, a Parisian interior designer who was in the circles around Igor Stravinsky, Sergei Diaghilev, Jean Cocteau, and Blaise Cendrars.*

---

* Though he used the *baron* title, it is not entirely clear whether de Meyer was entitled to it or just added it himself. Frank was from a wealthy but tragic Jewish family. Living in Paris but of German nationality, his father died by suicide in the war, and his mother died some years later in an asylum, having never recovered from the tragedy. Frank himself suffered severe lifelong depression. In the later 1920s, he came under the influence of the Chilean aesthete and champion of minimalism Eugenia Errázuriz, which later informed his interior design ethos. Frank died by suicide in New York in 1941.

Sebastian was yet another Peking jade obsessive in the 1920s, though, like Sassoon in Shanghai, with the funds to allow him to seriously collect. He knew the curio shops of Liu Li Chang and the morning markets. He had cultivated an appreciation of jade, an ability to instantly reject the inferior, the fake (clever green glass copies from Canton, or soapstone substituted for white jade), or the so-called Peking glass (transparent emerald and apple green and perfectly ideal for costume jewelry if priced right), developing skills at evaluating the age and value from touch and temperature as much as by sight. He had a sense of how to find the best transparent green jade—known as *fei tsui*.

Sebastian too was a keen interior designer, as Wallis would be (her notable interiors some years in the future still). Caroline Blackwood, who was commissioned by *The Sunday Times* to go to Paris to interview and write about the duchess in 1980, considered that Wallis had a "sharp decorator's eye" and that Chinese-style jade was around her all her life after Peking.[*] Wallis was keen to learn all she could from her friendship with Sebastian, whom Diana Mosley describes as "a man of taste and a perfectionist . . . a great influence upon her," while he was in Peking.[†]

However, in one lesson, she failed terribly. Sebastian suggested Chinese-language lessons to help her haggle and impress the dealers, if nothing else. But Wallis never really took to languages (Caroline Blackwood says Wallis never really mastered French so was lost

[*] Caroline Blackwood, *The Last of the Duchess* (London: Vintage, 2012), 38, 110. Though Blackwood met and interviewed Wallis in 1980, the text is scathing regarding the controlling behavior of her final (and highly controversial) representative, the lawyer Suzanne Blum (aka Maitre Blum), who had originally been married to Paul Weill, the Duke of Windsor's attorney in Paris. Therefore, the book was not published until after Blum's death in 1994.

[†] Diana Mosley, *The Duchess of Windsor* (London: Sidgwick & Jackson, 1980), 50.

when it came to Chinese).[*] Both Herman and Kitty took intensive daily Chinese lessons and had become quite proficient. They also encouraged Wallis to employ their tutor, a retired scholar, if she was planning to stay in China for a while. Wallis agreed, and the teacher, called Mr. Wu, was duly hired. He arrived at her wing of the Shih-Chia courtyard in his trademark language-teacher's garb of a long Manchu-style traditional *changshan* silk robe set off by a Western-style Borsalino hat and a black umbrella permanently under his arm. Wallis attempted two or three lessons a week and studied her Chinese character cards in between tutorials.

To all but the most dedicated, mastering the Chinese language in its spoken as well as its written form can be an insurmountable task. For most members of the Foreign Colony, their relative wealth and privilege meant they could bypass the process, while their servants, shopkeepers, waiters, and other Chinese they might interact with had enough understanding to get by. Robert Swallow, the Ningpo-born son of missionary parents, was in Peking at the same time as Wallis. He had learned Ningpo dialect, a form of Wu Chinese whose variations are found south of the Yangtze River, and so had had to learn Pekingese dialect when he based himself in the capital (for a time as a tutor to the sons of the Great War–era president of China, Yuan Shih-kai, and then as a businessman). In 1927, he published a lyrical book on hutong life, *Sidelights on Peking Life*, in which he described learning Pekingese as a tough and exhausting process "that involved a lot of tea and cigarettes, sugared peanuts and melon seeds."[†]

But, as Wallis told one of her biographers, the American journalist Ralph G. Martin, almost fifty years later, "I really tried to learn the language, but I was no good at it; I'm tone deaf, and Chinese

---

* Blackwood, *The Last of the Duchess*, 156.

† Robert William Swallow, *Sidelights on Peking Life* (Peking: French Bookstore, 1927), 32.

has different tones on different levels and they all have different meanings."* It does indeed seem that Wallis never managed to master more than a few basic phrases.

Traces of Wallis's life at this time are to be found in a rather obscure novel. Margaret Mackprang was from Nebraska. She married a Scotsman, Alex Mackay, who managed hotels in Tientsin and Peking. The couple settled in Peking a few years after Wallis left. Margaret became a fairly prolific poet, lyrically describing northern China in much of her work. She also wrote a now long-forgotten and out-of-print novel called *Lady with Jade*, originally published in 1939. Was Margaret thinking of Wallis, now embroiled in the abdication crisis and the fallout from the China Dossier at the time she was writing?

Lady with Jade is the tale of Moira Chisholm, a thinly veiled Wallis: "of medium height, fine-boned, and slim to the point of thinness so that she looked taller than she was." Moira is a young American woman who has come to China following her US Marine husband who turns out to be a heavy drinker, profligate with his salary, and fallen deeply in debt. He departs China for his next posting, deserting Moira in Peking, alone, broke, separated, feeling embarrassed about the failure of her marriage, and with barely the fare home to America. Like Wallis, Moira becomes entranced by jade. Entranced to the extent that she uses her last meager stash of dollars to open a small curio-dealing business run out of her hutong courtyard home, selling jade trinkets to foreigners. At first, "she loves jade in the distant impersonal way of one who can never hope to afford it—possessively, as one may admire the moon." But Moira is successful, her business does well, and she begins to seriously

* Ralph G. Martin, *The Woman He Loved: The Story of the Duke and Duchess of Windsor* (New York: Simon & Schuster, 1974), 89.

collect jade objets while becoming something of a celebrity within the Foreign Colony.

Moira is described as having a "windblown bob." She invariably wears "a white silk blouse, simple, round neckline, collarless." She has a helpful friend, Nat Purdy, an American who has lived in Paris and is a pretty good stand-in for Gerry Greene. But jade does not bring Moira happiness. She slowly withdraws into her collections, scorning the outside social world of the Colony. She refuses two proposals of marriage. She decides that no man can ever be a satisfactory substitute for the immaculate, classic perfection of jade to which she has given her life.[*]

It's an interesting question as to whether or not Mackay, having fled the Japanese invasion of northern China in the summer of 1937 and living in Honolulu in 1939, was modeling her character on Wallis as she wrote. There are certainly shades of Wallis's life and background in this ultimately rather bleak novel, but also elements of Helen Burton as well as the later sojourner and writer Helen Foster Snow (the wife of Edgar Snow, the first Western journalist to interview Mao Tse-tung and who wrote the bestseller *Red Star Over China* in 1937).[†]

Though Moira may share certain traits and experiences with Wallis, her withdrawal from human emotions into classical Chinese aesthetics is certainly not Wallis's Peking life. By contrast, Wallis enjoyed the process of buying and reselling jade, relished her time with the dealers of Liu Li Chang, and delighted in the extra funds

---

[*] Margaret Mackprang Mackay, *The Lady with Jade* (New York: John Day, 1939).

[†] It seems Helen Foster Snow (whose sometime pen name was Nym Wales) was perhaps aware of the similarities. She did model clothes for Helen Burton in the 1930s and hosted a popular Sunday salon at the Snows' courtyard home on Kuei Chia-Chang Hutong near Hatamen Street. Helen disliked the novel, describing it as too "pretty-pretty."

it brought to enjoy her Peking life. Her jade obsession was in many ways an extension of her busy social life.

As the worst of the Peking winter passed, outdoor activities picked up again. Though sweaters were still needed for Wallis and Herman's morning rides on the Tartar Wall, the sun would emerge each day a little earlier, a little warmer. The British legation's compound on Jade Canal Street (which every rickshaw puller in Peking knew as the Ying-Kuo-Fu*) was entered by a squat gray gateway, guarded by sentries, a constable's lodge to the righthand side. Included within the compound, which had formerly been Prince Su of the Qing dynasty's mansion, was a purpose-built clay tennis court. Wallis was keen on the game. It was a way to meet the British crowd in Peking (though she was reputedly supremely untalented at the sport), donning white dress while the men wore tennis flannels.† Herman also played at the British legation regularly, and the two formed a mixed doubles team on occasions. It was all very social with various British residents or junior staff mixing with invited Europeans and Americans around the edges of the court, where rattan chairs with bamboo tables were placed for the inevitable sundowner drinks and gossip.

Herman, wealthy and always one for the latest thing, filmed himself, Kitty, Wallis, and their friends on his Ciné-Kodak camera,

---

* In the Qing dynasty, a building referred to as a *fu* was invariably a residence associated with a prince of the royal bloodline. The British took over the compound in 1861. Despite the end of the Qing dynasty, it remained known to most Peking Chinese as the Ying-Kuo-Fu—Ying-Kuo (Yingguo) meaning "England." Jade Canal Street is now Zhengyi Road.

† Indeed, the tennis matches appear to have been more social events than sporting challenges. Wallis later told *The New York Times*, "I swim, but my only real exercise is running up and down stairs . . . I have never been one to take exercise." "After 25 Years France Is Home to the Duchess of Windsor," *New York Times*, July 19, 1964.

clowning around, laughing, and joking. Sometimes they donned fancy dress, the men in too-tight suits, stockings, buckled shoes, and high collars like Regency dandies, Wallis and Kitty in full-length dresses and boudoir caps or bandages wrapped round their foreheads. They acted silly for the camera, kissing one another, blowing kisses to the lens, dancing jigs. Cecil Beaton saw some of Herman's films later, in France at the Château de Candé, when he was photographing Wallis at her wedding to the Duke of Windsor. Beaton remarked that Wallis "seemed much less individual then," by which he perhaps meant she was more carefree, less considered, "her hair thicker, her head bigger, her body fatter."*

And now Wallis was able to indulge herself a little with her money made from the curio dealing and poker games. She enlarged her personal collection of miniature jade and ivory elephants, Chinese screens that took her fancy, and clothes. Peking was home to a wealth of highly affordable Chinese tailors able to run up anything from an American magazine or a fashion sketch, while Russian émigré seamstresses would call round anytime, day or night. The Indian Silk Merchants on Morrison Street sold beautiful material while the so-called Clock Store on Hatamen Street sold silk from large camphorwood chests. The milliners were only slightly more expensive at the European-run Aux Nouveautés on the Rue Marco Polo (Taijichang Street) or at Chic de Paris, run by Mesdames Dreyfus, Skorzewska, and Adamska, back on Hatamen, that employed Chinese seamstresses to replicate the latest European designs.

The first touch of spring in Peking is to feel the warming sun on your face for the first time in months, to see the yellow forsythia

---

* Cecil Beaton, *The Wandering Years* (London: Weidenfeld & Nicolson, 1961), 307. The impressive Château de Candé (which included an eighteen-hole golf course, tennis courts, and a solarium) was owned by a friend of Herman Rogers's, the Franco-American industrial millionaire Charles Bedaux. It was where the marriage of Wallis and the Duke of Windsor occurred. Beaton was the official photographer.

break into full bloom, announcing the change of seasons, to shrug off the Siberian furs, hats, and gloves, the Mongolian wool rickshaw blankets, and take your spring wardrobe out from protective camphor chests or call in the tailors and seamstresses for new spring garb.

Politically, things seemed to be improving in 1925. The seemingly ever-present threat of one or other of the northern warlords invading the city appeared to have receded, though the respite was to prove only temporary. The social life of the Foreign Colony resumed its annual outdoor activities, particularly weekend trips to the nearby Western Hills. And it was those hills and those weekends spent in remote rented temples with friends that were to form some of Wallis's most enduringly happy memories of China.

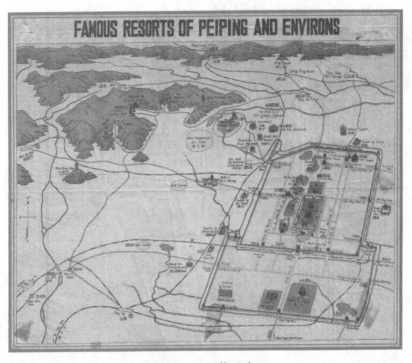

The Western Hills, Peking

9

TEMPLE WEEKENDS

THE WESTERN HILLS
PEKING
APRIL–MAY 1925

The lovely blue hills, lying light as veined bubbles upon the horizon. Taoist temples, Lama temples, Buddhist temples, temples of Confucius, temples of agriculture and of the azure clouds, temples to the god of fire, the god of war, the god of literature.

—Osbert Sitwell, *Escape with Me!*

The Western Hills change their appearance thrice a day and once a year put on their transient green; the lotus blooms, the willows turn to gold, and everywhere the splendor of the sun and frost is exercised.

—Ann Bridge, *Peking Picnic*

We lingered for a weekend, in surroundings that spoke of bygone splendour and ageless serenity. But when the sun went down and we were left in candlelight, the incongruity faded, and the spirit of the place settled down upon us.

—Wallis, *The Heart Has Its Reasons*

WEEKENDS IN THE WESTERN HILLS

The city of Peking sits in a flat, alluvial plain. This doesn't help when sandstorms so thick they paint the sky orange sweep in from the

Gobi Desert. But on clear days, it does afford the residents of the central city stunning views of Xishan, the Western Hills, sometimes known as the Fragrant Hills, that reach to the horizon. The hills are technically an extension of the vast Taihang Mountain Range that stretches back into Hopei (Hebei) Province. As the bitter cold of the long Peking winter ebbed, the cold, blustery weather receded. Slowly, lilacs started to bloom, high lavender and white boughs peeked tentatively above the gray walls of the hutongs, and geese flew noisily overhead. And so thoughts would turn to weekend excursions to the Western Hills. Trips up into the hills, to explore, to stay at rented temples, began around early April as the approaching summer heat began to envelop the city. By the final days of May, the humidity would be suffocating.

At their highest, the hills rise to nearly two thousand meters above sea level and can appear positively alpine in places, with shady white pines and edelweiss growing.* Though less than twenty miles from the Forbidden City, until well into the 1800s, they were effectively inaccessible to the casual visitor, as only rough tracks penetrated the area. Expeditions required careful planning.

Over the centuries, a great number (perhaps as many as four thousand) of Buddhist temples were constructed throughout the Western Hills, endowed by various emperors of China, including Kangxi, third emperor of the Qing, and Qianlong, fifth emperor of the Qing. Many smaller temples were supported by wealthy palace eunuchs, who had no heirs to whom they might leave their often quite substantial fortunes. A Western Hills temple could be a lasting

---

* In her 1920 guide to Peking, Juliet Bredon notes that this type of pine, *Pinus bungeana*, is almost unique to this area and a few other parts of northern China. Distinguishable by its large size and white bark, it was considered ornamental when planted adjacent to tombs and temples. For arborists not familiar with the white pine, Bredon advises reading Norman Shaw, *Chinese Forest Trees and Timber Supply* (London: T. Fisher Unwin, 1914).

monument to a man whose lineage ceased the day of his castration. An elderly eunuch might see out his twilight days in a house attached to a temple with grateful monks to care for him; an elderly scholar might retire from the city for the hills to compose poems contemplating nature; a retired imperial viceroy might retreat in his old age to the calm of the hills to write his self-aggrandizing memoirs or a tract or two. The influential and powerful Li Lianying, sometimes known as "the Last Eunuch," who had had great sway over the empress dowager Cixi, had been buried in the hills.

The more intrepid members of the Foreign Colony had discovered the hills back in the 1860s, finding the temples wonderfully cool retreats from the encroaching heat come late spring, with the bonus of being available for relatively modest sums. Their Buddhist monk inhabitants discovered that renting guest rooms to weekending foreigners was a useful source of income. Temples that had fallen into disuse were taken over completely and rented on long leases as weekend holiday homes.* The English and French claimed they rented the temples so as to have somewhere to garden, and indeed small vegetable patches were established to supplement and vary local supplies.

In the late nineteenth century, accommodations were spartan to say the least, modern plumbing totally absent. The Buddhist monks provided meals composed of eggs, stewed fruit, vegetables, scrawny chickens (no hen was ever eaten till it had laid its final egg), and millet pancakes. Life was fairly rudimentary, but the temples had undeniable charm. In the heat of a Peking summer, visitors often slept in the courtyards on camp beds (made slightly more comfortable by the addition of palliasses). To recline under

---

* Prices were considered affordable. The Italian diplomat Daniele Varè, who loved the Western Hills, quotes a price of thirty silver taels a month in his memoir, *The Gate of Happy Sparrows* (New York: Doubleday, Doran, 1937), 65.

the stars listening to the tinkling temple bells and Buddhist chanting of the monks was bliss.

By the turn of the century, reduced communities of Buddhist monks, lamas, and abbots remained in the temples. A few housed retired (or now redundant) eunuchs. As their residents died off, many of the temples became abandoned and dilapidated. But one thing that united them, whatever their age, origin, or condition, was that they were universally well located, nestled in the foothills, offering great views and access to nearby water. Most had beautiful architecture with elaborate decorations and gardens all with excellent feng shui. Though the structures were collectively known as "temples," they were in fact various types of monasteries, lamaseries, shrines, Confucian tombs, and multidenominational joss houses, where people could revere the gods of their choice along with their dear departed ancestors. Many were part commercial enterprise, the monks or lamas banging gongs all day to attract visitors to come and sample the food grown in the temple gardens or the fermented mead on offer, brewed using the temple's honeycombs.

One temple had been taken over by French Trappist monks, who lived solitary lives and rarely if ever ventured down into Peking. They maintained a cow or two, and so had milk, a product not required of the Taoist, and former court eunuch residents of the hills. Helen Burton rented a temple near their monastery and visited occasionally, as the monks made their own liqueurs for sale.[*] They were a mysterious order—the Legation Quarter gossips said they were men wanted back in Paris but who had found God (or at least sanctuary from the French police), ex-convicts of La Santé prison, men who had seen and done things in the Great War unimaginable to them

---

* Helen Foster Snow, *My China Years: A Memoir* (New York: Harrap, 1984), 95–97. They were still around in the later 1930s. Living in Peking in the mid-1930s, Helen Foster Snow purchased all manner of liqueurs from them, including crème de menthe.

before and unreconcilable except perhaps in this place, so far away, so cloistered, so well suited to inner contemplation. They traded spirits—brandy, cassis—for cash to buy essential supplies. Whatever the truth, the warlord troops and bandits that passed through the hills left them alone.

By the 1920s, better transport links into the Western Hills—twice-daily trains to the foothills, paved roads, private cars (still quite a rare thing in mid-1920s Peking), motorized taxis—meant that the Foreign Colony began to revive the fortunes of the temples, appreciating their picturesque decay and disintegration.

Some of the grander temples, or those closer to navigable roads, were well known and became popular day trip destinations. For instance, the Ta Chung Ssu, or Temple Where They Understand the Secret of Existence, was home to a great bell that kept time and could be heard throughout the hills for miles around. The Huang Ssu, or Yellow Temple, was popular with the Foreign Colony, being large and rambling and full of usually friendly lamas who welcomed weekend parties. Wan Shou Ssu, the Temple of Ten Thousand Longevities; the Wu Ta Ssu, or Five Pagoda Temple; the Ta Hui Ssu, or the Temple of the Big Buddha; the Lung-men Ssu, or White Pine Temple; the Tien-tai Ssu, or Temple of the Imperial Mummy; the Pi Yun Ssu, or the Temple of the Azure Clouds, and many, many more were all described lovingly in helpful guide books, such as G. E. Hubbard's *Temples of the Western Hills* (published in 1923 by Henri Vetch's French Bookstore in the lobby of the Grand Hôtel de Pekin) or Juliet Bredon's authoritative study of Peking, published in 1922.[*]

---

[*] G. E. Hubbard, *The Temples of the Western Hills Visited from Peking* (Peking: La Librairie Francaise & Tientsin Press, 1923). La Librairie Francaise was the publishing imprint of Vetch's French Bookshop; Juliet Bredon, *Peking: A Historical and Intimate Description of Its Chief Places of Interest* (Shanghai: Kelly & Walsh, 1931).

Though things had vastly improved since the first temple week-enders of the 1860s, the journey could still be difficult. Cecil Lewis, the Great War pilot and aircraft salesman living in Peking, visited in 1922 by catching a coal truck along the railway line from the north-west gate of the city, where sheep still grazed just beyond the wall, to the foot of the hills and Mentoukou, where there was a coal mine providing much of the city's needs. Then he embarked on a five-hour trek by donkey, led by "donkey boys" in blue tunics and straw hats, to Che Tai Ssu, the Temple of the Terrace of Ordainment.

But the curse of warlordism in northern China had taken its toll on the day-tripping vogue. The Buddhist monks fled warlord troops skirmishing in the hills for the city, while nervous foreigners avoided the remoter hills. By 1925, many of the temples had reverted to little more than deserted ruins. Bandits and warlord army deserters were far from unknown, and most foreign men venturing into the hills carried loaded revolvers, just in case of trouble.

By the time Wallis visited, it was estimated that of the original four thousand, there were perhaps only seventy potentially habitable structures scattered across the Western Hills. But dangerous or not, the Western Hills were to become one of Wallis's most fondly remembered Chinese excursions.

THE POOL OF THE BLACK DRAGON TEMPLE

Herman (with the sense of invulnerability that seemed to define his, and many other Westerners', time in China) found and rented his dream temple deep in the hills.* Frequently in biographies of Wallis,

---

* Quite what rent Herman paid is unknown, but Ellen La Motte, in her 1919 book *Peking Dust*, recalls renting a weekend temple some years previous and quotes a price of thirty dollars Mex for the entire season—not so very expensive and a fairly incon-sequential amount to a man of Herman's considerable means.

the Rogerses' Western Hills temple is mentioned as a favorite place of hers. Indeed, in her own autobiography, Wallis claimed that her weekends at the Rogerses' temple were "joyous" and the temple itself a "fabulous place" with a beautiful tiled roof of many colors, vermillion eaves with tiny Buddhist bells that tinkled in the wind. She recalled that the Western Hills "abounded in temples of every imaginable description and configuration, dozens and dozens of them, mostly empty and deserted."[*]

Most biographers of Wallis, while they note her weekends at the Rogerses' temple, do not name it. Where the name is mentioned (and Wallis herself waxes enthusiastically but also never specifically names it), it is usually Black Dragon Temple. In fact, it was actually the Hei-lung-t'an Ssu, or the Pool of the Black Dragon Temple (or sometimes Black Dragon King), although invariably known locally as the Hei-lung Ssu, the Black Dragon Temple, for short.

Despite the rather forbidding name, it is recalled in memoirs as a marvelous spot with a royal pedigree. Legend had it that Emperor Qianlong (who reigned from 1735 to 1796) enjoyed visits to the temple, and so subsequently, many Qing courtiers also visited as a form of pilgrimage. Whatever the legends—which were, of course, retold repeatedly to tourists by the local men who rented out the donkeys and ponies, acted as sedan chair bearers and porters, ran local provisions shops, or sold coal or firewood in the nearby villages—Black Dragon Temple was indeed charming, having been partially refurbished by Herman. And there was a central pool too. According to Juliet Bredon, who visited shortly before Herman took the lease, it was about ten feet wide by three feet deep. The temple priests thought swimming in the pool was bad luck, though they didn't discourage Western visitors who weren't so worried about the consequences of displeasing the black dragon.[†]

---

[*] Wallis Simpson, *The Heart Has Its Reasons* (London: Michael Joseph, 1956), 115.

[†] Bredon, *Peking*, 300–301.

However, it wasn't the most easily accessible temple. The main railway line from the city ran out from Peking's northwest gate through the stops of Huang-Tsun (Huangcun) and San-Chia Tien to the final stop at Mentoukou. Just a couple of years after Cecil Lewis's visit by coal train, things had improved dramatically with the establishment of chauffeured car services waiting at the train station to greet visitors. A newly built hotel for overnighters had been constructed adjacent to Mentoukou Station. Guests could then pause for tiffin or stay overnight and set out the following morning to the clusters of temples to either side of the mountain streams that cut up and through the Western Hills.

Wallis recalled that as the weather improved, it became their custom on Fridays, after lunch, to drive in a comfortable hired Chevrolet the fifteen miles out of the city to the Summer Palace. A recently macadamized road ran from the Hsi-Chih-Men Gate Tower (Xizhimen), just to the west of the Forbidden City, out to the old Yiheyuan, or Summer Palace, the vast Qing dynasty ensemble of lakes, gardens, and fantastical European-style structures partially destroyed by rampaging foreign troops in 1860. By the Summer Palace was a hotel that could valet park cars and provide overnight beds, and a shop for those last-minute Western extras, such as coffee and sugar, as well as treats, including small tins of lychees in syrup from Japan or lemon squash from Singapore. Beyond there, as Wallis described, "the road disintegrated into impassable ruts."[*]

The Rogerses' temple was approximately a three-hour trek through the foothills along ancient pathways. All had been organized in advance. Chinese servants would be waiting with donkeys or ponies to complete the journey. A typical weekend might mean bringing along a cook, a "table boy" and "house boy" to serve, a "traveling boy" to keep control of the luggage, an amah (if children were included in

---

[*] Simpson, *The Heart Has Its Reasons*, 113.

the party), and possibly a gardener from Shih-Chia Hutong to maintain the foliage at the temple. Wallis would pack clothes for dining but travel in breeches and leggings with a khaki jacket to protect against the dust and dirt of the trails.

They would set off in a long line, bells on the donkeys' manes jingling at every step, the donkey boys leading the way along narrow tracks, footpaths that followed streams and passed by forgotten and neglected tombs, ceremonial pailou arches, and the occasional small hamlet. The donkey ride could be quite unforgiving on the buttocks and spine, as it was often without saddles. But the views were worth it. As they rose up farther into the hills, they could look behind them and see Peking in the distance back to the east. Hedgehogs could be spotted as well as large grasshoppers. They would stop occasionally in the shade of old cypress trees for tiny cups of green tea, a cooling beverage in the spring heat, and to let the donkeys drink the fresh stream water.

Arriving at the temple was magical. By now, evening would be approaching, though the site would already be lit with torches and an open fire in the courtyard amid the gingko trees. Additional servants had been sent ahead the night before to prepare the temple and to serve food when the Rogerses' and any weekend guests arrived. It was unadulterated luxury after the trek through the hills—hot towels prepared and proffered upon arrival, cool jugs of water from nearby springs followed by white wine chilled in the temple's pool. Fresh clothes had been laid out. Everything was transported from Peking— food, table linens, glassware, silverware, ivory chopsticks, and even a wood-burning or charcoal stove complete with oven.

The main entrance of the Black Dragon Temple was formed by cracked, white balustraded steps bordered with bamboo groves to ward off earthquakes. The steps opened onto an inner courtyard entered through a moon gate festooned in ornate paper lanterns and surrounded on three sides by trellised porticoes covered in wisteria, with a garden of fern-clad rocks on the fourth side. Just beyond the rocks was the home of the reputed black dragon, a sparkling, blue-tinted pool (fed by a nearby spring). Old trees overhung the water while, in season, showers of fragrant white catalpa blossoms tumbled into the pool. Tubs of oleanders bloomed, and the wisteria from the porticoes drooped their masses of purple streamers, curtaining the edges of the pool. Nearby Chinese white pine trees (*Pinus armandii*) on the hillside slopes meant the scent of fresh resin was carried on the nighttime air and mingled with incense lit to deter mosquitoes.

The pool itself was ideal for bathing on hot nights (you could ignore the nonvenomous snakes that lay out on the sun-heated stones beside the water), though the more pious or superstitious believed that drinking or bathing in the water would greatly displease the black dragon.* The foreigners ignored this stipulation, but they did refrain from killing the sunbathing snakes, aware of both the Buddhist prejudice against taking any life and also the belief that the snakes were sent by the dragon king to announce the coming of the gods. Snakes were heavenly messengers and therefore to be left alone. Superstitions and sunbathing reptiles aside, it was an idyllic location, the surrounding trees home to bluebirds with their soft and low call tones and the rhythmic tap-tapping of woodpeckers.

In early spring, the Rogerses and their guests came to the hills most weekends, though they could never be completely sure whether the temple might not be partly occupied. The proximity of the Black Dragon Temple to the Summer Palace meant that General Feng, in 1923, had occupied it with his troops as a lookout across the valleys. Feng was poised to take the city and had announced his intention to expel Puyi, the last emperor, from both the Forbidden City and the Summer Palace. The warlord suspected that Puyi might try to escape before the city fell and so ordered his men to watch the foothills closest to the palace carefully.

---

* Hubbard, *The Temples of the Western Hills*, 59.

When he finally captured Peking in late 1924, Feng did immediately expel Puyi and his entourage and then opened the Forbidden City to the public. For the price of an admission ticket, ordinary Pekingers could now wander the gardens of the Summer Palace or the courtyards of the Forbidden City. However, a few of Feng's former troops, deserters—called *tao-ping* by the local Chinese—still in their once-white uniforms, beige trousers, and puttees up to their knees, continued to loiter around the temple.* Encountering them could be off-putting, though it seems that they decided to ignore the presence of the foreigners, and the foreigners decided to pretend they weren't camped nearby, and everyone peacefully coexisted.

While researching Peking for her guidebook, Juliet Bredon visited the Black Dragon Temple. As Bredon was a popular journalist writing in American magazines about her experiences in China, Wallis may well have read her articles on the Western Hills and its temples in *National Geographic* before ever venturing east, though she would not have recognized her name—Bredon submitted her pieces on China to the magazine under the pen name Adam Warwick, as the magazine was uneasy with a female contributor from China. Bredon recalled the Pool of the Black Dragon Temple's "golden roof that catches and reflects the sunlight like burnished mirrors from the crest of the Hua Mei Shan, Flowering Eyebrows Hill, behind." She remembered arriving by sedan chair, supported on two long saplings and with the four bearers chanting a parody of an old Han dynasty poem:

> *When the dragon comes, ah!*
> *The wind stirs and sighs,*
> *Paper money thrown, ah!*

---

* Now *taobing*—literally "escaped soldier."

Silk umbrellas waved.
When the dragon goes, ah!
The wind also is still.
Incense fire dies, ah!
The cups and vessels are cold.[*]

Moving into the temple, the central courtyard had wickerwork armchairs for relaxing. Dominating the space was a sizable statue of the Buddha, smiling and contemplative, seated on a lotus petal, "originally gilded but now peeling and leprously discoloured," as well as some plaster frescoes that had been damaged by General Feng's troops clattering about the year before when barracked there.

Along the back wall of the main bedroom was an emperor-size traditional northern Chinese bed, a *kang,* that could be heated with coals underneath, now covered in a brilliantly brocaded rug that Kitty had bought from Helen Burton at the Camel's Bell. Two other, smaller guest bedrooms contained cots or camp beds and blackwood folding chairs, with small petroleum stoves if the nights turned chilly. Kerosene-fueled hurricane lamps were provided for light. Although the plumbing was rudimentary to nonexistent at many temples, Herman had installed a toilet.

Throughout the mornings, itinerant vendors wandered the Western Hills from temple to temple with all manner of foods—candied fruit, fried bean curd, steamed buns (*mantou*), small cakes and confectionery, as well as cigarettes and hay for the horses—as did wandering barbers and sellers of pots and pans.

Daytime was for exploration through the foothills by pony or hiking. There were so many temples—often just ruins, becoming lost under the encroaching vegetation. It's fair to say that in her mem-

---

[*] Bredon, *Peking,* 349. The translation of the bearer's chant is by the prolific British-based Sinologist and linguist Arthur Waley, who curiously never visited China, afraid it would only disappoint him were he to see it with his own eyes.

oirs of the period (even if they were ghostwritten), it is recalling the temples of the Western Hills where Wallis's nostalgia for China seriously takes flight. The hills unsurprisingly made a profound impression on her. She writes, "Every eminence, every outcropping, was graced by some kind of temple—Buddhist temples, temples of Confucius, Taoist temples, Lama temples, most of them crumbling into dry ruin, their once lovely courts choked by weeds, their monstrous, obese gods toppled off their pedestals, and everywhere a silence broken only by the lonesome, forlorn tinkling of the surviving temple bells."*

At lunchtime, guests ate a preprepared picnic served by Chinese servants wearing blue cotton gowns and red satin waistcoats. Champagne, of course, and all manner of imported treats, expensive French cheeses, and canned Japanese lychees.

Wallis might also have recalled the smells of the Western Hills, often known as the Fragrant Hills. Daniele Varè, the Italian diplomat in Peking around the same time and an aesthete with a deep love for the traditions of old Qing China, recalled the distinctive smell of Chinese wisteria, a creamy vanilla-like smell, and the intoxicating scent of lotus in the humid spring night combining with candles floating in citronella oil.† These smells, mingled with the joss sticks, musk, and burning tallow, all worked to deter insects. Throughout the night could be heard the never-ending (and eventually unnoticed) buzzing chorus of cicadas as guests changed into their pajamas for the warm evenings and indulged in a little stargazing.

Despite the concerns over roaming bandits and former warlord troops—not to mention the savage "wonks," stray mongrel dogs loose in the hills—Wallis often wandered the foothills alone, allowing

---

* Simpson, *The Heart Has Its Reasons*, 116.
† Daniele Varè, *The Last Empresses and the Passing from the Old China to the New* (London: John Murray, 1938), 125.

Herman and Kitty some time together. She seems to have absorbed and adopted Herman's (and that of many other foreigners in China at the time) sense of privileged invulnerability.* Her destinations were enchanting—Wan Hua Shan, the Mountain of Ten Thousand Flowers; Hsiang Shan, the Perfumed Mountain; or local sights such as the Shih Tzu Wo, or Lion's Nest, that had been a retired eunuch's pleasure house. Otherwise, attired simply in a cotton dress, a straw hat, and a Chinese oil-painted parasol to keep the midday sun off her skin, Wallis would just sit, read, and relax.[†]

NIGHTS IN THE FRAGRANT HILLS

By nightfall, the scene was delightful. Large coal-fired braziers provided heat and light in the courtyard with an open wood fire in the middle. Lit candles were positioned around the edges of the pool and in the nearby shrubbery.

A typical temple weekend dinner would begin with caviar on toast served with glasses of sherry, followed by an entrée usually consisting of chicken or locally shot bustard bought in nearby villages. The Chinese chefs prided themselves on what they could achieve in

---

* A common thing, though not always sensible during this time, at least outside of Peking, as many foreigners in northern China were kidnapped by desperate bandits and former warlord troops for ransom. Most were returned relatively unharmed. But some did die, by accident, of disease, or at the hands of the bandits. See, for instance, Paul French, "How Chinese Bandits' Kidnapping of a Blonde British Bride and Her Pet Dogs Became a Global News Story," *South China Morning Post Magazine*, January 6, 2019.

† Ann Bridge, a regular visitor to the temples of the Western Hills on weekends in the mid-1920s, recalled in her book *The Ginger Griffin* that the Russian classics were extremely popular with the Foreign Colony at the time, Tolstoy's *Anna Karenina* in particular.

relatively basic surroundings.* The chicken would often be served with mustard and locally picked mushrooms as chicken á la Américaine with a premixed Russian salad. Daniele Varè recalled temple dinners featuring a starter of mousse de foie de olaille, followed by filets de lièvre aux champignons des bois, and concluded with a pêche Melba, courses served with wines, liqueurs, and fresh-brewed coffee.

A table would be set up with the requisite linen, china, and glassware, all brought from Shih-Chia Hutong. The Rogerses were modern and didn't insist on a full Western table setting, and Herman didn't insist on men wearing dinner jackets and black tie, as more formal European hosts at some other temples did. Herman wore white linens and ducks, Wallis and Kitty evening dresses, but nothing too elaborate. Herman enjoyed lecturing on Chinese history between courses and after dinner with glasses of the local *samshu* Chinese wine as a digestif. Though his intended book on China was never completed (or at least never published), Herman was knowledgeable about Chinese traditions and customs. There was always much gossip back in the Foreign Colony of opium pipes accompanying the temple weekends, but if Wallis sampled the *da yen*, big smoke, up in the Western Hills, she never told.† Mostly people drank, played a rubber or two of bridge while enjoying the red sunsets, ate grapefruit and kidney omelets at leisurely 8:00 a.m. breakfasts, enjoyed a

---

* Bustards are big birds, weighing up to forty-five pounds and having a wingspan of up to seven feet. They are the world's heaviest flying birds that nest on the ground and can reportedly run faster than a greyhound. They have been compared to turkeys, but Peking resident author Ann Bridge described them (in *The Ginger Griffin*) as looking like mutton, tasting like venison, and reminiscent of goose.

† Stella Benson, in her book *Worlds Within Worlds* (New York: Harper and Brothers, 1928), suggests opium smoking was a popular pastime in the Western Hills, though it was frowned upon if rumored to be indulged in back in the Legation Quarter. The term *big smoke* for opium was popularized later by Emily Hahn in her piece of the same name for *The New Yorker* (February 15, 1969) on her opium addiction in 1930s Shanghai.

final communal Sunday lunch club with people from adjoining and nearby temples before heading back to the city.

It was a sybaritic experience. Wallis wrote that it might have seemed indulgent to have lingered for a weekend in surroundings that "spoke of bygone splendour and ageless serenity. But when the sun went down and we were left in candlelight, the incongruity faded, and the spirit of the place settled down upon us.'"

Then, come Sunday afternoons, the whole process would begin in reverse. The Rogerses and Wallis would take their ponies and begin the three-hour trek back toward the Summer Palace. They would retrieve their car from the car park by the so-called Yufeng Ta, the Jade Fountain, a pagoda built on the site of a former Tibetan Buddhist temple with the Yu Chuan Mountain behind it, atop of which was the equally impressive Jade Peak Pagoda. Up on Mount Yu Chuan were the springs that ran down in cascading streams before being channeled all the way to the Forbidden City, providing a good portion of the fresh water supply for the imperial and other wealthy families in periodically dry Peking. They had to ensure they returned before the city gates were closed against invaders and bandits at 7:30 p.m. in the darker winter months and 9:00 p.m. sharp in the summer. Preapproved passes were required to gain access if late; without them, the guards were hard to bribe, and threats generally proved useless. Once back inside the old city walls, they were greeted by the familiar cacophony of Peking. On reentering the calm interior courtyard of Shih-Chia Hutong, away from the rattling trolley-buses, the hawker and peddler calls, the car horns receded.

The leisurely spring and early-summer weekends in the Western Hills, the charm of the Black Dragon Temple, the time spent alone wandering the foothill paths were all restorative and allowed for contemplation. A decade later, after the northern warlords had

---

* Simpson, *The Heart Has Its Reasons*, 116.

either been co-opted by Chiang Kai-shek's army or wiped out, the Western Hills that Wallis knew in the mid-1920s had become tamer. By the time the English aesthete and Peking sojourner Harold Acton found his "little temple" in the hills, ten years after Wallis's weekends, things were far more organized. Temples, according to Acton, became like country cottages, interiors were often Western-style, all chintz and cabbage rose patterns, horse and hound paintings on the walls, with modern cocktail bars installed.*

Looking back on these excursions, Wallis was to write that despite Herman's informative lectures, she never became an authority on Chinese customs and religions: "I did attain something that was even more important to me at that stage of my life: the nightmare of my last association with Win faded from my mind. For that I shall always be grateful to Herman and Katherine Rogers."†

Perhaps with thoughts of Win receding and old wounds—emotional and physical—healing, Wallis was feeling ready for a love affair. Later gossip spoke of a tall British cavalry officer met at the British legation tennis court, or was it a handsome chargé d'affaires at the French legation who was her "intimate"? But if either affair occurred, then the men's names and all details are lost to history.‡

Gerry Greene was ever present, but that appears to have been a friendship rather than anything else, a repeat of her squiring by Robbie in Shanghai—both charming, well-mannered, entertaining bachelors with a fondness for dancing. Still, all the socializing, dances, tiffins, and weekends in the Western Hills were bound sooner or later to bring Wallis into someone's orbit who attracted

---

* Harold Acton, *Memoirs of an Aesthete* (London: Methuen, 1948), 394.
† Simpson, *The Heart Has Its Reasons*, 116.
‡ Wallis mentions, but gives no details, of a "dashing British military officer" (*The Heart Has Its Reasons*, 117). Various biographers mention a British officer and a French chargé, both supposedly included in the China Dossier, though anonymously and with no further details to support any allegations. See Joe Bryan and Charles J. V. Murphy, *The Windsor Story* (New York: William Morrow, 1979), 22.

her and was available. Wallis was single—"semi-independent," she described herself—very sociable, and there was inevitably a degree of gossip and chatter, what the China coast slang would have called *walla walla*, concerning her. And indeed, she did meet someone with whom she would share one Peking spring and "who whirled briefly in and out" of her life.[*]

---

[*] Simpson, *The Heart Has Its Reasons*, 117.

10

CINDERELLA IN THE LEGATION QUARTER

THE ITALIAN LEGATION
VIALE ITALIA
PEKING LEGATION QUARTER
SPRING 1925

To be sure, the incidence of honourable men with dishonourable in-
tentions was undoubtedly higher than a Sunday-School teacher of
that period might knowingly have tolerated for long; but such perils,
if prudently recognised in advance, are readily manageable. The point
is that for women Peking could be and was perhaps not so much a
metropolis as a point in time where every woman could be Cinderella
and midnight never struck.

—Wallis, *The Heart Has Its Reasons*

The Peking diplomatic corps has created within the confines of the
Legation Quarter, its own very special, cocoon-like mode of life.

—Alexis Leger (aka Saint-John Perse)

They had come to the party because they had nothing else in the
world to do, but when the moment came that they could decently
take their leave they would go with a sigh of relief. They were bored
to death with one another.

—W. Somerset Maugham, *On a Chinese Screen*

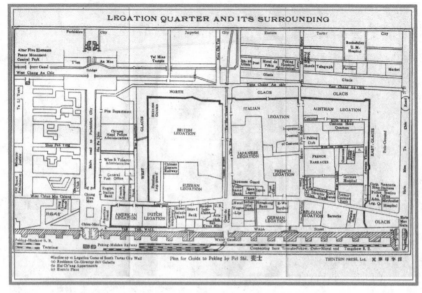

The Legation Quarter, Peking

DASHING DA ZARA

Comandante Alberto da Zara was certainly a man you'd notice. Indeed, he was known among the Legation Quarter cognoscenti as Dashing da Zara. Good-looking, tall, lean, elegant, slicked-back black hair with a fleck of gray at each temple. By day, he would be attired in the smart black uniform of the Italian navy, the Regia Marina; off duty, a well-cut linen suit. He had impeccable manners, was witty, had a charming smile, and was in possession of the only Fiat 510 sports car in Peking, a not inconsiderable asset. Da Zara was enjoying his life in China and was not overly stretched workwise. Where the couple met, we cannot be sure. But a love affair began in the early spring. In 1925, da Zara was a thirty-six-year-old bachelor. Wallis (as a sympathetic Kitty Rogers would let people know) was in the throes of a divorce from an unpleasant husband. Contrary to suggestions in the supposed China Dossier a dozen years later, their relationship was not particularly scandalous and was completely open. The couple did not need to be overly discreet. She called him Alberto; he called her Wally. It appeared that, despite Win's behavior, Wallis had not soured on naval officers completely.

Born in the northern Italian city of Padua into a military family of cavalry officers and supposedly of Jewish descent, da Zara had joined the navy in 1907 at eighteen.* He served in the Italo-Turkish conflict of 1911–12 and then the Great War, commanding torpedo boats. He was awarded two silver medals and elevated up the ranks to lieutenant. After the armistice, he briefly commanded a battleship in the Dodecanese before being posted to China in command of the gunboat RM *Ermanno Carlotto* on Yangtze Patrol.† He arrived in China in 1922 and was initially stationed at Shanghai. Da Zara was also a cultured man, a poet, and a disciple of d'Annunzio.

Italy's connections to China went back a long way and were hopelessly romantic, beginning, of course, with Marco Polo. Matteo Ricci had been the first European to enter the Forbidden City while his fellow Jesuit Giuseppe Castiglione had served as an artist to the imperial court of three Qing dynasty emperors.‡ Italy was a treaty port power and had its own leafy and shady concession in Tientsin as well as a presence in Chefoo on the Shantung coast. When da Zara arrived, Italian businesses were actively attempting to sell to China. The Banca Italiana per la Cina facilitated any deals. A growing community of Italians—over six hundred between Canton and

---

* The da Zara family's Jewish ancestry is debated, though *da Zara* is often a corruption of the Jewish surname Zadar, derived from the Croatian Dalmatian coast.

† The RM *Ermanno Carlotto* was named after an Italian lieutenant who had died during the suppression of the Boxer Uprising in 1900.

‡ Being the Kangxi, Yongzheng, and Qianlong emperors.

Chefoo—required protection and support.* Consequently, the Italians also had a Regia Marina (RM) naval patrol presence in China on both the Yangtze and the Paihe Rivers. Italy's handful of patrol vessels was nowhere near as large as the British China Station or the American Asiatic Fleet, but they still plied the coastal waters and rivers of China showing *il Tricolore*.

The gunboat RM *Sebastian Cabot*, stationed in Shanghai, led the Italian naval presence in China. It was backed up by several smaller craft designed primarily for river patrol duties. Da Zara's *Ermanno Carlotto* was not one of the more attractive crafts (it was not dissimilar in size and capabilities to Win's USS *Pampanga*). It had been built at the Shanghai Dock and Engineering Company with a low draft, allowing it to penetrate far upriver. But the *Ermanno Carlotto* had been a seriously good promotion for First Lieutenant da Zara. China was one of only a few overseas commands reserved for junior officers in the RM and meant a promotion to commander lieutenant. Da Zara got full command of his own gunboat at just thirty-three years of age and a posting to Shanghai.†

Yangtze Patrol meant venturing as far upriver from Shanghai as the riverside treaty port of Ichang (Yichang) in Hopei Province, the Gateway of the Three Gorges, a thousand miles inland from Shanghai. The gorges were tough to navigate, but essential if you were to venture farther upstream as far as Chungking (Chongqing), another four hundred miles past the gorges toward Tibet. In June 1923, da Zara became the first Italian naval captain to successfully navigate the rapids above Ichang, reaching Chungking (Chongqing), just north of the gorges. Getting back home proved

---

* Statistics on the number of Italians in China from Guido Samarani, "The Italian Presence in China: Historical Trends and Perspectives (1902–1947)" in *Italy's Encounters with Modern China: Imperial Dreams, Strategic Ambitions*, ed. Maurizio Marinelli and Giovanni Andornino (New York: Palgrave Macmillan, 2014), 51.
† Win Spencer was approximately the same age when awarded command of the *Pampanga*.

even tougher. The flood season was taking hold, water levels dangerously rising, and the tide flow faster, which made it perilous returning through the gorges, as the rocks of the rapids were now submerged and out of sight while the channels narrowed to less than a hundred feet at some points. But they made it. The *Ermanno Carlotto* arrived back just in time to be the stars of the 1923 Italian Consulate Ball in Shanghai, where the local Italian community applauded da Zara to the rooftops and carried him around the ballroom hoisted on the shoulders of his men.

Da Zara completed his command of the *Ermanno Carlotto* in March 1924 and was reassigned to Peking as commander of the guard. Since the Boxer Uprising a quarter of a century earlier, the RM had been the branch of the Italian armed forces assigned to the decidedly inland, and very dry, Peking to guard the Italian legation.

Wallis and Alberto would have probably first encountered each other at one Legation Quarter function or another, a Grand Hôtel dance, or perhaps a communal Sunday lunch club in the Western Hills. The Italians, and there were only about sixty or so in Peking in 1925, were a well-liked community. A major thoroughfare of the quarter was named Rue Marco Polo, reminding everyone of Italy's long involvement with China. Those Chinese government officials easy in the company of foreigners were regular visitors to the Italian legation. Many Italians lived near the Legation Quarter on Erh-Tiao Hutong (not far from Shih-Chia Hutong and very central), where a Signore Venturi had opened an Italian provisions store popular with Italians and non-Italians alike. Italian businesses were making inroads into the China market—Fiat trucks, Breda aircraft, the Compagnia Italiana per l'Estremo Oriente (CIDEO) was importing all manner of Italian-made goods, and there were a few Italian silk importers. Many of the musicians at the Grand Hôtel de Pekin and the Wagons-Lits and the first-class attendants on the Peking-Hanko Railway were Italian, while in Tientsin's Italian Concession, they ran cafés, hairdressers, and several trattorias. And, of course, not forgetting the Catholic missionaries, nuns, doctors, and nurses across China.

The Italian legation in Peking, off a stretch of Chang'an Avenue that was generally referred to as the Viale Italia by non-Chinese, was one of the larger compounds in the foreign enclave. It occupied much of the land around the Jade Canal at the northern end of the quarter, bordering a slice of the glacis to the north and the adjacent Japanese legation to the west.* After the original buildings were destroyed during the 1900 Boxer Uprising, the Italians increased the size of their legation compound significantly, from one to twelve acres. They built their embassy and adjoining buildings in a European style, as well as installing ornate entrance gates crowned by a pair of striking art nouveau lamps. In expanding and Europeanizing their legation, the Italians were doing nothing that the other Europeans, the Americans, and the Japanese were not doing too. George Kates, an American aesthete who lived in Peking, was an expert in classical Chinese decorative arts. He surveyed the newly rebuilt Legation Quarter that Wallis knew:

> The buildings of each Legation . . . looked as if lifted bodily from their own country to be set down here in China. Not only were the styles all different, but the very hardware on the windows would

---

* The glacis was a post-1900 feature of the quarter introduced after the Boxer Uprising and resultant siege of the legations. *Glacis* is a military term meaning a piece of land kept open to provide a buffer zone so that attackers are forced to expose themselves. It ran around the eastern edge of the quarter at the border with Hatamen Street and part of the northern boundary in front of the Italian legation. It was mostly used by foreign troops to drill, by polo players as a polo field, and by privileged foreigners exercising their horses.

also be French, or Dutch, or British. The plumbing, the tiling, all had been transported at the expense of the State to which the building belonged, to be combined with grosser Chinese materials at hand.*

Wallis would come to know the Italian legation well. The main building had four large halls for receptions, five guest bedrooms, and a large and impressive foyer. The ambassador's personal residence had two large halls with six floor-to-ceiling windows each, plus guest bedrooms with their own verandas. Furniture and art had been sent from Italy for the ambassador's use. There were further houses in the grounds for the first interpreter, the second interpreter, as well as a chapel, which had an ornamental ceiling that had been shipped from Italy. Daniele Varè (the legation's secretary during World War I and, after 1927, ambassador) described it as being "as big as most churches."† There was a stable for eighteen horses and a small private paddock in which to exercise them. Add to this a laundry, a greenhouse, an orangery, a servants' block, and barracks for up to three hundred men of the Marina Militare in their trademark *grigioverde*, olive-drab, uniforms. To support the legation, there were two mess halls (one for officers and one for ranks), legation offices, a small hospital, two prison cells, an armory, food storage sheds, a commissary, a cookhouse (the legation's soufflés were especially highly regarded),

---

* George N. Kates, *The Years That Were Fat: Peking 1933–1940* (New York: Harper & Brothers, 1952), 114.

† The detailed itinerary of the legation's buildings is from *Daniele Varè, Laughing Diplomat* (New York: Doubleday, 1938), 88. In the late 1950s, the foreign legations were relocated north of Chang'an to a new embassy district. The former Italian legation buildings and compound became the headquarters of the Chinese People's Association for Friendship with Foreign Countries. Several of the former embassy buildings were converted to houses for use by "foreign friends" who supported the Chinese revolution, including the American communist activist Anna Louise Strong and the New Zealander Rewi Alley.

yet more stables for the Marina Militare's use, and a water-distilling plant.

For Wallis, da Zara was her first real affair since Felipe Espil in Washington. Robbie had been a fun companion, Gerry Greene a dashing chaperone, but da Zara was her lover. Accusations of other relationships came much later, as part of the supposed China Dossier, with no evidence.[*] But da Zara was the real thing.

LEGATION QUARTER LIFE

Visiting the Legation Quarter in 1920, W. Somerset Maugham reported everyone to be bored out of their minds. Cecil Lewis described the quarter in the 1920s as mired in "ridiculous petty protocol."[†] Peter Fleming (travel writer and older brother of James Bond creator Ian) described the denizens of the quarter as living in a goldfish bowl, "fish in an aquarium going round and round . . . serene and glassy-eyed."[‡] The argumentative and gossipy writer who spent many years in Peking—and was eventually murdered in Tientsin—B. L. Putnam Weale, said the quarter was a ghetto-like fortress where

---

[*] For instance, Joe Bryan and Charles J. V. Murphy in *The Windsor Story* (New York: HarperCollins, 1979) allege that Wallis had an "open romance" with a "boyish ensign" (a junior commissioned officer rank in the US Navy) en route to Hong Kong. Apparently, in Hong Kong, the ensign told Win he wanted to marry Wallis, and Win threw them both out of the house. There is no evidence of this mysterious ensign, how Wallis would have known him, an argument with Win, or any details whatsoever beyond the vague source of unattributed "fellow passenger gossip."

[†] Cecil Lewis, *All My Yesterdays* (London: Element Books, 1993), 35. It was the case that dress codes were very strict. Indeed, American legation student interpreters (basically junior diplomats focused for several years on language learning) were still required between the wars to wear top hats and morning coats when outside of the legation compound.

[‡] Peter Fleming, *News From Tartary* (London: Jonathan Cape, 1936).

the Peking gossips feasted on scurrilous rumor.[*] Wallis herself described the Legation Quarter set as "not merely Victorian, but mid-Victorian."[†]

Perhaps, but the Legation Quarter, carved out by the foreign powers in the 1860s, was in many ways a very appealing fortress. An enclave of brick sidewalks lined with acacia trees, the substantial European-style buildings and manicured gardens hidden behind ornate gates and four- or five-meter-high gray walls. The quarter's roads were thronged with rickshaws (which required permits to enter the foreign enclave), a few diplomatic cars, and even a few of the old-fashioned glass-paneled carriages favored by older residents and leftover Chinese aristocrats of the old Qing dynasty who remained living in the district. Led by Mongolian ponies in harnesses with silver fittings, red leather reins, and drivers perched on small stools, they rang gentle bells to alert distracted pedestrians.

During Wallis's Peking sojourn, she always resided close to, though never wholly within, the Legation Quarter. The Grand Hôtel was just opposite the British and Japanese legations; Shih-Chia Hutong was nearby to the north, so the quarter was a regular destination. It had a range of services Wallis and the rest of the Foreign Colony depended on—foreign dentists and doctors if required, La Violette's beauty parlor (run by Italians, but staffed by young Russian émigré women with Italian noms de plume), American and European banks, Hartung's famous photo studio, the offices of Thomas Cook, American Express, and P&O, various banks, as well

---

[*] Bertram Lenox Simpson (aka B. L. Putnam Weale) came to China in the 1890s and was accused by the British embassy of looting in the aftermath of the Boxer Uprising. He strongly objected to the charge, causing a lifelong enmity with the British Establishment in China. He went on to work for several warlords while writing a number of rather scurrilous books, including *Indiscreet Letters from Peking* (1906). He was hatcheted and then shot to death on a Tientsin street by unknown assassins in 1930.

[†] Wallis Simpson, *The Heart Has Its Reasons* (London: Michael Joseph, 1956), 114.

as, of course, the American legation, where Wallis went for all matters passport related. But Wallis, though a regular visitor, was never really a part of the Legation Quarter clique—that is, until her love affair with Alberto da Zara.

The Legation Quarter clique was relatively small—white, privileged, well-heeled, invariably linked to the embassies. It was often incestuous, and the company could feel repetitive. In 1925, the corps of "dipsis," as the diplomats were colloquially known in Peking, was actually smaller than it had been a decade earlier. The defeated Germans were now excluded from the embassy circuit while the newly Bolshevized, and thus socially outré, Soviet Russians kept aloof from the bourgeois social circle. The usual Europeans, Japanese, and Americans were joined by the Brazilians, Uruguayans, Cubans, Mexicans, Peruvians, and the Mission of the Far Eastern Republic (the last remnants of the anti-Bolshevik "White Russian" exiles who were supported and indulged due largely to old friendships). This was the clique W. Somerset Maugham had thought shallow, tedious, and mostly bored with one another. He had encountered "the Chargé d'Affaires of Montenegro, who flattered himself he was the best-dressed man in the diplomatic body but was not quite sure whether the First Secretary of the British legation thought him so" and worried about that!*

Though dominated by the dipsis, the crowd was added to by the higher-ups at the Imperial Chinese Customs, the Postmaster General's Office, and the salt gabelle agency, as well as businessmen attached to the major foreign concerns in Peking—Jardine Matheson, British American Tobacco, the Standard Oil Company

* W. Somerset Maugham, *On a Chinese Screen* (London: Jonathan Cape, 1928), 27.

of New York, and Texaco, alongside the bankers from the HSBC, Standard Chartered, City Bank of New York, and the Banques Russo-Asiatique, Deutsche-Asiatische, l'Indochine et de Suez, and Sino-Argentine. Making up the numbers were representatives of locomotive manufacturers, the railway consortiums, shipbuilders, and (profiting greatly from the ongoing warlord skirmishing) assorted foreign arms dealers. Providing a uniformed presence, soldiers of second lieutenant rank and above were acceptable.* Those temporarily in town and of a better class—the occasional light opera singer, musician, or touring acting troupe, retired military types in town for a look-see, wealthy sojourning tourists— were welcome; missionaries less so (being universally, with one or two exceptions, considered boring).

The Peking Wallis knew was still largely devoid of Western-style nightclubs and cabarets, jazz was yet to arrive, there were no casinos, and only a cinema or two showed Hollywood movies. Consequently, entertainment was confined largely to hotels, private homes, or on the social circuit of the legations. Many of the Colony met one another again and again . . . and again . . . at social functions, dinner parties, national days, the Paomachang racetrack, and polo games; whispering in club libraries, gossiping in the beauty parlors, being seen at concerts, attending lectures of the Peking branch of the Royal Asiatic Society, or viewing exhibitions at the city's Institute of Fine Arts, which had the occasional recital or amateur dramatics production. For many, particularly the more modern Bright Young Things of the Legation Quarter, who loved

---

* For those American marines below that rank (privates and NCOs), there was the Enlisted Men's Club (founded 1910), which, while socially frowned upon, was visited by many Foreign Colony Americans, as it served home comforts such as steak and potatoes, ice cream, and Coca-Cola, and it showed Hollywood movies on a makeshift screen in the dining room.

to declare, "I am bored . . . the Foreign Colony is boring . . . ," the quarter clique rapidly became very claustrophobic.[*]

Still, for all the quarter's confines, it was undoubtedly a cosmopolitan society. In Peking in 1925, it would have been hard for any foreigner, including Wallis, not to have had a decidedly international group of friends. Indeed, as we have seen, Wallis was acquainted with fellow Americans as well as the British, French, Romanians, and Italians, among others. Inevitably, gossip centered on who was arriving, who was departing, any sojourners of interest passing through, the occasional celebrity visitor, who was having an affair with whom, who should be having an affair with whom, as well as, often woefully lastly, what was going on in China outside the Legation Quarter.

And the quarter was also where much of the old gentry of the departed Qing dynasty could still be found. Chinese aristocrats of the pre-Republican era were still invited to legation dinners. Their imperial world may have departed a dozen years before, but their anecdotes were still in high demand. They would arrive in padded winter robes of dark blue brocade, sleeveless jackets of plum-colored velvet, black satin skull caps, chains around their necks of carved amber beads and emerald-green jade thumb rings all wrapped up in sable furs from the Russian borderlands along the Amur River. Many of their wives had bound feet from their youth, their knotted hair held in place with jade-and-gold hairpins. They represented an earlier era many quarter denizens remembered, exoticized, and were romantically nostalgic for.

But it was also, so we can divine from the best novels that attempted to capture the ambience of the Legation Quarter, an often bitchy world. Ann Bridge's novel of manners, *Peking Picnic*, and Harold Acton's comic novel *Peonies and Ponies* (set in the 1930s)

---

[*] Damien de Martel and Léon de Hoyer, *Silhouettes of Peking* (Peking: Henry Vetch, 1926).

are instructive about its cramped minutiae and would have rung bells with Wallis. In her novel *Four-Part Setting*, Ann Bridge wrote that the quarter lacked a decent library, "the shortage of books was almost as acute as that of unmarried women," and so all that was left was "bridge and gossip, and drinks at the Club; and these endless dreary, dreary parties and the drab little flirtations."[*] Bridge returned to the Legation Quarter's "drab little flirtations" in several books. Her comment in *The Ginger Griffin*—her 1934 novel of a young Englishwoman falling in and out of Peking love affairs—that China was a reputational graveyard harked back to the sometimesharsh slanders of the 1920s. Bridge (who was English) also noted "the automatic glance of coquetry which seems to be as much a part of the female American's social equipment as a frock."[†] Reading Bridge and Acton, just as with Margaret Mackprang Mackay, we get a whiff of Wallis's Peking.

But perhaps Damien de Martel and Léon de Hoyer's comic novel *Silhouettes of Peking* is the closest literary evocation of the quarter Wallis knew. The authors, a diplomat and a banker of long residence in Peking, mercilessly lampoon the Peking gossips of the post–Great War period, the "silhouettes" of their title, who lead privileged and hedonistic lifestyles in the foreign clubs, hotels, and racecourse of Peking, yet do no more than touch the surface of Chinese society:

Peking is a city of officials, slightly formal and perhaps a trifle snobbish, but anyway clean-minded and agreeable to frequent. It is a casual and temporary agglomeration of people who have seen the world, have stayed in Paris and London; passed through Florence

---

[*] Ann Bridge, *Four-Part Setting* (London: Chatto & Windus, 1939), 74.

[†] Ann Bridge, *Peking Picnic* (London: Chatto & Windus, 1932); Ann Bridge, *The Ginger Griffin* (London: Chatto & Windus, 1934); Harold Acton, *Peonies and Ponies* (London: Chatto & Windus, 1941).

and Athens, played with politics in Petrograd or with finance in America; people who have crossed all the seas, made collections in the East and made love in Venice . . . but it is above everything else, a city that has given birth to a special type of human being . . . the Peking silhouette."[*]

Somerset Maugham, in his chapter "Legation Quarter Dinner" in *On a Chinese Screen*, recalls that quarter women were invariably described as "handsome" rather than "pretty." Gossip swirled. Maugham heard tell of one diplomatic wife with a past on the stage of the London music hall and another ambassador's wife rumored to have been a "cocotte," a prostitute, or *grande horizontale*, in Paris before the Great War.[†] Dinners featured lots of uniforms and medals unless deemed *en petite comité*, thus allowing attendees to relax the formal dress codes slightly.

It was a job in itself to remember the affiliations of each diner over cocktails and canapés of toasted cheese and red caviar on triangles of black bread.[‡] And a major task to keep everyone's names, ranks, titles, and social allegiances straight all the way through to the after-dinner brandies, let alone who was engaged in a liaison with whom, had quarrelled with whom, was about to enter into an illicit relationship with whom. According to Maugham, each nation was distinctive in some way—the French always late, the Swiss always early. Everybody seemed to be able to switch between French and English effortlessly. Apart from those required to do so for their jobs—the student interpreters, senior military, some at-

---

* De Martel and de Hoyer, *Silhouettes of Peking*. It should be noted that although published in 1926 the novel was written around 1916 or 1917.
† Maugham, *On a Chinese Screen*, 26.
‡ Canapés were usually described by the Russian term *zakuski* in the Legation Quarter, which until the Bolshevik Revolution had seen the imperial Russian legations be one of the major centers of sophisticated quarter social life.

tachés (though rarely the ambassadors themselves)—nobody spoke Chinese. Why bother when, if required, an interpreter was a paltry twenty-five dollars a month?

Cocktails morphed into multicourse dinners; pink gins into endless rubbers of bridge seated around mahogany tables. Still, Maugham, a keen bridge player (and who would later play with Wallis when she became the Duchess of Windsor on the French Riviera) was unimpressed.* Norwood Allman, the Shanghai lawyer who had been a student interpreter at the American legation in the early 1920s, would occasionally have to attend dinners when "more important fry" dropped out. He recalled that the "dinners were fearsome affairs, consisting of course after course, and the conversation, if one were able to converse, ran to questions such as, 'how long have you been in Peking? Do you like it? Isn't the dust dreadful?' When conversation became really animated the weather was included."†

Perhaps worst of all, you couldn't escape a Legation Quarter dinner once you'd arrived. Following cocktails, chitchat, and some early rounds of bridge, dinner might not be served until as late as 9:00 p.m. It was considered extremely bad form to make an exit before the senior diplomat and his wife took their leave. If they were night owls, drinkers, or keen bridge players, that could mean the wee small hours. Dinners, and after-dinner bridge, regularly went on until 2:00 or 3:00 a.m., perhaps even as late (or early) as 5:00 a.m. Warlord battles in the surrounding countryside often kicked off at dawn, and it

* Maugham is rumored to have claimed: "Bridge is the most diverting and intelligent card game that the wit of man has so far devised. . . . You can play bridge so long as you can sit up at a table and tell one card from another. In fact, when all else fails—sport, love, ambition—bridge remains a solace and an entertainment."
† Norwood F. Allman, *Shanghai Lawyer* (New York: Whittlesey House, 1943), 31.

was not unheard of for departing guests to hear the artillery fire of various factions facing off against one another beyond the walls of the city as they traveled home.

One exception to the overformal, hierarchical Legation Quarter party was to be invited to dine with the coterie of stylish international Chinese in Peking. These included China's own dipsis as well as scholars, Peking opera singers, and overseas Chinese who had returned home having made fortunes in Europe, America, or Southeast Asia. The most sought-after dinner invitation among this group was to the elegant hutong home of Wellington Koo and his wife, Oei Hui-lan, Madame Koo.

Koo Vi Kyuin was better known to everyone as Wellington Koo (and now often Gu Weijun in China). He had grown up in a well-to-do Shanghai cosmopolitan family and was educated at Shanghai's St. John's University and at Columbia in New York. In 1912, he had returned to work for President Yuan Shih-kai and then, at just twenty-seven, was appointed China's ambassador to the United States. In China and abroad, Koo was best known for having been the Chinese diplomat who refused to sign the Treaty of Versailles at the 1919 Paris Peace Conference over objections to Japan's Great War land grab in Shantung. He had since served as both China's foreign minister and finance minister. He had survived at least one assassination attempt.

In 1924, Koo, often working his extensive American contacts, was trying to bridge the divides between Sun Yat-sen's Southern Government in Canton and the various northern warlords. He was still only thirty-seven and married to Oei Hui-lan, the beautiful daughter of a Chinese-Javanese sugar baron. They were the most celebrated couple on the Peking circuit, and Wallis attended a dinner at their home at least once in the company of da Zara. How they got along is not recorded—at the time, Oei Hui-lan was apparently exasperated at the number of dinners she was having to arrange in their home. Some went better than others. Shortly before they hosted da Zara and Wallis, Wellington and Oei Hui-lan had both been violently sick after one of their dinner parties. What first appeared to be a bad case of food poisoning turned out to be potentially fatal arsenic poisoning. Several servants disappeared that night, never to be traced. Northern warlord machinations, with one or the other side unhappy with Koo as foreign minister, had managed to infiltrate a Legation Quarter dinner.[*]

Twenty years later, Madame Koo was in London, as her husband was the wartime Chinese ambassador to Britain. Wallis was now the Duchess of Windsor, and the infamous China Dossier had spread a great deal of gossip about her China time. Madame Koo made the comment that Wallis knew only four words of Chinese: "Boy, pass the champagne."[†] This is a somewhat catty story in a rather catty memoir, not to mention the phrase being actually unrenderable in the exact form Oei Hui-lan suggests. Still, it became a staple part of the legend of Wallis's China years, and whether Madame Koo truly remembered Wallis Spencer on the arm of an Italian naval officer at one of their many, many dinner parties two decades previous is not entirely clear. Nevertheless, it does indicate the elevated circles in which Wallis was moving while sojourning in Peking.

The Koo home is worth recalling, as an invitation there, to lunch or dinner, was the most desired in Foreign Colony society, and Wallis, by now immersed in Chinese style, would have appreciated getting to see it. Their hutong courtyard was in the shadow of the Forbidden City. The walls of the public rooms were paneled with intricately

---

[*] Jonathan Clements, *Wellington Koo* (London: Haus, 2008), 114.
[†] Madame Wellington Koo [Oei Hui-lan], *No Feast Lasts Forever* (New York: New York Times Book Company, 1975).

carved, honey-colored sandalwood. Roof supporting beams were stained a rich brown and embossed in gold leaf. The upholstery was covered in gold brocade amid mirrored cabinets, lacquer-topped tables, and modern central heating, cleverly installed behind brass fixtures resembling traditional incense burners. The ceilings were covered in embossed paper decorated with phoenixes and peonies. Attached to some of the walls were much-admired silk panels from Manchuria. In the warmer spring months, the Koos usually entertained in their summer dining room, which was less ornate though lined with wooden chests that, on hot days, could be filled with slabs of ice—Peking-style air-conditioning in 1924. Guests drifted out on to the verandas to admire an artificial pond and landscaped garden scented by mauve lilac trees.

Madame Koo had returned to China obsessed with the current vogue for mah-jongg and recalled in her memoirs that every dinner party ended with games of mah-jongg (rapidly replacing bridge among many of the more fashionable in Peking) played with sets of beautifully carved ivory tiles. It seems Wallis never took to mah-jongg, sticking with bridge and poker all her life. However, Madame Koo was yet another avid jade collector, so maybe there was a subject for small talk?

CAUTIONARY TALES AND THE MURDEROUS MARCHESA

Wallis was publicly separated from Win. Still based in Hong Kong, he appeared to accept that their marriage was over and was not raising any objections to their divorcing. It was simply a technical matter of Wallis or himself being in a jurisdiction capable of finalizing the decision, signing some paperwork, and ratifying the process legally. So, for all intents and purposes, Wallis was a free woman, her reputation intact.

But there were cautionary tales. Occasionally, the claustropho-bia and incestuous nature of the Legation Quarter, the frenzied love affairs, would explode spectacularly. When later in the 1930s tales were told of Wallis's supposedly bizarre behavior in China, hyped up in the China Dossier by those seeking to derail any marriage to the king, some of the rumors may have been based on a vaguely re-membered cause célèbre from 1920s Peking that sounded a lot like it might have been Wallis—the case of the marchesa Durazzo, wife of the Italian ambassador to China, and her ill-fated lover Captain Pitri.

During Wallis's time in Peking, Alberto da Zara's boss was the popular Italian ambassador Vittorio Cerruti. Cerruti, a Piedmon-tese, was just forty-four. He was urbane, stylish, and well-liked. He had recently married his equally popular and very witty wife, Elis-abetta de Paulay, a Budapest-born Jewish-Hungarian actress who had appeared on both the stage and in silent movies. Cerruti was no social snob. He didn't disapprove of da Zara's relationship with Wallis; he was close to both Wellington Koo at the Chinese For-eign Ministry and Gerry Greene at the American legation, who was a sometime confidant. Wallis, through da Zara, came to know the Cerrutis well.

When he arrived in 1922, Cerruti had needed friends in the Lega-tion Quarter. His entire career prior to China had been in Europe, with a brief posting to Buenos Aires during the Great War. China was some considerable way out of his sphere of knowledge, experi-ence, and interest. It had all happened so quickly. He had received an urgent order from Rome to pack his bags and head to Peking, where he would be the new ambassador. The reason for the haste—Ambassador Durazzo and his wife.

The marchese (or marquis) Carlo Durazzo had been appointed Italian ambassador to China in 1920 after a successful posting as an attaché in Washington. Durazzo was a handsome, perfectly man-nered, and socially popular professional diplomat. Perhaps a little too much the diplomat. Stella Benson recalled him as "pleasant, but rather too polite to be interesting."* Accompanying him was his wife, the marchesa (marquess) Amanda Durazzo, younger than her husband, considered a great beauty, and having lived for many years as a child in Tokyo, where her father had been the Austro-Hungarian ambassador. Within weeks of arriving, the marchesa had begun a passionate affair with a dashing Sicilian, Captain Alfredo Pitri, the Italian legation's naval attaché. The affair soon became the worst-kept secret in the Foreign Colony. Perhaps most intriguing, it seemed Carlo Durazzo wasn't particularly bothered about it all.

Things might have carried on without any great scandal, the affair might have fizzled out, another of Ann Bridge's "drab little flirtations," but for Signora Maria Cioci—Captain Pitri's mistress and alleged fiancée. She had boarded a ship from Naples to Tientsin to claim her man. Pitri rushed to Tientsin and persuaded her to return home with promises he would follow as soon as possible. She agreed and made the journey back to Italy, after which Pitri promptly forgot her and resumed his affair with Amanda Durazzo.

Had Maria Cioci been a less determined woman, there would have been no problem. But realizing Pitri wasn't following as promised, she returned once more to Tientsin in the summer of 1921. This time, she got the train to Peking and checked into a suite at the Grand Hôtel des Wagons-Lits, announcing to the whole Foreign Colony who she was. It seems the marchesa exploded with rage, stormed into Cioci's suite, and attacked her with a set of very unladylike knuckle-dusters, or a horsewhip, or a broken water decanter, or her fists and boots?—it all becomes very unclear what happened at this point except that the hotel was in total uproar. Cioci was rushed to the hospital, covered in

* *The Diaries of Stella Benson, 1902–1933*, Cambridge University Library.

blood, and the marchesa hurriedly secreted behind the shut-fast gates of the Italian legation.

Despite attempts by Italian diplomats and officials of the Catholic Church in Peking to cover up the scandal, word of the incident got back to Rome. Durazzo was recalled. The marchesa was reportedly declared "unbalanced." Pitri apologized to Maria Cioci at her hospital bedside, returned to his barracks at the legation, and shot himself in the head. Distraught at her fiancé's death, Cioci returned to Italy and anonymity. The Foreign Colony was bemused by the rapid turn of events—Legation Quarter "drab little flirtations" were not supposed to end like this. Cecil Bowra, the rather snobby English secretary of the Imperial Chinese Customs, was perplexed by it all, writing: "Captain Pitri was an uninteresting individual of commonplace type; and why two women, one at any rate of unusual charm and attractiveness [Bowra meant the marchesa], with a delightful husband and nice children, should have cared sufficiently about him to go to these extraordinary lengths is a mystery buried in the dark depths."*

The scandal rocked the goldfish bowl of the Legation Quarter. The Durazzos hurriedly gone, the Cerrutis soon arrived and sought to recover Italy's reputation in Peking. They did so by being excellent hosts and bridge players—the two primary attributes of a successful Legation Quarter couple. The story of the marchesa Durazzo and Captain Pitri was never mentioned publicly in polite circles in Peking, though it's hard to imagine, certainly after she began her affair with Alberto da Zara, that Wallis had not heard tell of the murderous marchesa of Peking.

The events had been reported in the British and American newspapers in 1921 to an intrigued international readership lapping up

---

* Quoted in Julia Boyd, *A Dance with the Dragon: The Vanished World of Peking's Foreign Colony* (London: I. B. Taurus, 2012), 126.

scandal in far-off Peking. One of the clever elements of the China Dossier gossip circulated about Wallis is that the allegations and suggestions often had root in a real event. In this case, an affair within the Italian legation and a scandal involving a naval attaché. It was all too easy to conflate half-remembered, barely reported stories with fact. The marchesa's story, even if not directly, merged with Wallis's in some minds, muddied the waters, confirming the idea that Peking was, as Ann Bridge had written, "a graveyard of reputations."*

When Wallis came to write her autobiography, Alberto da Zara was one subject she was coy about. She remembered him fondly, though, writing in 1956, "The Italian, who later became an admiral, is now dead; among his effects was found a poem written during his youth which he left to me 'the sea, the sky, and the sun'—surely the noblest of bequests."† As the Duchess of Windsor, she wasn't about to start gossiping about her exes, beyond the ones to whom she had been married and divorced. Nor was she going to revive any gossip from the supposed China Dossier. But it was a real affair.

They were caught on camera (pretty much the only photo we have of Wallis in China) looking relaxed together, easy in each oth-

---

* If Wallis knew the story of the Durazzo scandal, she might have been interested to note that, finally, in 1925, the case came to court in Ancona, Italy. The press gathered, hoping for some juicy gossip to emerge. The Durazzos were either "reconciled" or had apparently separated, depending on which newspaper you read, his diplomatic career derailed, and she finally out of the "private nursing home" (the press invariably called it an "asylum") she had been sent to after arriving back in Italy. Dramatically, just before the trial began, Maria Cioci (who had lost the use of her right hand) withdrew the case. The marchesa Durazzo was released from any further investigation. The press speculated, but could not prove, that Durazzo had used his influence to end the trial and that Cioci had either been paid off or put under pressure from Rome. Either way, the Durazzo scandal fizzled out. Paul French, "An Affair to Remember: The Murderous Marchesa of 1920s Peking," *South China Morning Post Magazine*, August 28, 2022.

† Simpson, *The Heart Has Its Reasons*, 117.

er's company, a handsome couple. But where to conduct their affair? Wallis was ensconced with the Rogerses on Shih-Chia Hutong; da Zara had quarters inside the Italian legation. Both places might be a little awkward. But da Zara was also the keeper of the keys to one of the most romantic and ancient locations in northern China—the fort at Lao Long Tou, the Old Dragon's Head—where the Great Wall meets the Yellow Sea.

The Narrow Guage Railway to Shanhaikwan (Courtesy: David Noyce and Special Collections, University of Bristol Library)

11

ROMANCE AT THE END
OF THE GREAT WALL

LAO LONG TOU FORT
(THE OLD DRAGON'S HEAD)
SHANHAIKWAN
EAST OF PEKING
SPRING 1925

China is apt to be a graveyard of reputations . . . most girls who come
to Peking leave it engaged, generally to the wrong man; and nearly all
women leave Peking with a broken heart.
—Ann Bridge, *The Ginger Griffin*

Nearly anything's proper in Peking. No one will be surprised.
—J. P. Marquand, *Ming Yellow*

There was never in the world such a place for rumours as Peking.
—Ellen Newbold La Motte, *Peking Dust*

WEEKENDS AT THE OLD DRAGON'S HEAD

Warmer weather meant you could feel the hot sun on your skin.
Peking was perfumed by lilac and wisteria. The city's legion of
poplar trees shed their fluffy catkins, filling the air with tiny white

tufts—the Chinese were said to believe that every willow fluff represented a wandering soul.

As spring progressed, the Foreign Colony was beset by rumors of a renewed conflict between the warlords Chang Tso-lin, aka the Old Marshal, and the ever-unreliable Betrayal General, Feng Yu-hsiang. The city was on tenterhooks; newspapers issued special editions with almost hourly updates. Newsboys on street corners shouted terrifying predictions of Peking's imminent invasion, each new edition more alarming than the last. And Peking residents were right to be concerned. The skirmishing would escalate in northern China throughout the spring and summer, finally breaking out into open war in September—the so-called Second Chihli-Fengtian War— with armies battling across China from Shanghai to Manchuria.* The Old Marshal was to eventually retake Peking in the autumn.

Trying to make sense of warlord politics and allegiances was impossible. Feng and his so-called National Army had already betrayed his former Chihli clique ally, the warlord Wu Peifu. Feng had then, predictably perhaps, switched sides and joined with the Old Marshal. Just months later, the two warlords fell out, to nobody's great surprise, and Feng was now defending Peking from Chang's renewed onslaught. To confuse matters further, Wu Peifu joined Chang to seek vengeance against the disloyal traitor Feng. The machinations of the northern warlords were labyrinthine and incomprehensible to the vast majority of outsiders. By the time news of freshly brokered alliances reached the newspapers, these agreements had already been broken and deadly enmities with former friends now declared. The legations all had their political officers attempting to work out which

---

* Chihli, or sometimes Zhili, was the area of China now known as Hebei Province. Fengtian, now part of what is known as Liaoning Province, was the area around Zhang Zuolin's power base of Mukden (Shenyang). The First Chihli-Fengtian War was in 1922 and saw Zhang and the Fengtian clique defeated. Zhang was expelled from the coalition Zhili-Fengtian government in Peking by the warlord and Chihli strategist Wu Peifu.

side to favor, possibly even arm . . . but most admitted they were at a loss to know what was going to happen or even if China would hold together and not splinter off into multiple fiefdoms and self-governing territories run by warlords. Sun Yat-sen seemed unable to bang heads together; little had come of the American-brokered Tientsin peace conference the previous Christmas.

At street level, all this chaos meant nervous panic and uncertainty. Inflation meant spiraling food prices and wildly fluctuating exchange rates between copper, gold, and silver, as well as hard and paper currencies. Depositors fearing the disappearance of their life savings caused long queues and runs on banks (institutions never much trusted at the best of times). Everyone was hoarding rice, cooking oil, wheat, and kerosene. Thanks to exchange rates remaining generally in their favor, most foreigners could weather the inflationary storm. But some decided that, this time, the streets of Peking might finally become a battleground, that the old walls could well be breached by one warlord army or another, and blood—Chinese and foreign—would be shed. Many moved their families south to the Shanghai International Settlement, or even as far as Hong Kong, for safety. Both the Shanghai Express train and the coastal steamers south from Tientsin were fully booked for weeks ahead. The streets and hutongs were unnaturally quiet. Rickshaw pullers and street peddlers stayed indoors. Many of the Foreign Colony decamped early that year for their extended stays at the nearby coastal resorts.

When it came to seaside resorts accessible from Peking in which to escape the unremitting summer heat (and the possibility of warlord siege), the British and American contingent favored Peitaiho (Beidaihe). Then a slow and often disrupted nine-hour journey from the city, Peitaiho had originally been a summer retreat for missionaries. Now it had long found favor with the British and Americans of the Foreign Colony, as well as the wealthier Chinese, including the ever-fashionable and trendsetting Koos, who all rented villas and bungalows in the so-called West End of town. The big Peking and Tientsin department stores opened temporary summer shops to keep the Foreign Colony supplied with everything from swimsuits to new gramophone records. The Tung-Chau Dairy brought milk supplies from the city; the Greek-run Galatis Tobacconists opened a beach front stall; the Tientsin Bakery ensured supplies of bread and pastries. The German pharmacy on Hatamen Street opened a summer-long shop front offering rose water, boric acid, castor oil, quinine, bismuth, and disinfectant tablets—the Foreign Colony lived in constant fear of hepatitis, diarrhea, dysentery, typhoid, various mosquito-borne diseases, ptomaine poisoning, and all manner of serious upset stomachs. Even the bigger curio stores opened summer shops in the resort. Fresh copies of the *Peking* and *Tientsin Times* arrived daily. Herman and Kitty regularly spent time at Peitaiho, renting a beachfront bungalow each year since they arrived in China in 1922. They were among those looking into securing a bungalow at Peitaiho again that summer.

However, in 1925, northern China's Italian community favored the coastal town of Shanhaikwan (Shanhaiguan), slightly to the north of Peitaiho. This was the area known as the Shanhai Pass—the First Pass Under Heaven—where the Great Wall meets the Gulf of Pechili (Bohai Gulf) and the Yellow Sea. Three miles outside Shanhaikwan was the large, impressive Ming dynasty fort Lao Long Tou, literally "the Old Dragon's Head." It sat at the very start (or end, depending on your perspective) of the Great Wall of China. By road, Shanhaikwan was about 180 miles from the capital. Trains ran regularly from Peking to Tientsin, where you transferred to the narrow-gauge coastal line onward to Peitaiho and finally the small European-style Shanhaikwan Station. From there, the ride to the beach was on a mule-pulled trolley with your luggage following behind along a single track dubbed the "one-mile-an-hour-engine."

While Peitaiho's appeal for the Foreign Colony was enduring (and would be for some time until the Japanese invasion of China in 1937), in 1925 Shanhaikwan was becoming a fashionable alternative, helped by the fact that it was the summer retreat of choice of Vittorio and Elisabetta Cerruti. Despite widespread warlordism in the surrounding area and a general spate of kidnapping of foreigners, little untoward ever seemed to happen at laid-back Shanhaikwan, where there was a small garrison of Italian troops. Along with Peitaiho, Shanhaikwan was billed by travel agents, rather hopefully given the political situation, as northern China's Riviera. The Cerrutis and the Italian diplomatic crowd were soon joined by the wider Italian community from Peking and the Tientsin Italian Concession as families rented or built villas for the spring weekends and summer months. The Italians made Shanhaikwan their own.

Lagging behind the French and British, Italy had long wanted to expand its territory in China. In 1899, Rome had tried to lease San-Mun Bay (Sanmen Wan) on the southern tropical island of Hainan. But China refused, saying, "Italy is not so important in China to allow it to be given treatment like the other Powers."* This unforgivable slight set Rome and Peking on a collision course. Italy contributed nearly two thousand soldiers and sailors to the Eight-Nation Alliance that suppressed the Boxer Uprising, relieved the siege of the legations, and then promptly sacked and looted Peking in 1900. As part of the post-Boxer settlement, Italy got its own concession in Tientsin, as well as the right to maintain a military garrison within the Peking Legation Quarter and another one at Shanhaikwan (on condition of the payment of two thousand lira

---

* Orazio Coco, "Italian Diplomacy in China: The Forgotten Affair of San Men Xian (1898–1899)," *Journal of Modern Italian Studies* 24, no. 2 (2019).

a year).[*] In the mid-1920s, a small detachment of Italian marines guarded Lao Long Tou and prevented any warlord occupation. As the Regia Marina's most senior officer in northern China, Alberto da Zara literally had the keys to the Old Dragon's Head.

The fort had little strategic importance by 1925 but was a major tourist attraction.[†] It was possible to walk along the impressive last section of the Great Wall, through the ancient fort, and out to sea on what effectively became a wide stone pier. There was an Italian-run International Officers Club (where visiting foreigners could get a drink), two churches, a hotel built when the railway line arrived (unimaginatively called the Railway Hotel but noted as "comfortable" by Carl Crow in his 1921 *Travelers' Handbook for China*), as well as a decent beach close by.[‡]

And so it was to Shanhaikwan that da Zara brought Wallis to escape the threatening atmosphere of warlord violence, as well as the early-summer dust and crowds of Peking. He had full access to the Old Dragon's Head fort and the better appointed and more comfortable officers' rooms there. The ranks were in a nearby garrison block. The fort was lightly manned, and so when da Zara visited, he usually had the officers' quarters to himself.

The suite of rooms was decorated with lacquer furniture, faded old yellow silk brocade, and Chinese porcelain vases that dated back to the initial Italian occupation of the fort in 1901. The ceilings were painted with dragons and other symbols of the Chinese astral world,

---

* Averaging fluctuating Italian exchange and inflation rates over the 1920s, we could assume an exchange rate of US$1 = 19 Italian Lira (Lit). Therefore, Lit2,000 would be approximately US$38,000 in the mid-1920s, which would be roughly US$663,000 in 2023.

† Shanhaikwan had been strategically important during the Boxer siege when foreign troops landed close by before marching on Peking. The town had been occupied by foreign troops, and afterward, a small permanent, Italian-manned garrison remained.

‡ Carl Crow, *Travelers' Handbook for China* (Shanghai: Hwa-Mei Book Concern, 1921).

supported by painted pillars of intermingled greens, reds, and blues. The bedrooms had traditional northern Chinese kang beds supported on fired clay that could be heated underneath by hot coals if the nights were chilly. The Cerrutis—and before them, the ill-fated Durazzos—had stayed in the suite when visiting. Over the years, various ambassadors had added Cantonese blackwood chairs and comfortable sofas imported from Europe. The bedrooms were carpeted with rugs from Bokhara, Persia, and Turkestan. Mosquitoes were a plague, but the scents of gently burning sandalwood and camphor incense kept them at bay. The fort had never been electrified, so candles in lanterns hung from the ceilings. A small Chinese staff prepared breakfast, lunches, and dinners, or food could be delivered from the Railway Hotel. The Cerrutis had ensured there was a well-stocked wine cellar.

On warm early-summer evenings, cool breezes blew through the rooms, gently flickering the candles. Outside could be heard the sound of the waves lapping against the base of the Old Dragon's Head and the distant noises of the bustling town. Sunrises and sunsets were equally impressive. The Lao Long Tou was, despite being a little basic on the amenities, decidedly romantic. It must have reminded Wallis of the verandas and beach cabanas of the Repulse Bay Hotel in Hong Kong. She could have no idea that these idyllic breaks from the hot city on the balmy Yellow Sea coast would later be used to suggest she was an unfit consort for a king.

THE QUEEN OF PEKING

That idea of Ann Bridge's, in her bestselling 1934 novel *The Ginger Griffin*, that "Peking was a graveyard of reputations" would come back to haunt Wallis. Bridge's novels of Peking Foreign Colony manners had all been widely read in England. And in America too;

Peking Picnic won the *Atlantic Monthly* prize of $10,000 in 1932.* This was one reason the compilers of the China Dossier, alleging all sorts of misconduct in China a decade or more earlier, had such an easy target. And while memories were hazy and sources difficult to check in the late 1930s, wasn't there an American woman living in Peking back then who had indulged in multiple affairs and trashed her reputation?

There was. But it wasn't Wallis Spencer. Instead, it was an American woman known for some years as the Queen of Peking— Constance Coolidge.

Coolidge (a distant relative of the former president Calvin Coolidge) was just a couple of years older than Wallis. A Boston Brahmin who had lived in Paris, she was considered extremely beautiful—an "it girl" of her time. From her teenage years, she had been a wild child with a penchant for horse racing, gambling, and scandalous affairs. In France, she met fellow Bostonian Roy Atherton, an architecture student at the Beaux-Arts de Paris. Though he was a decade older than she was, a whirlwind romance and marriage followed. During the Great War, Atherton became a diplomat, was posted to Tokyo in 1917 and then, in 1919, to Peking as second secretary at the American legation. Constance accompanied him. Prohibition-free China, her trust fund, his salary, and favorable exchange rates meant life was good. Constance drank, gambled, and almost immediately upon arrival in Peking became notorious. She bought a share in a Mongolian gold mine that ultimately yielded little precious metal. She bought several Mongolian ponies that won regularly at the Paomachang racetrack. But then she lost a lot of money, including some of her trust fund and her Paomachang winnings, when the French-run Banque Industrielle de Chine, where

---

* Not to be sniffed at—US$10,000 in 1932 is equivalent in purchasing power parity to about US$229,000 in 2024.

she'd deposited large sums of cash, collapsed. Like Wallis, she was fascinated by Peking:

> Every time you go out it is an adventure for the streets are so fascinating with hens & camels & donkeys & thousands of coolies & rickshaws in a hopeless confusion. The tiles on the Emperor's Palace are all yellow & shine & glitter in the sun like gold. The Temple of Heaven has blue—deep blue—tiles & oh the architecture is so beautiful.*

Her marriage to Atherton had quickly gone stale, and Constance had begun a series of quite overt and often ill-judged affairs. A married American businessman was followed by an official of the Banque Industrielle de Chine, who convinced her to put her money in his failing bank! The American died of cancer shortly after the affair began; the Frenchman fell off his horse and never regained consciousness. In the spring of 1922, Atherton was transferred home, to the State Department in Washington. Constance decided to stay on in Peking (declaring it was so she could sell her stable of racing ponies). The scandals that had naturally gripped the Legation Quarter goldfish bowl's rapt attention meant she was now known mockingly as "the Queen of Peking."

With Atherton on a boat back to America, Constance began an affair with a diplomat, the Shanghai-born Eric Brenan, a student interpreter in the British legation. Brenan was from a family of diplomats all of whom saw service in China—his father was with the Chinese Maritime Customs Service, his uncle a consul general in Shanghai, while his older brother would go on to be consul general in both Shanghai and Canton in the 1930s (he had a younger brother who died at Ypres). Brenan had everything going in his favor before

---

* Andrea Lynn, *Shadow Lovers: The Last Affairs of H. G. Wells* (New York: Perseus, 2001), 233. The ampersands are Constance's.

he met Constance Atherton: Cambridge-educated, survived service in the Great War unscathed, eased into the diplomatic corps thanks to family connections, a member of the exclusive Peking Club, and living in comfortable British legation bachelor quarters. Brenan was a man expected to go far. But the affair with Constance Atherton derailed his fledgling career. The goldfish bowl of 1920s Peking meant everyone knew, and while mild flirtations were permissible, an open and flagrantly conducted affair with another member of the diplomatic corps (as the marchesa Durazzo was to discover around the same time) was just too scandalous for Legation Street.

Constance departed China for France, promising she would divorce Atherton and marry Brenan. But she began another affair in Paris with Felix Doubleday (the adopted son of Frank Nelson Doubleday, founder of the publishing empire Doubleday).* Doubleday was devoted to her, but she soon began yet another illicit liaison with Harry Crosby, the wealthy Bohemian archetype of the American lost generation in Paris. Constance eventually divorced Atherton in 1924.† Brenan, his fledgling diplomatic career in tatters, sailed to America hoping Constance would reunite with him there. He wrote desperate letters to her, threatening to kill himself. The whole thing was an awful mess, heartbroken beaus and wrecked relationships trailing in Constance's wake. Caresse Crosby, the Paris-based avant-garde publisher and wife of Harry Crosby, while he was engaged in

* Felix Doubleday did not join the family publishing business but worked as a broker in Europe. His affair with Constance contributed to his divorce from his first wife in 1924. He died at just fifty-three after a long period of ill health caused by having been gassed while on active service in World War I. In a link to China, his adoptive mother, Neltje "Nellie" Doubleday, died in 1918 in Canton of a sudden cerebral hemorrhage while on a tour of the Philippines, Hong Kong, and China for the American Red Cross.

† Ray Atherton's career does not seem to have unduly suffered despite the scandals around Constance, and he went on to be US Ambassador to Canada, Greece, Bulgaria, Luxembourg, and Denmark, as well as an alternate US delegate to the newly formed United Nations.

his affair with Constance, wrote of the Queen of Peking's time in China: "She had lived in a temple, raced Mongolian ponies, defied convention and was generally an exciting pagan."[*]

Wallis arrived in Peking two years after Constance left, but she could not fail to have heard tales of the Queen of Peking, Constance's story told repeatedly over the long nights of bridge or round Legation Quarter dinner tables. And not least because, in the summer of 1922, Constance had met and befriended the newly arrived Herman and Kitty Rogers, then spending their first summer at Peitaiho in a bungalow adjacent to Constance. Constance wrote of encountering the couple on the beach, "I don't know who they are, but they are very good looking and attractive."[†] And so perhaps the later confusions with a number of Wallis's biographers asserting the two had known each other in China, which was not in fact possible. The conflation of Wallis and Constance undoubtedly prompted the rumors and conjecture of the China Dossier whispered in polite society.

A decade after China, in the 1930s, Wallis was actually introduced to Constance in France by Herman and Kitty. Constance later became an occasional part of the Windsors' circle—dining with the Rogerses and the duke and duchess on the Riviera, all attending the horse races at Longchamp and Auteuil, or Schiaparelli and Balenciaga fashion shows in Paris. It had been easy for many to confuse Constance and Wallis—both American, both Peking sojourners, both keen equestriennes and aficionados of the Paomachang racetrack, both divorced a number of times and finally settled in Europe. But they were not the same, and Wallis's time with Alberto da Zara was a very different affair from those Constance Coolidge indulged in.

And considering Wallis's time with da Zara, there's another

---

[*] Caresse Crosby, *The Passionate Years* (New York: Dial Press, 1953), 113.
[†] Lynn, *Shadow Lovers*, 240.

rumor from the China Dossier, one that has long continued to be circulated and repeated, that needs to be dismissed.

FALSE RUMORS

Later, during the abdication crisis, one of the charges laid against Wallis was of being sympathetic to fascism. Certainly as war drew closer in 1939, questions could legitimately be raised concerning both the duke and duchess's political leanings. After the abdication and during World War II, aspects of their conduct and with whom they chose to communicate were clearly ill advised.* The roots of this, at best curiosity, and at worst open support for fascism, were sometimes said to be traceable to Wallis's China sojourn. And so the notion of a liaison with an Italian was raised as part of the supposed China Dossier and as a link between Wallis and Italian fascism.

In 1924, Mussolini's new fascist state had yet to fully corrupt the Italian foreign service. Inside the Italian legation in Peking, loyalties were divided. Ambassador Cerruti appears to have been loyal to the Italian nation, but ambivalent as far as Mussolini's state was concerned. Though he remained in the foreign service, he was often at odds with the more virulent fascist elements. Additionally, many older Italian China Hands were loyal to the widely admired senior diplomat Carlo Sforza, who had until Mussolini's coup been a guiding light on Italian foreign relations. Sforza had been a consular secretary in Peking at the start of his career. He had then returned as ambassador between 1911 and 1915, navigating both the collapse of the Qing dynasty and negotiating the statutes governing

---

* For more on the subject of the Duke and Duchess of Windsor's flirtation or involvement with fascism, see Andrew Lownie, *Traitor King: The Scandalous Exile of the Duke and Duchess of Windsor* (London: Bonnier Books, 2021).

the new Italian Concession in Tientsin. Leaving diplomacy for politics, Sforza led the anti-fascist opposition in the Italian Senate until being forced into exile in 1926. Among many Italians with China connections—diplomatic, commercial, military, academic—there was strong support for Sforza.[*]

Of course, major questions of loyalty and allegiance, tests that would affect everybody's lives and careers even in faraway China, were soon coming, and those found wanting in their allegiances would be purged (or forced into exile, like Carlo Sforza). The position of the Regia Marina, the army's Italian battalion in China, and their officers would soon become more complicated, and men like da Zara would be watched closely for their ideological leanings and associations. But not quite yet, in spring 1925, in China. There's no evidence da Zara was particularly political or that he ever talked politics, fascist or otherwise, with Wallis.

For the record, when Mussolini marched on Rome and took power in late 1921, da Zara was already on his way east to Shanghai and his posting in command of the *Ermanno Carlotto*. He was posted back to Italy in late 1925 to the Venice Naval Command. After Peking, there are some inconsistencies in his career. In 1936, he was placed in command of one of several Regia Marina ships shelling Republican-held Valencia at the start of the Spanish Civil War. Later, he commanded Italian troops in Albania (a key Italian imperial objective). In 1937, da Zara returned to China as the situation between China and Japan deteriorated. He was given command of the cruiser RM *Raimondo Montecuccoli*. Mussolini instructed him to protect Italian citizens, but also to display "Nippophilia," a generally supportive attitude toward Japan. However, many who knew him at this time believed that while da Zara carried out his

---

[*] In exile, Sforza did get his experiences of China published as *L'énigme chinoise* [The Chinese enigma] (Paris: Payot, 1928).

immediate orders to protect Italian interests, he was generally decidedly pro-Chinese in his outlook. He returned to Italy in late 1938. He served as a rear admiral during the war, and after the armistice with the Allies was proclaimed, he complied with the orders and surrendered his ships at Malta. After the war, da Zara was able to continue in the peacetime Italian navy until his retirement and was not subject to any particular censure by the allies.

But from the first rushed biographies of Wallis in the 1930s and still often today in biographies and articles, da Zara is often written out of the story.[*] His position during Wallis's China sojourn as lover was assumed by another, far-better-known Italian who spent time in Shanghai and Peking. The man who would become Mussolini's foreign minister, as well as his son-in-law, Count Galeazzo Ciano.

It has been asserted and then repeated again and again that, while in China, Wallis had an affair with Ciano.[†] As well as the fling, it is also suggested by some that she became pregnant by him and had a botched abortion. This rumor has been repeated in book after book, and even in memoirs by people looking back on the time and convinced they knew this to be the case. But they are confusing their Italians in China. And it's important not to. If Wallis ever sympathized with Italian fascism later in life, then it was not

---

[*] In part perhaps because Wallis mentions "a gallant Italian naval officer" in *The Heart Has Its Reasons*, but does not specifically name him.

[†] For instance, by Higham in his biography. He has Wallis visiting Shanhaikwan with Ciano, becoming pregnant by him there, and then going to Hong Kong for an abortion. But he has no sources for it being Ciano or the alleged Hong Kong abortion—which is impossible, as Wallis never returned to Hong Kong after leaving in late 1924. Many other sources repeat this or variations of the Wallis-Ciano story. For instance, in her memoirs of her youth in China, Diana Angulo (born 1919), the daughter of a US naval attaché assigned to the American legation in Peking and then Shanghai, is insistent Ciano and Wallis met in China, though this would have been impossible. Diana Hutchins Angulo, *Peking Sun, Shanghai Moon* (Shanghai: Old China Hand Press, 2008).

due to having had an affair with Count Ciano in China. If Wallis ever did have an abortion or miscarriage, then it was not the result of an affair with him.

A hard-core supporter of Mussolini, Galeazzo Ciano (six or seven years younger than Wallis) had taken part in the march on Rome shortly after graduating from university. He then began a diplomatic career, first as an attaché in Rio de Janeiro and then for a time in Peking under the returning, and very popular, ambassador Daniele Varè. Ciano's first posting to China began in May 1927, well after Wallis had left the city, never to return. Ciano's and Wallis's paths never crossed in China.

Ciano did have the reputation of a lothario. Varè recorded that Ciano enjoyed Peking and thought him possessed of an "easy bourgeois charm." Elisabetta Cerruti commented that "although he was not attractive, being too fat for his age and somehow unhealthy, he had a certain unrefined handsomeness and thought himself quite irresistible to the ladies."* Harold Acton dismissed him as a "lounge lizard."† In 1930, Ciano married Mussolini's daughter Edda, and Il Duce became his father-in-law. He was appointed Italian consul general to Shanghai and served there in 1931 and 1932. He was considered to have had many liaisons and affairs while in the city. And so the story was spun a dozen years later. Ciano was Italian, he had been in Peking at some point in the 1920s, and he had returned again as consul general in Shanghai, where he was a serial adulterer.

For her part, Edda had an affair with the Chinese warlord Chang Hsueh-liang (Zhang Xueliang), the Young Marshal and son

---

* Cerruti quoted in Tobias Hof, *Galeazzo Ciano: The Fascist Pretender* (Toronto: University of Toronto Press, 2021), 58, 71.

† Harold Acton, *Memoirs of an Aesthete* (London: Methuen, 1948), 289. Acton also described Edda (Mussolini) Ciano as "button eyed and with a massive jaw that gave her a striking resemblance to her father."

of Chang Tso-lin, the by-then-assassinated Old Marshal.* Edda and Chang took long walks along the Tartar Wall together, where Wallis had once ridden with Herman and Kitty. Edda liked to visit Peitaiho and Shanhaikwan. She also gave birth to the couple's first son, Fabrizio, while in Shanghai. She did also reputedly develop a bit of a gambling problem in Shanghai.† Did people confuse rumors regarding Edda with those being circulated about Wallis?‡ It has been suggested that the story was first put about by Billy Miles, the wife of Milton E. Miles, a fellow naval officer of Win's at the time (Milton was a lieutenant with the US Asiatic Fleet) who later ran naval intelligence operations in China during World War II and ended up a vice admiral.§ Though whether this was a genuine confusion or malicious intent by Billy Miles is unclear.

Ciano did eventually encounter Wallis—in Venice, in June 1937, while she was honeymooning with the Duke of Windsor. In some

---

* In June 1926, Chang managed to capture Peking. It was rumored that he was planning to proclaim himself an emperor. He settled for being termed *generalissimo*. Chang found himself caught between the increasingly aggressive Japanese in Manchuria and Chiang Kai-shek's advancing army aiming to unify China under the Republic. In June 1928, he left Peking for Mukden. En route, his train was bombed and derailed in Manchuria by the Japanese army (known as the Kwangtung Army). Chang died several days later. He was succeeded as warlord of the Manchuria government by his son Chang Hsueh-liang, the Young Marshal.

† Caroline Moorehead, *Edda Mussolini: The Most Dangerous Woman in Europe* (London: Chatto & Windus, 2022), 168.

‡ To be fair, it is largely Wallis's less scrupulous biographers and detractors who claim she had an affair with Ciano in China. His biographers find no evidence of it, and some—for instance, Ray Moseley in *Mussolini's Shadow: The Double Life of Galeazzo Ciano* (New Haven, CT: Yale University Press, 1999)—disprove the rumor. There is also the possibility that Wallis having stayed at the Repulse Bay Hotel in Hong Kong with Win may have confused some, as this was also a hotel that Ciano and Edda stayed at some time later.

§ This suggestion has appeared in several books, though quite why Wilma "Billy" Miles would make this allegation is unclear. It is true, however, that Miles E. Milton was commissioned as an ensign and lieutenant junior grade with the US Asiatic Fleet between 1922 and 1927.

instances, the inference that Wallis and Ciano had a liaison in China is considered deliberate—to portray her as a longtime sympathizer with fascism under the sway of a man closely connected to Mussolini.[*] For others, though, it seems to have become an urban legend, a fabrication they came to believe, repeated, and asserted right down to the current day. But it was not true.

The balmy Shanhaikwan weekend over, the couple had to return to the city. The bumpy, narrow gauge train ride, then the hopefully bandit-free haul to Tientsin and back to Peking. Da Zara returning to duties at the Italian legation. Wallis to the hairdresser's, at least if the novelist Ann Bridge is to be believed. "The first concern of those who return from a sojourn at Peitaiho to Peking is—in the case of women, at least—to get their hair set." The salon at the Grand Hôtel de Pekin was very social, "not to say matey," and hair appointments were accompanied by manicures, face massages, and a lot of gossip.[†]

With Wallis's personal situation well known and da Zara a bachelor, there was no reason for them to hide their relationship within the confines of the Italian legation or stay stashed away on weekends at the Old Dragon's Head. They could appear in public together if they wished. And there was one ever-popular Peking Foreign Colony pastime, an obsession for just about every Westerner in the city, that Wallis and da Zara also shared—the racetrack . . .

* Moorehead, *Edda Mussolini*, 168.
† Ann Bridge, *Four-Part Setting* (London: Chatto & Windus, 1939), 59.

The Main Stand, Paomachang Race Course, Peking (Courtesy: Charlotte Thomas and Special Collections, University of Bristol Library)

12

CHEERING PONIES AND CHERRY BRANDY

PAOMACHANG RACETRACK
PEKING
LATE SPRING 1925

Peking's such loads of fun. Jugglers, fortune-tellers, acrobats, puppet-shows, temple tiffins, treasure hunts and Paomachang picnics—not to speak of costume jamborees, galas and fancy-dress affairs—always something original. Home-made natural fun, not imported or artificially manufactured as in Shanghai. And there's always a delicious slice of the unexpected.

—Harold Action, *Peonies and Ponies*

Social position is a delicate structure, which sometimes rests on strange foundations.

—Daniele Varè, *The Maker of Heavenly Trousers*

AMID THE PAOMACHANGITES . . .

Horses—or, to be more precise, Mongolian ponies—had been part of Wallis's Peking life since she had moved in with Herman and Kitty at Shih-Chia Hutong. They enjoyed morning rides on the Tartar Wall (now at 6:00 or 7:00 a.m. with the arrival of lighter mornings), weekend treks up to the temples of the Western Hills, while another social highlight of the Legation Quarter were the polo matches on the glacis. And then, of course, there was the start of the seasonal meetings at Paomachang—the Peking Race Club.

Since arriving in Peking, Wallis had turned out to watch polo, which was a year-round sport. She was familiar with the game—having occasionally escaped the drab confines of the Coronado naval air station, and Win's temper, to travel up the coast to friends who lived close by the Del Monte polo fields near Monterey. In Peking, Herman was a regular player, always had been as a young man in the States, and he tried never to miss a match. There were chukkers three times a week with the scrubland of the glacis, grandly dubbed the Peking Polo Grounds, for those occasions. But it wasn't much of a pitch. The glacis was what was known as a "skinned field," a mix of silt, clay, cinder, and broken brick, with a layer of Peking dust on top. Coming off your mount meant nasty scrapes to exposed skin. Broken arms and collarbones were not infrequent.

Polo was an American-dominated affair in Peking. Traditionally, the chairman of the Polo Club was an American, often the naval attaché. Many players were US Marines with plenty of horse-riding experience back where they came from but usually little acquaintance with the more rarefied game of polo. Still, they threw themselves into the game, making for an often rather rough-and-tumble chukker. As the Peking Polo Club, which played in imperial yellow with a blue dragon on their shirts, they were considered "quite fair class players," according to *The Cavalry Journal*.* The highlight of the season was the much-coveted Inter-Port Cup between Peking, Shanghai, Tientsin, and teams from other treaty ports around China, including one composed exclusively of Chinese army cavalry

---

* "Polo in Peking," *Cavalry Journal*, no. 68 (1928): 267–72. The article is written by "Chien-men," obviously a pseudonym. However, though published in 1928, the now long-anonymous author is referring to his time in China in 1925–26.

officers.* As well as liking horses, Wallis was connected to many of the players through Louis Little of the Legation Guard, who, as a regular player himself, reputedly swore at you in a mix of English and Chinese if you fouled him.†

But though she enjoyed the fast and furious excitement of the polo, it was the social milieu of Paomachang, the Peking Race Club, that Wallis most enjoyed.

As the race season commenced in late spring, the Paomachang (literally "Horse Running Field") became Wallis's regular destination. She was usually accompanied by the equally equestrian-minded Alberto da Zara. Paomachang in the late spring was essentially the Legation Quarter at play, and those who went regularly—which was just about anyone who was anyone—were dubbed (at least by Harold Acton) "Paomachangites."‡ Race seasons were twice a year in Peking, first in mid-spring and then again in the late fall. Peking horse racing was actually a winter and spring sport—by June, the climate would become too hot and dry, with the horses unable to see anything in the clouds of dust unless they were in the lead. Then the summer rains came, reducing the Paomachang track to a mud bath, making racing impossible until the drier, colder, late-autumn months came again and the ground hardened up.

Wallis rarely missed a spring race meet during her Peking sojourn. Along with other Paomachangites, she became a regular passenger on the small—but on race day always full and festive—train that pierced the Tartar Wall to the west of the city and ran along

---

* Norwood F. Allman recalls playing against the Chinese cavalry polo team, who were, he thought, skilled. He also notes that all these men died fighting the Japanese in Shanghai in January 1932 when the Japanese army attacked the Chinese portions of the city to the north of Soochow Creek following a staged provocation.

† Norwood F. Allman, *Shanghai Lawyer* (New York: Whittlesey House, 1943), 151–55.

‡ Harold Acton, *Peonies and Ponies* (London: Chatto & Windus, 1941), 157.

outside the wall for a while before arriving twenty minutes later in Paomachang, barely six miles from the Legation Quarter.

It was said of the British Empire that when the English pitched up anywhere—and this was certainly true of Hong Kong and Shanghai—they built a club first and a racecourse second. The British had taken control of Hong Kong Island from the Chinese at the end of the First Opium War in 1842. They opened the Happy Valley racetrack, built on land that had been a pestilential swamp, in 1845. Similarly in Shanghai, within a few years of occupying the treaty port, the British had a race club up and running by 1850.

Peking wasn't far behind. Paomachang held its first race in 1863. It was a fairly egalitarian sport among the Foreign Colony compared with back home. Those with money kept horses. As we've seen, Constance Coolidge kept a stable of racing ponies, as did Herman. But great wealth wasn't a prerequisite. Many could affordably own a pony or two through shared ownership schemes. If they didn't, like Herman, have their own stables, then they could keep them out at Paomachang for a small rent. Every season horse traders would come down from the north with herds of stout, strong ponies, fed and reared on the grasslands of Mongolia. Ann Bridge's rather pompous British diplomat Nugent Grant-Howard in *The Ginger Griffin* notes of his Peking posting, "The riding is first-class and the cheapest in the world. Quite average ponies for a tenner, and plenty of polo."*

Many foreigners also owned or rented weekend bungalows out by the course and hosted race parties every meeting. Alberto da Zara was a dedicated race fan and never missed an event. Wallis attended with him, sharing his binoculars, exchanging tips. At the races, they mixed with the less stuffy elements of the Legation Quarter set. Most of the younger dipsis attended. Since taking up with da Zara,

---

* Ann Bridge, *The Ginger Griffin* (London: Chatto & Windus, 1934), 3.

Wallis knew this set now and had become part of it, and Paomachang was where they gathered on spring weekends.

Many of the Italians in Peking were horse-racing fans, Vittorio and Elisabetta Cerruti among them. So too the Americans. The popular US ambassador Jacob Gould Schurman—known as "the dining diplomat"—always attended Paomachang. So did the Chinese Koos, the recently arrived Spanish ambassador Don Justo Garrido y Cisneros and his wife, and the Portuguese ambassador José Batalha de Freitas. Senhora de Freitas was, like Wallis, a keen jade collector, which ensured they got on immediately. Among the most coveted race-day picnic tiffin invitations were those hosted by Lady Evelyn Macleay, wife of the British ambassador Sir Ronald Macleay. The Macleays were considered to be a little less stuck-up and more fun than some of their predecessors at the British legation had been. Some of the Legation Quarter set decamped to Paomachang semipermanently when the races were on. Madame de Martel, the Parisian wife of the portly, gossipy, epicurean French ambassador the comte Damien de Martel, lived and entertained in a villa adjacent to the track throughout both the spring and fall race seasons, not bothering to return to the Legation Quarter between meets.

RACE DAY

Sunday was race day. The Foreign Colony gathered at their slightly rackety but charming country weekend bungalows around the edge of the track, lunching with friends. Others rented the few temples in the area for group picnics. Wealthy Chinese turned out for the races too. Several had built sumptuous new multistory villas close to the track.

The first activity of the day was the cross-country paper chase (or paper hunt)—an all-male affair, except for the last of the season, which was traditionally an exclusively ladies' hunt. The riders followed a pre-laid paper trail for ten miles or so across the open countryside, the whole pack moving as quickly as possible, jostling for position. Wallis liked to ride, but the paper hunt was a rougher gallop than she was used to. Although, as with polo, there were a fair number of broken bones from nasty falls, it was considered fun by most participants. Invariably, the English led the way, dressed up as if on a fox hunt in Berkshire or Surrey in scarlet jacket and jodhpurs, hunting horns echoing across the countryside. The Chinese farmers detested the paper hunt—the ponies churned up their sorghum fields, broke down mud walls, smashed their carefully woven fences of kaoliang straw, and, more distressingly, disturbed sacred burial mounds. A race club official was forced to follow the hunt around its random course, sorting out compensation payments on the spot with the aggrieved farmers.

The afternoons were devoted to racing on the track. Shanghai and Hong Kong ran almost exclusively flat races, but Peking also featured jumps. Though Paomachang had a grandstand of sorts, it was never to be as grand as the Shanghai Race Club or Hong Kong's Happy Valley. In the winter season, the stands were a sea of men in greatcoats and ladies in sable furs covering satin dresses, the chill winds whipping around their silk-clad ankles. Detractors described it as standing about, freezing, waiting for a cloud of dust to appear and then disappear while attempting to ascertain if one's husband, lover, or sweetheart had managed to stay on his mount. Herman raced his own ponies and was considered a good jockey, taking it seriously, blanketing his ponies between races, studying the hastily Gestetner-printed form sheets. Louis Little also rode at Paomachang and won regularly.

Race day was a seriously social event. Those not participating in the paper hunt sipped champagne on the grandstand's veranda, waiting for the ponies and their riders to return. Upstairs was a spacious dining room, rather austere with whitewashed walls. After large lunches, everyone massed in the grandstand's lower floor on long benches, which in the spring were pleasant enough. There was an airy veranda, though inevitably you were enveloped in a dust cloud as the ponies raced past, leaving everyone coughing and shielding their eyes.

Betting, which was reportedly quite furious, was on the pari-mutuel system.* During the races, cups of cherry brandy (distilled by the French Trappist monks of the Western Hills), accompanied by ginger cookies, were handed around. There were three races before a break for an afternoon tiffin back up in the dining room. Then a few more races before a mad scramble back to the city. Juliet Bredon, a regular at Paomachang every Sunday in the season, recalled, "The moment the last race was run, all hurriedly packed themselves into their conveyances and dashed back along the ruts of the roads or the furrows of the fields to catch the gate of the Tartar City before it closed for the night."†

And they hurried to attend the Grand Hôtel de Pekin's post-race party, where the tables of the roof garden were decorated with vases of roses and sprays of lilies, to enjoy more champagne or gin and bitters, as well as crème de menthe (from those Trappists monks in the Western Hills again), music from a Russian émigré band, and dancing till late.

Race season was fun, but somewhere along the way, Wallis's affair with da Zara petered out. He recalled their brief time in his postwar memoir, *Pelle d'Ammiraglio (The Skin of an Admiral)*, written in 1949, reminiscing about that Peking spring as a very pleasant time and remembering Wallis with great fondness.‡ Still, neither ever broached the question of why they separated or whether either

---

* A betting pool in which those who bet on competitors finishing in the first three places share the total amount wagered minus a percentage for the race club. Much off-track informal betting occurred too.

† Juliet Bredon, *Peking: A Historical and Intimate Description of Its Chief Places of Interest* (Shanghai: Kelly & Walsh, 1931), 75.

‡ Alberto da Zara, *Pelle d'Ammiraglio* [The skin of an admiral] (Verona: Mondadori Editore, 1949).

of them had ever thought to take it further. Wallis remained technically married; a formal separation would have to wait till she returned to America to file the divorce petition. But she wasn't expecting Win to contest it. Da Zara was an Italian, a naval captain, unmarried. Marriages to foreigners were no problem—Ambassador Cerruti had married a Hungarian actress; Daniele Varè married a Scottish woman; the marchesa Durazzo's family came from Austria-Hungary. Perhaps da Zara wanted an affair and nothing more, knowing he would move on at some point to another posting, another ship, another command. Perhaps Wallis concurred in this, knowing her time in China was always to be a sojourn. It had been a fling, harmless fun, a mutually pleasant adventure with no recriminations.

Charles Higham includes in his biography some comments of Lieutenant Giuseppe Pighini, who in the 1930s was an aide-de-camp to da Zara. Higham had many details of Wallis's China sojourn wrong, and sadly doesn't adequately source this interview, but says that Pighini told him:

> Mrs Simpson and da Zara had a very close relationship which from love developed into lasting friendship. Da Zara used to say about her that although she was not beautiful she was extremely attractive and had very refined and cultivated tastes. Her conversation was brilliant and she had the capacity of bringing up the right subject of conversation with anyone she came in contact with and entertaining them on that subject. The quality of conversation and her great knowledge and love of horses were things she had in common with da Zara.*

As the spring progressed toward summer, Wallis remained at Shih-Chia Hutong, heading out to scour the markets and curio

---

* Higham quoting Pighini, *Wallis: Secret Lives of the Duchess of Windsor* (London: Sidgwick & Jackson, 1988), 43.

shops for bargains, riding along the top of the Tartar Wall at day-break, playing bridge at Peking's endless round of nightly dinner parties and "at-homes." But Win and the need to start divorce proceedings were hanging over her and would have to be dealt with at some point. Wallis knew that eventually she would have to move on, return to America. She was about to turn twenty-nine in a few weeks, on June 19. The milestone of thirty loomed and she was far from home, estranged from a husband she wished to divorce, and with no significant long-term prospects in China. However, as temporarily idyllic her life in Peking was—her self-declared Lotus Year—a decision would have to be made. In the end, forces far beyond her control made the decision for her. Events in China were about to take a turn for the worse.

A Busy Market Just South of the Qianmen Gate, Peking (Courtesy: Special Collections, University of Bristol Library)

13

THE LOTUS-EATER'S DREAM SHATTERED: LEAVING CHINA

HATAMEN STREET
TARTAR CITY
PEKING
JUNE 1925

There can be no summary and dramatic end to a marriage—only a slow and painful unravelling of a tangled skein of threads too stubborn to be broken.

—Wallis, *The Heart Has Its Reasons*

I have only this to say to you. You are far too brimming with vitality and demand far too much of life for this worn out land. China is nothing but dust, powdery loess blown in by the west wind, a land worn down to the bone by age.

—Alexis Leger (aka Saint-John Perse), "Letter to a European Lady"

It was my good fortune to live in Peking at a time when she was permitted to remain faithful to some of her centuries-old traditions. . . . When I knew her she resembled a deposed empress, still clad in the remains of her imperial wardrobe, making ineffectual attempts to pose as an ordinary housewife.

—John Blofeld, *City of Lingering Splendour: A Frank Account of Old Peking's Exotic Pleasures*

A PEKING SUMMER

By June, the heat starts to rise sharply in Peking, and temperatures reach ninety-five degrees in the shade and more. The humidity can become stifling. In his reminiscences, *Memoirs of an Aesthete*, Harold Acton recalled that the coming of the June heat encouraged thoughts of departure, reminding one that the next few months would be unbearably hot as well as having to endure the combined sound of "four million cicadas."[*]

The heat brought forth the smells of the city—a sort of "sweetish sourness," as Ann Bridge described it, mixed with the pleasant sandalwood and citronella wafts of the lit green incense coils that slowly smoked away, deterring mosquitoes.[†] But also the stench of open sewers; the buckets of night soil yet to be collected or in the process of being transported by "honey cart" to the countryside as manure. Everyone wanted to escape to Peitaiho or Shanhaikwan— and some did decamp for the entire summer in the *saison morte*. The Western Hills were also a popular escape, or just up onto the city's rooftops. The Grand Hôtel's roof was open nightly while the Chengkwang cinema moved double-bill screenings of American movies up on to the roof to allow patrons to benefit from at least the occasionally moving air. Wallis became a regular at the newly built open-air swimming pool in the American legation where marines, dipsis, and the American contingent of the Foreign Colony cooled off.

Wallis and the women of the Foreign Colony bought Japanese silk kimonos and soft cloth espadrilles to wear around their courtyard houses or apartments. Cold-water sponge baths were a treat. At Shih-Chia Hutong, electric fans blew softly over bowls of ice to refresh the air, vases of tuberoses scented the rooms, and goldfish swam in earthenware basins. Kitty and Wallis lunched in negligées

---

[*] Harold Acton, *Memoirs of an Aesthete* (London: Methuen, 1948), 286–97.
[†] Ann Bridge, *Four-Part Setting* (London: Chatto & Windus, 1939), 55.

in the courtyard outside, the vermillion walls covered in century-old wisteria. In the courtyard gardens, persimmon trees were in full bloom, as was golden forsythia, with the seasonal hum of cicadas a constant backdrop. The itinerant hawkers and visiting curio vendors came in the cooler mornings, and so the cries of peddlers selling bean curd and dumplings, cats' meat sellers, tradesmen offering all manner of repairs and knife grinding were largely absent after midmorning as the heat intensified.* With everyone taking siestas, the afternoon hutong lanes became still and calm, feeling Mediterranean in their warm lethargy, the preserve of cats lazing in sunny spots, yellow-haired hutong weasels traversing compound walls, emerald dragonflies occupying the courtyard gardens, while above were azure-winged magpies, larks, and thrushes.†

Guests relaxed in rattan rocking chairs in the precious shade of gingko and jujube trees, sipping predinner cocktails. The heavy meat courses of winter gave way to cold buffet suppers, gazpachos served with small, hard-boiled pigeon eggs, cold chicken, buttered cobs of sweet corn, iced soufflés or macédoine of any available fruits with cream mousse, accompanied by iced tea or chilled liebfraumilch.

In the hot summer months, large mats of bamboo (known as *pongs*) were hung across the courtyard to provide some additional shade and carpets of golden straw laid across the hard earth of the hutong, which was regularly sprinkled by Peking city employees carrying large wooden buckets of water and wooden shakers to limit the

---

* In his memoirs of 1930s Peking and his comic novel of Foreign Colony manners, *Peonies and Ponies* (London: Chatto & Windus, 1941), longtime Peking and hutong inhabitant Harold Acton notes that cats' meat sellers were actually selling horsemeat from the abattoirs around the city, considered suitable for feeding pet cats or dogs.

† The so-called hutong weasel is actually the Siberian weasel, nicknamed for its common lane habitat by foreigners and known as the "yellow rat wolf" (*huang shu lang*) by the Chinese. In general, foreigners thought them rather cute, while Chinese proverbs see them as metaphors for sneaky and ill-intending characters. They can still be seen occasionally, though wider roads, heavier traffic, and the eradication and truncation of the hutongs have all combined to reduce their number.

dust.* As evening temperatures cooled, nighttime excursions were made out to the almost-forgotten Temple of Heaven, where once emperors led prayers for good harvests, but now its abandoned walls were smothered in ivy and honeysuckle. Beyond, along the barren Imperial Road, was little more than farmland and rubbish dumps in 1925, the edge of the outer city giving way to smallholdings, fields of kaoliang, maize, and soybeans—and the piles of haphazardly dumped city waste scavenged by snarling packs of yellow "wonk" dogs.

Herman and Kitty conducted their summer evening outings in style as ever, taking picnics of duck's liver pâté, egg sandwiches with stuffed olives, and tournedos with béarnaise sauce. Sitting on the steps of the Temple of Heaven, they drank champagne and hot chicory coffee as they watched the reddish glow of the horizon fade as the sun went down over the Western Hills, the noises of the city behind them and just the high-pitched buzzing of the ever-present cicadas and the barking of farm dogs to break the silence.

Morning horse rides on the Tartar Wall continued. Female riders purchased Manila straw hats to keep off the early-morning sun. One learned to walk through the Legation Quarter on the shady sides of the streets, cool under the shelter offered by the acacia and London plane trees. Life in China was still pleasant for Wallis, yet about to be brought to a dramatic halt.

Wallis's self-termed Lotus Year, her China idyll, would be shattered by the sound of gunfire that occurred on a late-May afternoon outside a police station 750 miles away from the calm of Shih-Chia Hutong in the Shanghai International Settlement. The so-called May Thirtieth Incident isn't remembered much outside China any-

---

* Pongs are mounted on bamboo poles and adjusted to provide shade throughout the day or over windows to cool rooms. They are then rolled up at night.

more. But every Chinese schoolchild can explain the events of that gruesome day.

The shooting happened at a demonstration staged by thousands of civilian students and workers in front of the Louza Police Station near the Settlement's main thoroughfare of Nanking Road. They were protesting the arrest of six Chinese students who had criticized foreign imperialism, the treaty ports, and the stationing of foreign troops in China. Some in the crowd reputedly chanted, "Kill the foreigners." The Shanghai Municipal Police ordered the crowd to scatter. A white police officer, Inspector Edward Everson, addressed the crowd in Shanghainese dialect, telling them to disperse or he would shoot. The actual sequence of events remains sketchy and contested, but according to eyewitnesses, several seconds later, Everson fired into the crowd and then ordered his Sikh and Chinese constables to do likewise. The policemen fired a total of forty rounds and, though the numbers are disputed, killed at least four protestors and wounded many more.

Almost immediately, or at least as fast as the telegraph wires could disseminate the tragic events in Shanghai, protests erupted across China, in Peking, and particularly in Canton, where things went from bad to worse. Membership of the fledgling Communist Party, only founded in 1921 with a few dozen members, exploded. In Shanghai, British soldiers fired on demonstrating students, workers, military cadets, children, and uniformed Boy Scouts, killing fifty-two. Follow-up strikes and demonstrations were held in Canton, Chungking, and many other Chinese cities, as well as in Hong Kong, continuing throughout the year. In Hankow, a protest descended into a riot and led to further Chinese deaths and subsequently a renewed wave of protests and strikes across the country. In Tientsin, Clarence Gauss, whom Wallis had known briefly and who by mid-1925 had been appointed US consul general in the treaty port, cabled Washington that warlord troops had invaded the city and demonstrations were breaking out along with the looting of shops in the foreign concessions. The disturbances were to last the rest of the year.[*]

The reverberations of the May Thirtieth Incident were inevitably felt in Peking too. Herman reported back all the news from the Peking Club in the Legation Quarter, which issued a typed Reuters sheet reporting events from Shanghai, Tientsin, Amoy, Canton, and Hong Kong. Foreigners had to be careful; the atmosphere turned threatening, the city on edge. The main agitation was against the British and Japanese. A hastily handwritten sign posted outside the Forbidden City read:

DOG JAPAN MEN AND BRITISH NOT
ALLOWED TO ENTER

At the Paomachang railway station, two large signs were nailed up, warning the British to leave the country or risk being killed.[†] In order to distinguish themselves from the main target of the demonstrators' ire, some non-British nationals took to flying their countries' flags from their homes, offices, cars, and rickshaws in the hope they would avoid any trouble.

Kitty and Herman thought this cowardly and that a united front needed to be shown by all the Foreign Colony. The Rogerses were also, as Wallis well knew, committed Anglophiles, refusing to turn their backs on their long-standing British friends in a time of adversity. No Stars and Stripes appeared on Herman's, Kitty's, or Wallis's rickshaws when they went out from Shih-Chia Hutong. In her memoirs, Wallis admitted that she wasn't quite as staunch in her beliefs or as courageous as Herman and Kitty, and though she did venture

---

* "Foreign Quarter in Tientsin Is Attacked," *Free Press Evening Bulletin* (Winnipeg, MB), December 25, 1925.
† "China: Unrest," *Time*, June 15, 1925.

out during the demonstrations and boycotts, she really "felt quite uncomfortable."*

The American travel writer and novelist Harry Hervey was in Peking at the same time. He wrote home to friends in Savannah that his train into the city had been heavily guarded and that marines with machine guns were lined up along the walls of the US legation to protect it against attack.

> In the Tartar City the atmosphere was very hostile. Flamboyant posters, picturing wounded, and dead Chinese, were all along the walls bearing the legend "SHOOT TO KILL." This was the order given by the [Shanghai Municipal] Police. Frequently, as we rode along, students would make gestures pantomiming a slit throat. On the corners soap box orators declaimed against foreigners. There were numerous parades and demonstrations.†

TROUBLE ON LANTERN STREET

In the first week of June, Wallis was out visiting the cluster of curio stores around Lang Fang Tou Tiao Hutong (Lantern Street) in the heart of Liu Li Chang, the Western Lanes. After six months in Peking, Wallis was familiar with the bewildering networks of hutongs and the thoroughfares of the city, traversing them with her rickshaw puller (even throwing in a little Peking dialect she'd picked up— *wang tun* / *wang pei*—turn east / turn north).‡ She was by now

---

* Wallis Simpson, *The Heart Has Its Reasons* (London: Michael Joseph, 1956), 119.
† Harlan Greene, *The Damned Don't Cry—They Just Disappear: The Life and Works of Harry Hervey* (Columbia, SC: University of South Carolina Press, 2018), 55.
‡ A major skill to be acquired to survive Peking life, then and now, was to understand the city in terms of compass points rather than simply left and right.

accomplished at the tricky dip of the knees required to elegantly exit the rickshaw as she pulled up at her destination.

While inside one of the curio stores, Wallis and the Chinese proprietor became aware of a noise, a large crowd over toward Chang'an, Eternal Peace Street. Alarmed, Wallis left the shop as the proprietor began hurriedly clearing away the wares displayed outside and pulling down his shutters. Other nervous shopkeepers throughout the Western Lanes followed suit, avoiding eye contact with Wallis. A full-scale riot had broken out along Chang'an Avenue close by the Grand Hôtel de Pekin. A large demonstration had degenerated into chaos. Police moved in, trying to disperse the crowds, and the young students began to escape through the narrow lanes of the antiques-and-curio district. Batons were swung liberally and high-pressure water hoses turned on the young people.

Some protesting students running north into the myriad lanes and hutongs of Chienmen paused long enough to write anti-British slogans on Wallis's rickshaw in chalk, despite her anxious puller trying to tell them that Wallis was a "Melican lady."[*] Often, Harry Hervey recalled, passports were rudely demanded by protesting groups to prove someone was American and not British.[†]

As Wallis stood outside the shop, the students stared at her harshly, but fortunately decided against any more direct action despite Americans, normally known as "Mei-Kuo-Jen" (*meiguoren*), often being referred to in decidedly derogatory terms as "second chop Englishmen." Wallis, not a little panicked, headed into the safety of the Legation Quarter and made straight for the nearby American legation. She asked Louis Little of the marine guard to translate the chalked slogan. She was relieved to discover that they were rather mild curses and not at all bloodthirsty.[‡]

---

[*] Simpson, *The Heart Has Its Reasons*, 119.

[†] Greene, *The Damned Don't Cry*, 55.

[‡] Simpson, *The Heart Has Its Reasons*, 119.

Others were more theatrical. That same month, Harry Hervey recalled, "Riding out to the Summer Palace we encountered a mob of students. They stopped the motor car, and numbers of them jumped on the running-board. One fellow slit his finger and made several Chinese characters in blood on a piece of paper. Our chauffeur translated them; it seems they thought it would be a pleasant idea if they killed us."[*] Dramatic, indeed, and rumors did swell of Boxer-like massacres out in the hinterlands, of "Bolshevist" agents operating covertly to stir things up and a Japanese fleet sailing for Shanghai.[†] Though reprisals against foreigners in China in 1925 were overwhelmingly restricted to insults and gestures rather than any actual slit throats, the Foreign Colony was extremely nervous. The Boxer Uprising and the events of 1900 were still reasonably current in the Colony's collective mind; survivors were still around. Nervousness was to be expected.

Needless to say, the boycotts, daily protest marches by the city's students, and strikes by many Chinese staff working for foreigners put rather a dent in the usually carefree atmosphere of the Foreign Colony. The road out to the Paomachang racetrack was, according to Ann Bridge, draped with a sign proclaiming:

GOD DAMN BRITISHERS—GET OUT THIS ROAD

Business was terrible too. Continuing warlord machinations as well as the strikes and boycotts following the May Thirtieth Incident

---

* Greene, *The Damned Don't Cry*, 55.

† Newspapers in England and America reported the possible death of an Italian missionary in Kaifeng in Henan Province, Russian agents in Canton, and a Japanese "destroyer flotilla" heading to Shanghai. For instance, "China Situation Grave— Great Demonstration in Peking—Japanese Destroyers Under Orders," *Staffordshire Sentinel*, June 15, 1925, 4.

were scaring away the tourists. Increasingly, the ocean liners bypassed northern China, continuing directly to safer, better-protected Shanghai. If liners did dock at Tientsin, then the tourist passengers stayed on board. Consequently, the dealers from Peking went to the ships and got all the business on the ship without the passengers having to leave.

One night, Wallis turned up for dinner at the home of an attaché at the British legation to hear that the number one boy (despite his title, a fully grown man) had just resigned and walked out in protest. She saw the humorous side in the English attaché's remonstrating with his servant, saying, "I say, you can't do that. I have people coming to dinner you know!"*

Herman and Kitty—and, by extension, Wallis—tried to carry on as normal, but there had been a fundamental sea change in attitudes. Sun Yat-sen had been diagnosed with liver cancer at the Rockefeller-funded Peking Union Medical College (PUMC) in January 1925. He had been treated with radium, but had died, aged just fifty-nine, in March while staying in the hutong home of Wellington Koo and Oei Hui-lan. Dr. Sun left a country in mourning and a potentially dangerous power vacuum in China's Kuomintang, or Nationalist Party. A week after his death, there had been an enormous funeral cortege in Peking that had brought the city to a respectful and total halt. It seemed as if the entire city, including all the diplomatic corps in full mourning attire, had turned out to see the leader of the republican revolution pass by.†

Since Dr. Sun's death, the turmoil around Chiang Kai-shek's attempts to divide the Nationalist groupings in Canton had been ongoing. With the May Thirtieth Incident in Shanghai, the related

---

* Simpson, *The Heart Has Its Reasons*, 119.
† Sun Yat-sen remained buried in Peking until his coffin was entombed on June 1, 1929, in a massive marble mausoleum constructed at the foot of Purple Mountain in Nanking, at that time the capital of the Republic of China.

strikes and boycotts in Peking, political machinations in Canton, and Sun's death causing stasis, it seemed that China was once again, as perhaps it persistently seemed to foreigners throughout the 1920s, about to collapse into irrevocable fratricidal civil war. The northern warlord chaos was continuing unabated and was, Wallis rightly predicted, likely to continue for quite some time. Things seemed at least as bad as, if not worse than, when Wallis had arrived in the autumn of 1924 and found herself on a heavily guarded Shameen Island, or weeks later in a Shanghai surrounded by warring warlord cliques.

Strikes and boycotts were called by hastily assembled coalitions of students, workers, and some merchants, then opposed vociferously by other businessmen, other workers, other student groups. Evening parades along Peking's main thoroughfares in remembrance of those shot dead in Shanghai were on again, off again; initially allowed, then banned, finally violently dispersed by the Peking police. When the demonstrations did happen, though, they were well attended. The city's Chinese Chamber of Commerce decided to support the boycott and organized roving pickets to search shops for boycott-busting British and Japanese goods.

THE SEVERE VOICE OF CONSCIENCE

Despite the unrest, one mid-June weekend, with the summer heat starting to gather pace, Wallis found herself once again in the Western Hills above the city enjoying the peace and tranquility of the Black Dragon Temple. It must have been around the time of her birthday—June 19—and she was turning twenty-nine. Herman insisted on business as usual; his relaxing weekends at the Black Dragon Temple would not be disrupted.

Wallis sat on a mossy wall, looking across the rolling countryside to the Fragrant Hills and the village of Haitian (Haidian), a vista eventually stretching back toward ever-tumultuous Peking. The sun was setting. Night, which was pitch-black out in the countryside, was coming in fast. Wallis recalled later that she heard an "inner voice," one she thought to be her conscience, speak to her. It had a severe and reprimanding tone; it told her she was deluding herself. It told her that, in her own words, "I was beginning to confuse a lotus eater's illusion for reality," and that she had better return to America, to her family, and finally deal with the unfinished business concerning Win and their failed marriage.*

Wallis was entering her thirtieth year that June. She was estranged from a husband she did not love and whom she knew would never forsake the bottle for her. Another reconciliation was not a possibility. Win had had a fairly eventful six months or so since Wallis had left for Shanghai, though the couple had apparently not communicated during that time. Canton had remained in a state of chaos with repeated strikes, boycotts, demonstrations, and warlord skirmishing. The South China Patrol had headed to Whampoa, then just outside the city, to deliver supplies to American missionary–staffed Canton Christian College. There, the *Pampanga* was fired upon by soldiers of one or another warlord group (it was never quite clear who) and returned fire. They eventually resupplied the beleaguered college and evacuated some staff who wished to leave.† This was to be Win's last action with the *Pampanga*. His tour with the South China Patrol was over, and as Wallis herself prepared to leave Peking, Win was also on his way back to a new posting in the United States.

She was a long way from home and, she felt, not getting any younger. Her life had been on hold for a while, but that could not remain the situation indefinitely. Wallis felt she could not continue

---

* Simpson, *The Heart Has Its Reasons*, 120.

† "American Gunboat Pampanga Fired Upon," *Town Talk* (Alexandria, LA), June 11, 1925. Whampoa is now known as Huangpu and is one of Guangzhou city's eleven urban districts. The Canton Christian College eventually became Lingnan University.

to live a frivolous life of morning horse rides, curio hunting, tiffins, Paomachang paper chases, and temple weekends forever. So she resolved to make a firm change. She plucked up the courage to tell Kitty and Herman that she was leaving.

Wallis knew the Greek myth of the lotus-eaters, a race of people living on an island in peaceful apathy. After they eat the lotus, they forget their homes and loved ones. They wish only to stay where they are, with their fellow lotus-eaters, indulging in pleasure and luxury rather than facing mundane life and practical concerns. Wallis in China clearly identified with the lotus-eaters of ancient myth. But outside events, fractious Chinese politics, and violent colonial excess impinged upon her otherwise idyllic Lotus Year.

Some biographers of Wallis have suggested that she disappeared from Peking abruptly, that she left the Rogerses on Shih-Chia Hutong puzzled, hurt, and with no explanation for her sudden flight from China. As ever, it wasn't quite as simple as that, although that explanation would later fit the picture that some wished to paint of Wallis as self-centered and concerned only with herself. In reality, Kitty and Herman were quite cognizant of Wallis's life in Peking, its vicissitudes, that it had always been a sojourn, that there were matters to be dealt with. They were aware that they were hosting her for what would be a limited period of time, that she needed to resolve the issue of her failed marriage, that she would need to move on. They all remained good and close friends from that time until the end of their lives.

Paperwork determines that it was no "midnight flit." In her autobiography, she says, "I finally told the Rogers that, hard as it was to leave them, the time had come for me to start back home."* But there

---

* Simpson, *The Heart Has Its Reasons*, 120.

was a slight bureaucratic delay. Wallis needed to extend her passport so as to be able to travel again. She had applied for and received a new passport in America in July 1924 prior to sailing for Hong Kong (and paying the requisite fee of ten dollars). However, it was due to expire a year later—July 8, 1925. She needed an extension.

And so to the American legation and its passport office—a large room with a portrait of George Washington and a loud grandfather clock. She was recorded as residing at #4 Shih-Chia Hutong, being the "Wife of American Naval Officer," and extended her passport to July 8, 1926. In fact, Wallis visited the American legation on the same day, July 1, 1925, that back in Canton the Kuomintang had proclaimed itself China's new National Revolutionary Government (as opposed to the former "Southern" government) and announced its determination to reunite all of China and rid the republic of the scourge of warlordism, however brutal that suppression might have to be. There was to be a "Northern Expedition," and the warlords were put on notice—join with the Kuomintang government or prepare to be wiped out. It looked very much as if all-out civil war was coming to northern China.

In her memoirs, Wallis wrote simply, "So, in early summer, somewhat in the mood of a female Ulysses, I left for Japan to take a ship to the West Coast."[*]

It was to be a slightly roundabout journey.

HOMEWARD BOUND FINALLY

Wallis departed Peking as the first summer rains came. The *meiyu*, or Plum Rains, herald the beginning of East Asia's rainy season. They usually start around the fourth or fifth lunar month, June, and last

---

[*] Simpson, *The Heart Has Its Reasons*, 120.

until the end of August or into September. Moist air over the Pacific meets the cooler continental air mass, and when the rain does come, the heavens open, and then it seriously descends. Peking often flooded. The Shanghai-based satirical magazine *The Rattle* had long dubbed Peking in the Plum Rains time "the City of Dreadful Dirt."* In the Plum Rains of 1925, nine inches of rain fell in twenty-four hours one June day. The showers were preceded by high winds. The next day came more, maybe another fifteen inches of rainfall, then more, and everyone, realizing terrible floods might be coming, began sandbagging their homes. The roads, lanes, and hutongs of Peking turned to muddy swamps, unpassable for rickshaws or mule carts. In 1925, only a handful of Peking roads were asphalted, hardly any outside the privileged citadel of the Legation Quarter, and only a couple properly macadamized.

The rains did bring the closest thing to a riot of color in Peking. Spring flowers were a rarity in northern China due to the dry, but freezing, winters. Flowers only came after the Plum Rains. It was now getting seriously hot, uncomfortably so—hitting over ninety degrees. This was the *ta shu* (the Great Heat), as Pekingers called it. The city was becoming a furnace, and the only places to escape the energy-sapping heat were the fanned and block-ice-cooled dining rooms of the Grand Hôtel de Pekin, the Hotel du Nord, the Grand Hôtel des Wagons-Lits, as well as the refined environs of the Peking Club. At #4 Shih-Chia Hutong there was no electric air-conditioning, of course, but it did have shaded areas and some fans. Herman could order ice from vendors (for cooling, not for ice cubes in drinks, of course, unless you wanted hepatitis!) that was placed into lacquered boxes around the house to chill the rooms day and night.

Wallis finally departed Peking as the *meiyu* downfalls began and the *ta shu* heat ratcheted up. Nevertheless, it was a more comfortable

---

* Noted first in *The Rattle*, published by Kelly & Walsh of Shanghai, August 1896 edition.

departure than her arrival had been on that freezing, stop-starting train from typhoid-hit Tientsin the previous December. The Rogerses had agreed to keep several trunks for her and send them along later as cargo to America—the purchases from the Camel's Bell, the Golden Dragon, Yamanaka, the Western Lanes, and markets. Those Chinese screens, lacquerware, the collection of jade and ivory elephants, winter clothes, a fur coat, and the other knickknacks sent up from Shanghai the year before.

Tickets were booked at American Express in the lobby of the Wagons-Lits. But there was no avoiding that it was going to be a slog of a journey. Wallis had hoped to take the famed Blue Express, the luxury international train from Peking to Shanghai that took thirty-six hours but had a bar, dining, smoking, and card cars, as well as comfortable fan-cooled couchettes to get some sleep. Unfortunately, the railway workers were on strike.

She managed to find a train that crept across to Tientsin; never getting above forty miles per hour due to fears of broken track. Just as with her journey the previous winter from Tientsin to Peking, the journey was only eighty miles or so but fraught with danger. Trains between Peking and Tientsin were still repeatedly being robbed throughout 1925. Clarence Gauss was still warning US citizens to avoid the line; things had become so bad, with Americans being robbed and, in several cases, shot at too. The Chinese responded by putting armed soldiers on all the trains to repel bandit attacks.[*]

Wallis boarded the train at the Chienmen station and rolled out, back through the Tartar Wall, and then watched the city disappear behind her, the distinctive rotunda of the Temple of Heaven, Paomachang in the distance, the Western Hills on the far horizon. For Wallis, the great fifty-foot-high wrought iron gates of the Lega-

---

[*] "Americans on Train Robbed by Chinese," *Chattanooga Daily Times*, January 3, 1925.

tion Quarter, which closed nightly at 9:00 p.m., clanged shut for the last time.

In Tientsin, the dockworkers had come out on strike. She would have to carry her own luggage aboard the liner bound for Shanghai. It was the *Empress of Canada*, the same ship that had originally taken her from Manila to Hong Kong the previous September. The ship arrived in a hot and steamy Shanghai on August 29 in the midst of a massive rainstorm and yet another citywide strike. Pedestrians rolled up their trousers and waded along Nanking and Bubbling Well Roads. In the French Concession, below-stairs rooms had to be cleared of servants and any possessions as they flash flooded. Poor Chinese drowned as the waters rose rapidly after the city's myriad snaking creeks—the Soochow, the Sawgin, the Siccawei, the Yangshupu—all burst their banks and flooded nearby basements so fast that the occupants, with nowhere else to go, were drowned.*

Despite having enjoyed her visit the previous winter, Wallis did not tarry more than a few days in Shanghai. She may have looked up Robbie for old times' sake, and she certainly attended the race club at least once.† But it was a claustrophobic city in August, uncomfortable in the heat of a Shanghai summer; the rains and flooding relentless; the strikes paralyzing the city with newspapers not being printed, shops and restaurants closed as store clerks and waiters struck, taxi drivers and rickshaw pullers staying home.

The brutal Shanghai summers alone were easily enough to encourage the sojourner to move swiftly on. Some years later, Harold

---

* The Suzhou, Shajin, Zikawei or Xujiahui, and the Yangtszepoo, or Yangpu, Creeks.
† Though Wallis never refers to her brief return to Shanghai en route back to the United States, there does exist a Shanghai Race Club complimentary member's badge in her name, most likely obtained for her by race club member Robbie to allow her to access the members' stand.

Acton, firmly a fan of Peking over Shanghai, traveled south to visit friends and see the sites of Shanghai. On arrival, Acton was stunned by the difference in climate compared to the drier, dustier north: "Humidity saturated the atmosphere," Acton recalled. "The walls were sweating, and everything one touched was sticky; the humming of electric fans stunned one into listlessness till evening beckoned to a furtive and hesitant breeze."*

Wallis pushed through the crowds, crossed the flooded Bund waterfront, the Whangpoo River running dangerously fast and high, and entered the offices of the Dollar Steamship Line. There she booked passage—a first-class cabin—on the *President McKinley* via Kobe, Yokohama, Honolulu, and finally Seattle.

Even once her ship had made it out of the Whangpoo, past the Woosung Bar into the Yangtze, and eventually out into the China seas, the adventure continued. As she docked in Japan, the coastal city of Nagoya had an earthquake causing widespread panic; there were terrible floods in Osaka, with bridges swept away and several hundred dead. The weather continued to be apocalyptic all the way home. Heavy rain and thunderstorms dogged Wallis's voyage as if the *meiyu* were pursuing her from China across the Pacific. She hit another big rainstorm in Hawaii that almost wiped out the islands' annual sugar crop. Eventually, the *President McKinley* reached Victoria, the compact capital of British Columbia nestled on the tip of Vancouver Island, on September 8. The liner then completed the last leg of its transpacific voyage and finally docked at Seattle on September 13.

Wallis was home after approximately a year away. However, she was not well. Her tendency to severe seasickness was compounded by a flare-up of her "obscure internal ailment" (that had afflicted her in Canton the year before and seen her hospitalized in Hong Kong

---

* Acton, *Memoirs of an Aesthete*, 287.

and then treated in Shanghai by Dr. Friedlander). She was put in the care of the ship's doctor and then taken to a Seattle hospital for an undefined operation. But she was back on American soil.

THE LOTUS YEAR COMPLETED

Wallis's time in China had given her the excitement of a new world. There had been awful moments—Win's drunkenness and violence, the threats of bandits and warlord fighting, proximity to outbreaks of disease and social strife. But the bad had been leavened by the extraordinarily beautiful—the restful environs of the remote temples of the Western Hills, the sea breezes at Shanhaikwan, the morning rides atop the Tartar Wall, the evening picnics at the Temple of Heaven. It is worth noting (given how many foreigners did recall suffering some sort of illness in China at the time) that, despite her hospitalization in Hong Kong, Wallis never seems to have been ill. She didn't fall prey to the typhoid, jaundice, beriberi, rheumatic fever, hepatitis, cholera, or any of the other maladies from which so many foreigners suffered. She appears to have remained robust and healthy throughout.

In the course of the months spent in Peking, the prospect of leaving Win, of becoming a divorced woman, had become more bearable. Where she had feared being unable to support herself, she now knew she could find ways to earn money, that she could confidently mix in an elevated level of society. She had no intention of returning to Win. She had moved on from the days (barely eighteen months previous) when her family had persuaded her that she must be the one to work to save her marriage, to acquiesce to Win's moods and temper. She could now be confident she was desired by others and that there were better, more charming men to be had, men like Alberto da Zara. Her time in Peking had convinced her she didn't want to be a navy wife with the long years of postings to dreary ports, forever moving and attempting to make the most of drab naval accommodation, the loneliness when husbands were at sea or on active duty and the seemingly inevitable arguments and fighting when they were ashore. No more China Birding for Wallis.

She was a different person now; her time in China had changed her. Anyone who still thought Wallis Warfield Spencer was just another delicate Southern belle, all polite manners and nothing more, would have been amazed at her exertions on the British legation tennis courts, her early-morning canters on the Tartar Wall, how she rode donkeys through the precarious paths of the Western Hills, scrambled on foot over rocks looking for hidden temples, explored the pre-dawn Thieves' Market, and haggled prices in the curio stores of Liu Li Chang.

Of course, Wallis still had all the charm and good manners of a Baltimore debutante, but she also now had experience of looking after herself and moving in cosmopolitan society. She was more sophisticated, knowing, and worldly-wise as well as tougher, more determined, and focused. Wallis was quite simply not the same woman who had boarded the USS *Chaumont* the year before. She was perhaps not yet the woman who would find herself at the center of the greatest ruction in the British royal family's history and at the heart of the twentieth century's greatest love story, but . . . that would all come after marrying into money and conquering London society. But after her Lotus Year, after her China experience, she was on her way to new adventures.

14

A NEW START

AFTER CHINA

The winter days were especially beautiful; sometimes the skies over Peking were incredibly blue; other days winds off the Gobi Desert would permeate the atmosphere with a thin yellowish film of dust through which the sunlight would fall as through a golden filter.

—Wallis, *The Heart Has Its Reasons*

In later years I was to reflect on how I missed China.

—Wallis, *The Heart Has Its Reasons*

The story of Wallis after she left China is, of course, well known. Back in America, she stayed in New York for much of 1926 with her childhood friend Mary Kirk and her husband, the French aviator turned stockbroker Jacques Raffray. Wallis and Mary visited Baltimore together in early 1927 before Wallis sailed for Europe in the summer. Arriving in France, she received news that she had finally obtained her divorce from Win. Wallis had charged him with desertion. Win did not contest it. He went on to marry three more times. None were great successes, and his subsequent divorces saw his drinking and temper raised frequently in court. He died in 1950 at just sixty-one. Spencer never published a memoir or talked publicly of his relationship with Wallis, its breakdown, or his time in Hong Kong and Canton.

At the Manhattan home of the Raffrays, Wallis had been introduced to a successful American-born British shipbroker, Ernest Simpson. They met again in Europe. In July 1928, Wallis became Mrs. Simpson. She wrote in her memoirs of her initial impression of him: "Reserved in manner, yet with a gift of quiet wit, always well dressed, a good dancer, fond of the theatre, and obviously well read, he impressed me as an unusually well-balanced man." She added, recalling having left China and returned to America, "I had acquired a taste for cosmopolitan minds."* The Simpsons settled in London, where, in 1931, Wallis met the Prince of Wales, who, after the death of his father, King George V, became Edward VIII. They fell in love. And so to the abdication crisis.

The Simpsons divorced in May 1937 (soon after which Ernest married Mary Kirk, who had herself recently divorced Jacques Raffray). After abdicating his crown, Edward married Wallis in June the same year. Bessie Wallis Warfield-Spencer-Simpson became Wallis, Duchess of Windsor. The couple became the subject of intense media fascination and bilious resentment in English Establishment circles. But they were also celebrities capable of rivaling and surpassing Hollywood stars and the reigning royal family in the newspapers. Their story caught the public imagination like no other romance. Elisabetta Cerruti, Wallis's occasional dinner companion at the Italian legation in Peking, was right when she commented in her memoirs that, in abdicating his crown, the king had paid Wallis the greatest compliment possible—to give up a throne and an empire.†
It perhaps took the coronation of the young Queen Elizabeth II in

---

* Wallis Simpson, *The Heart Has Its Reasons* (London: Michael Joseph, 1956), 125.

† The full quote was "I met the Duchess casually many years before in Peking. She had been Mrs Spencer then and a great success with men, but I never imagined her to be a woman for whom a King of England might leave his throne. His abdication had been the greatest compliment ever paid to a woman. Greeting her, I thought she had not changed at all since I had met her in Peking." Elisabetta Cerruti, *Ambassador's Wife* (London: George Allen & Unwin, 1952), 216.

1953 to eclipse the story of Edward and Mrs. Simpson, though it has never been far from the gossip pages and remains firmly lodged in the public imagination a century on from Wallis's China sojourn.

Wherever they went, immediately after their marriage, during the war years, and then the long years of exile in Paris, the Windsors got top billing. Wallis was photographed with just about everyone.

There is a photo from 1962 taken on the Spanish set of *55 Days at Peking*, Nicholas Ray's epic movie of the 1900 Boxer Uprising and the siege of the legations. Charlton Heston (who plays a US Marine) and the British-Chinese child actress Lynne Sue Moon (who played an orphaned girl he takes under his wing) are snapped on set chatting with a visiting Duchess of Windsor. Heston and Moon appear to be listening with interest to the duchess, then in her midsixties, who was wearing a headscarf and an enormous bejeweled bracelet on her wrist. The photograph is a curiosity, the confluence of royalty and Hollywood. But you can't help wondering if Heston knew enough of Wallis's past lives to ask her how their re-creation of Peking, on the outskirts of Madrid, matched the original she had known.

Also there to be found among all the photographs at balls, on holidays and traveling, the ephemera of opening nights, galas, dinner parties, the thousands of tabloid social page columns are Wallis's longer-term contacts. Wallis's China network proved stalwart as she navigated becoming the Duchess of Windsor. Fleeing London, she had stopped briefly with the former Queen of Peking, Constance Coolidge, in Paris, before bolting with Herman and Kitty Rogers on the Riviera. Soon after their marriage, the Windsors went to the races in Paris with Coolidge, dined with Elisabetta and Vittorio Cerruti, spent time with her old jade teacher, Georges Sebastian.

Despite being gay, in 1929 Sebastian had married a wealthy American heiress; he was thirty-three, and she was fifty-two. Together, they built the stunning modernist villa Dar Sebastian, near Hammamet in Tunisia. In July 1938, the Windsors and the Rogerses took a private cruise down the west coast of Italy. However, the British Foreign Office discouraged them from sailing to then fascist Italian–dominated Tunisia, where Wallis hoped to see Sebastian. Diana Mosley claims that when the duke and duchess were in Madrid in 1940, Wallis considered buying a house for them to settle in neutral Spain and was planning to consult Sebastian about the décor.* Churchill, concerned the Nazis might kidnap the duke, insisted they return home. The couple left for Lisbon and eventually the duke's wartime job as governor of the Bahamas.

In 1927, Colonel Louis Little left Peking to become director of operations and training for the US Marine Corps in Washington. He held that post until 1931, when he went to Haiti to serve as commanding general of the First Marine Brigade. In 1937, he was made commanding general of the Marine Corps base at San Diego, and in 1939, he began his last tour of active service as commanding general of the marine barracks in Quantico, Virginia. He retired in 1942 and died in 1960. He is buried at Arlington National Cemetery. Elsie Cobb Little restarted her interior decorating career after the Littles' Peking posting. She prospered and was highly regarded until the Depression put a stop to big spending on interiors, even among Elsie's generally wealthy clients. She died in 1949 at seventy-three.

Elbridge Gerry Greene stayed in Peking for nearly a decade before moving on to a number of diplomatic posts in Ottawa, Vienna, and finally Helsinki in the 1930s. He died in July 1946 of a heart attack in Boston at fifty-seven.

Mary Sadler remained a navy wife for the rest of her life. Her husband, Frank, was made a rear admiral by President Roosevelt in 1935. He oversaw the security of the Panama Canal Zone at the outbreak of World War II. Sadler left the navy in 1943, and the couple retired to Rhode Island, where Mary had grown up. Mary died in 1951, aged sixty-eight. Frank died in 1962 at eighty-one.

---

* Diana Mosley, *The Duchess of Windsor* (London: Sidgwick & Jackson, 1980), 50.

Clarence Gauss's diplomatic career in China continued to ever-greater heights. In the 1920s and 1930s, he served as consul general in Shanghai, Tientsin, and then Shanghai again. During this posting, Gauss was the leading American in Shanghai at the time of the Japanese attack on the city. After a brief diversion as ambassador to Australia, he returned to China to be ambassador, stationed in the heavily bombed wartime capital of Free China at Chungking from 1941 to 1944. Clarence Gauss was considered one of the State Department's best China Hands. He died in 1960 at seventy-three.

Alberto da Zara retired from the Italian navy in 1946. He later published his autobiography, *Pelle d'Ammiraglio* (*The Skin of an Admiral*). Da Zara died in 1951 at sixty-two. He never married, and to the end of his days retained the reputation of being a ladies' man. He never spoke publicly of his affair in Peking in 1925 with Wallis Spencer.

The fortunes of Herman and Kitty Rogers are crucial to Wallis's post-China years. On returning from China, the Rogerses lived between New York, London, and the South of France. It seems Herman forgot all the Chinese he'd tried so hard to learn and never did find a publisher for his book. They were friends with Wallis in England and guests at Fort Belvedere when she was the prince's mistress; later, they offered her sanctuary during the abdication crisis at their villa. Herman gave Wallis away at her wedding to the former king and later put the Villa Lou Viei at their disposal when the couple wished to escape Paris after their honeymoon in September 1937. They all remained close friends until the end.

Kitty suffered a protracted and painful illness and eventually died from cancer of the larynx in 1948. Wallis was often with her and regularly wrote to her if away. In 1950, Herman married the widow of a wartime British Spitfire pilot; the Duke and Duchess of Windsor acted as their witnesses. In his book *The Secret Life of the Duke of Windsor* (which does not discuss Wallis's time in China at all), Michael Bloch, who came to know Wallis later in her life, describes Herman and Kitty simply as "the best friends of the Windsors' on the Côte d'Azur."* But it was a much more long-lived relationship.

Wallis, of course, outlived them all, including the former king. The Duke of Windsor died in 1972 at seventy-seven. Wallis died in Paris in 1986 at eighty-nine. It was not an easy end—long, drawn out, and isolated. The couple are buried together at the Royal Burial Ground at Frogmore in Windsor.

AND THAT CHINA DOSSIER . . . ?

No China Dossier has ever been revealed. No document discovered moldering in the archives or an attic somewhere. Some suggest it may be hidden away, in the possession of the security services or the royal family, beyond public reach. It is safe to conclude that it never existed. Yet so many biographies and sensationalist newspaper articles on Wallis have repeated the tropes and rumors.

It was all the lascivious fabrication of someone in Special Branch or MI5. Most probably, as noted previously, the former head of the SIS in Shanghai, Harry Steptoe. Certainly, as argued here—with Count Ciano, with the marchesa Durazzo, with Sir Victor Sassoon, Constance Coolidge, and others—there were cases lingering in the minds of people that could be confused with Wallis. No doubt the continuing exoticization of the Far East enlivened by Hollywood, pulp fiction, and tabloid journalism stirred the mental pot of the time. The long-term clinging to these ideas in repeated biographies and newspaper articles demonstrates how prevalent racist stereotyping of China, East Asians, and anyone or anything associated with China remains.

---

* Michael Bloch, *The Secret File of the Duke of Windsor* (London: Bantam, 1988).

MAN RAY'S STUDIO, PARIS

Wallis was photographed by the American artist Man Ray for the first time in Paris in July 1935. It was a big deal. He was no mere jobbing society portrait photographer. Man Ray had been defining the photographic avant-garde for over a decade. For the appointment, Wallis wore a light-colored dress, her face set off by a halo-shaped hat. It was to be a seated portrait in profile, nothing fancy, but requiring concentration from both photographer and sitter. A ten-second exposure in those days could easily see a beautiful face freeze and turn to unflattering granite.

The two met again in March 1936 in Paris. Wallis happened to be in the French capital visiting an old friend, Josephine Gwynne Armstrong. Josephine had been an artist's model back in the States and, in Paris, worked as a mannequin for the couturier Jean Patou (whose Asian-inspired scents were favored by Wallis). This time around, the photographs were much more interesting, creative, and reflected Wallis's China past. She wrote from Fort Belvedere, the Windsor home of the Prince of Wales, to her aunt Bessie in Baltimore on March 16, the day of the shoot, telling her that "I had some rather good pictures taken for *Harper's Bazaar*—I don't know what issue they will appear in." The society photographer Cecil Beaton, who came to know Wallis in 1936, when she and Ernest Simpson were living on Cumberland Terrace overlooking Regent's Park, found her "alluring" and commented that "her skin today was incredibly bright and smooth like the inside of a shell, her hair as sleek as only the Chinese women know how to make it."[*]

Man Ray's second portrait of Wallis appeared in the June 1936 issue of *Harper's Bazaar*. It showed Wallis posed by a statue of

[*] See Hugo Vickers, *Cecil Beaton: The Authorized Biography* (London: Weidenfeld and Nicolson, 1985), 194.

Guan Yu, the god of war, wearing a Chinese-style dress clearly inspired by the *qipao* and designed by the Chicago-born, Manhattan-based couturier Main Rousseau Bocher, known professionally as Mainbocher. Her hair was styled in the kind of sleek chignon referred to in the fashion pages as "Chinese style." Cecil Beaton described it as "brushed so that a fly would slip off it." Her hairdresser of thirty years, Alexandre de Paris (Louis Alexandre Raimon) was once asked about her distinctive chignon. He said, "She learned about her hair from her days in China."[*]

The full-page photograph accompanied an article about American women then resident in London, and it was captioned:

> Mrs Ernest Simpson, the most famous American in London,
> wears a Chinese dinner dress.

Quite how the decision to style this photograph was taken—fashion journalist Suzy Menkes described the pose as "à la chinoise"—is not clear.[†] Man Ray had posed pictures with Chinese statues before, as in the mid-1920s, Chinese style was all the rage.[‡] However, Wallis was notorious for wanting to control her image, even before she became the Duchess of Windsor. She once said, "I'm not a beautiful woman. I'm nothing to look at, so the only thing I can do is dress better than anyone else."[§] The portrait obviously references her long-term and ongoing fascination with Chinese and Asian style despite what the current trends might be. Menkes has

---

[*] Suzy Menkes, *The Windsor Style* (London: Grafton, 1987), 142.

[†] Menkes, *The Windsor Style*, 44.

[‡] For instance, see the front cover of *Vu*, April 18, 1928, headlined "*La Tête d'un Bouddha d'Angkor été Volée.*"

[§] Reputedly to the American gossip columnist Elsa Maxwell. See Elsa Maxwell, *I Married the World* (London: William Heinemann, 1955), 249.

written that, with this "surreal study" Man Ray "caught the exotic, oriental taste of Wallis Simpson."[*]

The Mainbocher dress (the designer would later name a color, Wallis Blue, for her), the signature chignon hairstyle, the Chinese knickknacks, the midnight-blue screens, lacquerware, and, of course, the love of jade (eventually trading up to Cartier in Paris from Liu Li Chang in Peking), all became constants of Wallis's post-China life.

While I was researching this book, a small, embroidered cushion with a chinoiserie pattern featuring bamboo and other familiar Chinese touches came up for auction at an East Sussex sales house.[†] It was described as having been previously owned by Wallis Simpson. We know she continued to buy Chinese, chinoiserie, and *Japonois* items for both her homes with Ernest Simpson in London and then around the world with the Duke of Windsor. In her home in the Bois de Boulogne, she kept a latticed Chinese pagoda stand and a Chinese escritoire in her dressing room.[‡]

Wallis was a regular customer at Yamanaka & Co., a dealer in Japanese and Chinese art objects she had first known in Peking. The family business also had a showroom on New Bond Street, run by founder Sadajiro Yamanaka's son. Among Wallis's remaining paperwork is a letter from January 1932 regarding the purchase of an "Oriental" table and clock from Yamanaka in London.[§]

---

[*] Menkes, *The Windsor Style*, 99. The shoot was less memorable for Man Ray, who wrote, "My meeting with Mrs Simpson was purely commercial . . . she is only one of a thousand women I have photographed. It was routine work." Quoted in Neil Baldwin, *Man Ray: American Artist* (Boston: Da Capo, 2001), 204.

[†] The cushion, which had previously been sold at auction by Sotheby's in 1997, went for about UK£600 in 2021.

[‡] Menkes, *The Windsor Style*, 44, 47.

[§] See Michael Bloch, ed., *Wallis and Edward: Letters, 1931–1937* (New York: Summit Books, 1986), 60.

And then, of course, the pug dogs the duke and duchess consistently favored. Pugs are an ancient breed of dog that most canine historians agree originated in China, where they were bred as companion animals for the wealthy elite.

So there we have Wallis Simpson, later the Duchess of Windsor, dressed in a Mainbocher twist on the *qipao*, with either traditional Chinese butterfly knots or other ropework designs as adornment, her hair up in a chignon style, jade brooch adornments, trailing wafts of Jean Patou Asian-inspired fragrance, with the ever-present pug dogs nestling at her feet.

Though she was never to return, China was never far from Wallis's thoughts.

ACKNOWLEDGMENTS

This biography presented a rather unique set of challenges to the researcher/writer. Of course, when previously writing about the lives of foreigners in China between the world wars, I have encountered problems—the upheavals of modern times in China have not been kind to archives, and many have been destroyed, have vanished, or remain closed and off-limits. The perceived ephemeral nature of many sources—for instance, the old China coast foreign language press, records of now defunct entities such as those of the authorities of the Shanghai International Settlement and the Peking Legation Quarter, and the throwaway gossip-mongering "mosquito press" (Chinese language tabloids)—has meant much is lost. These problems can be attributed to the vicissitudes of history and that, after 1949, many local records were systematically destroyed or "lost" for reasons of political expediency or personal protection.

Unlike the Freedom of Information Act and regulations in the UK, USA, and elsewhere, no similar laws exist in China. Archive access, even when technically possible, is often subject to bureaucratic whim and encounters with overly protective local officials and librarians.

But Wallis adds another, and major, problem to the researcher—namely, the continuing and seemingly intransigent secrecy surrounding the British royal family and many of those deemed close to it. This secrecy is presumably in place explicitly to discourage dogged and unauthorized research into the royals, especially if that research may not reflect well on the family, their opinions, finances, and close associates. This still includes Wallis and any actual details of her China sojourn, as should be repeatedly apparent in the text. Essentially, independent biographers are not encouraged or welcomed to research the royal family and its wider clan, and far too much remains closed and hidden away without any reasonable explanation or near-time hope of public access.

Therefore, I would like to acknowledge the persistent campaign to encourage greater openness of the royal archives by the author Andrew Lownie, who has himself added to the shelf of "Wallis studies" with his book *Traitor King: The Scandalous Exile of the Duke and Duchess of Windsor* (London: Blink Publishing, 2021).

Many thanks to:

Beijing: Alan Babington-Smith and Melinda Liu at the Royal Asiatic Society in Beijing, Andrey Denisov, Kathleen Duignan (formerly with the US embassy in Beijing), Matthew Hu (China representative, the Prince's Foundation School of Traditional Arts, the Beijing Cultural Heritage Protection Center and attached to the Shijia Hutong Museum), Jeremiah Jenne at Beijing by Foot, that amazing cinematic re-creator of the hutong world of old Peking Jiang Wen, Sarah Keenlyside of Bespoke Beijing, Alex Pearson, Jenny Niven, Kadi Hughes, and Peter Goff of the (sadly now defunct) Beijing Bookworm for being such fun hosts on numerous occasions, Lars Ulrik Thom of Beijing Postcards, and Ying Wei of Clouds Intelligence. Additionally, the management and staff of the NUO Hotel Beijing (formerly the Grand Hôtel de Pékin) for repeatedly being such gracious hosts.

Hong Kong: David Bellis at Gwulo.com, Dave Besseling at the *South China Morning Post* magazine, Gary Brown at VIBE Books on Lantau Island, Doug Clark, Michael Duckworth at Hong Kong University Press, Annemarie Evans and the RTHK3 *Hong Kong Heritage* radio show, Michelle Garnaut, Rupert McCowan of the Royal Geographical Society in Hong Kong, Jo Lusby and all at the Hong Kong International Literary Festival, Shonee Mirchandani of Bookazine, Mark O'Neill, Peter Spurrier of Blacksmith Books, and Phil Whelan at RTHK3.

London: Phil Baker, Robert Bickers, Julia Boyd, Andrew Lownie, Caroline Moorehead, Michael Nakan at Envision Entertainment, Jon Riley, Anne Sebba, Hugo Vickers, Edward Wilson, and Frances Wood, the former keeper of the Chinese Collection at the British Library. I am very grateful to the Society of Authors' Foundation for awarding me a small but extremely helpful grant to help with research costs.

Shanghai: Patrick Cranley and Tina Kanagaratnam at Historic Shanghai, Gabor Holch and Rachel Rapaport of the Royal Asiatic Society in Shanghai, Tess Johnston, Ned Kelly at *That's Shanghai* magazine, Lynn Pan, and Bill Savadove.

USA: Adam Brookes, Jeremy Goldkorn, Kaiser Kuo, and Anthony Tao at the China Project, Ed Lanfranco, Lisa See, Scott Seligman, and Amy Sommers.

Also the staff at the Hong Kong University Library, the London Library, the UK National Archives at Kew, and the Royal Asiatic Society China Library in Shanghai.

Many thanks also to Charles Spicer and Hannah Pierdolla at St. Martin's Press in New York, Robin Harvie and Pippa Crane at Elliott & Thompson in London, copy editors Sara and Chris of ScriptAcuity Studio, and my agent, Clare Alexander, at Aitken Alexander Associates.

And finally, special thanks to my first, last, and most critical reader, Anne Witchard, who initially encouraged me to write about Wallis in China, did so much work on this manuscript, and was never anything less than totally supportive.

INDEX

ABOUT THE AUTHOR

Sue Anne Tay

Paul French was born in London and lived and worked in Shanghai for many years. His book *Midnight in Peking* was a *New York Times* bestseller and a BBC Radio 4 Book of the Week. He received the Mystery Writers of America Edgar® Award for Best Fact Crime and a Crime Writers' Association (UK) Dagger Award for Non-Fiction. His most recent book, *City of Devils: A Shanghai Noir,* received much praise with *The Economist* writing, "... in Mr. French the city has its champion storyteller." Both *Midnight in Peking* and *City of Devils* are currently in development for film.